Reality Orientation

PSYCHOLOGICAL APPROACHES TO THE 'CONFUSED' ELDERLY

Una P. Holden BA ABPsS
Principal in Neuropsychology,
St James's University Hospital, Leeds

Robert T. Woods MA MSc ABPsS
Lecturer in Clinical Psychology, Institute of Psychiatry
De Crespigny Park, London

CHURCHILL LIVINGSTONE
EDINBURGH LONDON MELBOURNE AND NEW YORK 1982

CHURCHILL LIVINGSTONE
Medical Division of Longman Group Limited

Distributed in the United States of America by Churchill Livingstone Inc., 19 West 44th Street,
New York, N.Y. 10036, and by associated companies branches and representatives throughout
the world.

First published 1982

ISBN 0 443 02276 3

British Library Cataloguing in Publication Data
Holden, Una P.
  Reality orientation.
  1. Geriatric psychiatry
  I. Title   II. Woods, Robert T.
  618.97'689   RC451.5.AS

Library of Congress Catalog Card Number 81-68078

Printed in Singapore by Selector Printing Co Pte Ltd

Preface

This book owes its existence to MIND – the National Association for Mental Health – who brought us together to lead a workshop on Reality Orientation at a conference in May 1979 in London on 'Positive approaches to mental infirmity in elderly people'. We realised then that there was no single publication on the theory and practice of RO to which we could refer the large number of people from a variety of disciplines who were expressing interest at the conference. The accounts that had been published were in a variety of journals, with often only a superficial description of the methods employed. We resolved then to attempt to meet the need for both a practical guide to RO and for a review of the relevant research.

We have aimed to cover all aspects of RO and related methods. This does mean that different parts of the book are particularly relevant to different groups of readers. Those interested in the research on RO will find this covered in Part I of the book – in chapters 2, 3 and 4 – while those whose interest is more directly practical will find Part II a more useful starting point. Chapters 6, 7 and 8 constitute an RO therapist's manual, in effect, while Chapter 9 develops some of the issues and problems that arise in the practical implementation of RO. Those attempting to implement RO will also find Chapter 5, on assessment methods, helpful in considering selection and monitoring of change. Conclusions regarding the research evidence are presented in the relevant chapters, whilst Chapter 10 represents our attempt at a feasible, practical future direction for work in this field.

The two parts of the book differ in their approach as well as content. Whereas in Part I constructive criticism of research studies is undertaken, in Part II there are fewer qualifications, fewer references and much more effort to provide 'best guesses' – from the literature and from our experience – for people to be able to use RO in a practical setting. In this – and in the whole endeavour – we are motivated by the knowledge that RO is being used in more and more settings, and that interest is expanding rapidly. We are concerned that there is a danger of RO being used inappropriately, of it being distorted, or of it being established on the wrong basis with resultant disappointment when the programme collapses. We hope that this book may help those setting up, monitoring and carrying out RO to be more aware of all that is involved in it, so that when it is established there is more chance of it having a useful part to play. We have also been concerned to place RO within the context of other psychological treatment approaches that have been developed for use with the confused elderly, and have attempted to show how the various approaches can complement each other.

We owe a huge debt of gratitude to all those over the last few years who in many different ways have contributed to the ideas and research in this book. It would require several pages to name them all individually – colleagues, students, caring staff from all parts of the UK at conferences, workshops and seminars, RO group leaders in the hospitals and old people's homes where we have been privileged to be involved in programmes – we trust they will accept our thanks for their support, stimulating ideas, questions and shared experience as well as for the hard work they have put in! We are particularly grateful to our colleagues who have been kind enough to share their findings with us prior to publication, which we hope will lessen the effects of the inevitable delay between writing and publication of this book. Our typists – Lucille Gray with help from Barbara Stead – deserve many thanks for producing the final manuscript, and we are grateful to Joan Woods for helping to type the early drafts. The Medical Illustration and Photography Department at Leeds University has provided valuable assistance with photography and graphics. Audrey Daniels of Kirklees Social Services kindly gave us permission to print two of

the photographs. Finally, we could not have completed this project without the help and support of our families – who have had
to live with RO for several years now!

We are happy to acknowledge appreciatively the many people
who have given us so much; however we wish to dedicate the
book to the elderly people who are its inspiration – to Danny,
Annie Mac, Mary, Charlie, Catherine . . . . . . , to all those who have
been labelled old and 'confused', but have managed to teach us a
great deal.

Various visual aids – video tapes, tape-slide package, etc., can
be obtained from the authors.* Memory aids, signs, orientation
boards etc. are available from S V Hanley, 'Orientation Aids',
Eddleston, Peebles, Scotland.

1982   U H
                                                                         B W

*Una Holden
  Department of Clinical Psychology
  St James's University Hospital
  Beckett Street
  Leeds   LS9 7TF

*Bob Woods
  Department of Psychology
  Institute of Psychiatry
  De Crespigny Park
  London   SE5 8AF

Contents

They're lucky here Lord,
    they each have a wardrobe and a dressing table,
    and the large dormitory is divided so that
        there is some privacy when they go to bed,
        there is space to keep clothes, a few photographs,
        some books, a box of chocolates:
        yes they're lucky here, not like some of the others:
            the first day Mrs Lawrie went to the
            Old Folk's Home they emptied out her handbag
            to make sure there were no valuables in it –
            nobody had ever touched her handbag before;
            Carrie lay in a bedroom with nine others,
            one tatty bedside locker each, and a jam jar
            with flowers in it to share between them,
            a transistor crackled somewhere,
            but nobody was listening,
            they stared at each other,
            stared, and said nothing;
            they let Vi have her canary and kept it
            in the living-room,
            but she couldn't keep books by her bedside,
            and she loved books;
            Bill used to sit with his buttons undone,
            he was beyond pride and caring
            and nobody seemed to mind,
            clothes were something to shamble in and out of,
            morning and evening.

Lord, those who care for the aged do a job I couldn't do,
    give them the strength and kindness,
        patience and cheerfulness
        to do it;
    and may those who organize the care of the elderly,
    government, local councils, hospital boards,
    voluntary agencies, trustees –
    may all of them create conditions in which
    people can grow old with dignity,
    enjoy the life that remains to them,
    and die, cradled in love.

(Reprinted from 'The old folk's home' by Michael Walker, with the permission of the publishers, Arthur James Ltd.)

PART | # ONE

The theory of
reality orientation

'Old age is for life what the evening is for the day. So one may call the evening the old age of the day and old age the evening of life.' *Aristotle*

Introduction

Although the evening of life has arrived for the elderly it does not follow that old age is something to be feared, dreaded and regarded with distaste. Glorious sunsets only occur in the evening which is also the time when the problems and pressures of the day are eased with relaxation and peace. Many elderly people *are* unhappy, but many more are not. A number of factors are involved in determining a person's reaction to advancing years – social, economic, health, personality and so on. Generalisations about 'the elderly' should then be made cautiously.

This book concerns itself primarily with a section of the elderly population often described with such terms as 'confused', 'senile' and 'demented'. These people could be said to be ageing abnormally; they form –as we shall see below – a minority of elderly people. However those working with them day-by-day may lose sight of what constitutes 'normal ageing', of what the evening of life can be. To provide a context for the abnormal, some psychological findings on normal ageing will be briefly discussed. Those interested in pursuing this area further are referred to Miller (1977a), Chapter 2 for a brief review and to Birren & Schaie (1977) for in-depth coverage.

NORMAL AGEING

Intellect

Intellectual ability in the past has been thought to reach a peak in early adulthood. A decline in functioning from this time on accelerated as the seventh and eighth decades were reached. This view is reflected in standardisation data for commonly used intelligence tests (see Miller 1977a, p 15). It adds support to the general belief that most elderly people suffer from deterioration of intellect.

However the reality is more complex than this straightforward notion of progressive decline would suggest. The American Psychological Association Task Force on Aging (1973) stated that 'many studies are now showing that the intelligence of older persons as measured is typically under-estimated.' The suggestion is then that age-related decline has been over-estimated in the past. Several factors are important here:

Cross-sectional differences

The early studies that showed progressive deterioration were cross-sectional in nature. Results of, say, groups of 20, 30, 40, 50 and 60 year olds would be compared on a particular measure. The problem here is that the groups differ in many other ways apart from age per se. Educational opportunities in 1920 and 1960, for example, were considerably different, and may have restricted the education and intellectual development of today's 60 year olds.

Differences in nutrition, culture, environment and medical care in the early years of life could also significantly disadvantage the older groups. At the time of assessment differences between age groups in physical health, economic status and social contact could be present – all of which could have some impact on intellectual test performance. Intelligence tests often seem to be designed for younger people; the older person may be less motivated and less competitive and so not perform as well as a younger person. The 80 year old in a wheel-chair may fail to see the relevance – to take an extreme example from Wechsler's Adult Intelligence Scale – of what one should do if lost in a forest in the day time!

Ideally (but impractically) longitudinal studies over a person's life-span would be needed to map out intellectual changes with age – although even here practice effects from repeated testing would complicate interpretation of the results obtained. Schaie & Strother (1968) and Schaie & Labouvie-Vief (1974) report a combination of the cross-sectional and longitudinal approaches. Groups of subjects at different ages from 20–70 years were administered the Primary Mental Abilities Test in conventional cross-sectional fashion. These groups were then followed up 7 and 14 years later and the testing repeated. Confirmation of the overestimate of decline by cross-sectional methods was obtained, but some deterioration in performance did seem to occur as groups reached the age of 60 or so.

Differential relationship of age with various aspects of intelligence

In the Schaie & Strother (1968) research, mentioned above, it was noted that some aspects of intellectual performance showed decline at an earlier age than others. In particular, tests with a large speed component show deterioration most rapidly; tests of verbal knowledge, on the other hand, may well show improvements, at least to the age of 60. These findings have been repeated many times, and have been related by Savage (1973) – among many others – to the notion that intellectual abilities can be subdivided into 'fluid' and 'crystallised'. Fluid intelligence is involved in adapting to novel situations, grasping new ideas, reasoning rapidly and so on. Crystallised intelligence reflects the person's acquired knowledge or accumulated wisdom. Fluid intelligence then is seen as declining more rapidly with age, while crystallised intelligence may well increase.

The whole question of intellectual changes with age remains the subject of much – often technical – controversy (see Botwinick 1977). However, it can be concluded at this stage that decline in intelligence has been over-estimated in the past; that some functions, especially where speed is involved, decline more rapidly than others. The size of these changes should also be emphasised; there remains considerable overlap between younger and older people on many functions, so that some older people will still perform better than some people 40 or 50 years younger! Finally, the importance of other factors which affect performance on tests apart from intelligence per se should be remembered. For example, the older person may be less prepared to take risks and may be more cautious in responding. The older person is more likely to suffer from ill-health, which may well have an impact on test performance.

Memory and learning

The old adage that 'you can't teach an old dog new tricks' reflects the stereotypical view of the elderly person's memory and learning ability. They are thought of as living in the past, with excellent recall for years gone by, but inability to recall the events of the previous day!

Research evidence, however, gives similar findings to those in the area of intellectual ability. There have been fewer longitudinal studies involving memory skills, however, and so the above mentioned difficulties with cross-sectional studies have to be borne in mind. Craik (1977) reviews the evidence; generally deficits in memory performance are found in older subjects. However, these deficits vary according to the type of memory involved and the experimental conditions. Immediate memory span (that part of memory where, for example, telephone numbers are rehearsed between finding them in the directory and dialling) is very little affected. Recall of new material after a longer period of time has elapsed is generally more impaired. If, however, memory is tested by a recognition method (e.g. 'was this word one that you learned?') then the deficit is less. Similarly if retrieval cues are given (e.g. 'some of the words were flowers') performance is similar to that in younger subjects.

Regarding memory for past events, there is conflicting evidence. For example, Warrington & Sanders (1971) found no evidence that old people remembered past events better than recent events. On tests of memory for past recognition of well-known faces, older people generally performed worse than younger subjects. Botwinick & Storandt (1980) reported that memory for past famous events was generally good with all ages, and suggested that discrepant results have been obtained when the 'past' events did not go as far back as the 60 year period in their study.

The memory loss that has been described is again relatively small. Older people tend to be more variable in their performance, and a large overlap remains with the performances of younger people. Normal elderly people are able to learn and remember new things; the conditions under which learning and recall take place are much more important, however. They are differentially affected by fast rates of presentation of information and differentially helped by retrieval cues, for instance. A study in Australia showing that a group of 65–85 year olds were able to learn German for the first time as proficiently as 16 year olds (Naylor & Harwood 1975) affirms the capabilities of normal elderly people!

Personality and adjustment

Assessment of personality at any age is fraught with difficulties. With the elderly, conventional personality questionnaires often seem inappropriate, having been designed for college students. As Neugarten (1977) points out this area 'reflects the .... disarray .... in the general field of personality'. However some points can be salvaged which may at least help question stereotypical views of the elderly person's personality.

Neugarten (1977) states that the best replicated and most consistent finding is that older people tend to be more introverted and inward-looking than younger people. This is an 'average' finding, and does not imply that all elderly people necessarily become introverted. Disengagement theory – first stated by Cumming & Henry (1961) – proposed that the decreased social interaction often noted in old age was not simply inflicted by society on the elderly. It was thought to be a mutual withdrawal, part of a normal ageing process, and necessary for successful adjustment to old age. The opposite view is that the well-adjusted elderly person will be the one who maintains his previous activities or develops new ones, despite the external disengaging forces of retirement, bereavements, loss of mobility, economic hardship and so on. Neither view seems to be universally applicable, however. The evidence suggests that some well-adjusted people remain busy and active, others disengage and are perfectly happy to sit back and relax. Conversely elderly people of both types show poor adjustment. The activity theory probably applies to more elderly people, however (Havighurst et al 1968). Neugarten (1977) stresses that it is life-long personality which is important in relation to how a particular elderly person will find satisfaction in old age, under the same social, financial and medical conditions. Continuity of personality seems to be an emerging theme, interacting with the vicissitudes of old age, but not being essentially changed by advancing years.

Conclusions on normal ageing

In this extremely brief review three major areas of psychological functioning have been considered. It has been suggested that changes do occur, but that these are usually relatively small. The diversity of the elderly must be stressed; their performance and personality show a great deal of variability between different elderly people. Normal ageing can be rich and full; it can be empty and sad. The whole range exists and cannot be constrained into any stereotype or image, whether blissful or miserable.

The importance of other factors – rather than change in the person themselves – relating to poor performance should be noted. Physical health is particularly important here; Eisdorfer & Wilkie (1977), for example, review the relationship of raised blood pressure to impaired cognitive functioning in elderly people. It could indeed be argued that many apparently age-related changes may be brought about by the increased incidence of ill-health in the elderly. This serves as a reminder also that the passage of time itself does not bring about any changes in functioning. It is other processes – of disease, environment or whatever – also varying in time, that actually lead to changes in behaviour.

DEMENTIA

Dementia is defined by Marsden (1978) as 'the syndrome of global disturbance of higher mental functions in an alert patient'. It should be distinguished from delirium, where the patient is not alert, having clouding of consciousness, usually arising from having an acute illness. Dementia is otherwise described as chronic brain failure, chronic brain syndrome and organic brain syndrome. Both dementia and delirium are sometimes described as 'confusion', particularly by non-medics. Where the term 'confusion' is used in this book dementia is implied. The major treatment approach to delirium is medical treatment of the underlying cause – infection, drug intoxication or whatever.

An arbitrary age limit – usually 65 years – divides pre-senile and senile dementias. Senile dementias are further sub-divided into two main types – arteriosclerotic (or multi-infarct) and senile dementia. Arteriosclerotic dementia results from a number of small strokes damaging cerebral tissue; its progressive decline is sudden and step-wise, rather than slow and steady. It probably accounts for a fifth of senile dementias (Blessed et al 1968). Senile dementia has been shown to be associated with brain changes (found at post-mortem) indistinguishable from those found in the most common pre-senile dementia, Alzheimer's disease. These include senile plaques and neurofibrillary tangles. The frequency of plaques has been found to correlate with deterioration in intellectual and behavioural function (Blessed et al 1968). Pearce & Miller (1973) and Constantinidis et al (1978) review these pathological changes. Perry (1980) reviews recent biochemical research, suggesting deficits in certain neurotransmitters in the brains of demented people. This research has led to some hope of a pharmacological therapy for dementia, but there remains as yet no proven medical treatment for senile dementia. Medical assessment of such patients has as its primary aim the exclusion of other potentially treatable causes for the person's condition (see Marsden 1978).

The first signs of dementia are often memory difficulties. These impair new learning ability particularly. Well established habits and memories from the past are usually retained – initially at least. Those affected may forget an appointment, or arrive on the wrong day. They may become lost in unfamiliar surroundings or arrive at the shops and forget what they had intended to buy. The person loses the ability to grasp complex ideas, and reasoning becomes less abstract. Self-neglect may occur, and as the dementia progresses the person may lose the ability to look after such personal needs as washing, dressing, toiletting and even eating.

The pattern of dysfunction varies from person to person; some may have particular difficulties in speech or in perceptuo-motor tasks, like drawing or dressing. The rate of deterioration is also variable – although the progressive nature of the disease is an important feature in distinguishing it from specific brain injury. The rate of deterioration often seems slower when it begins in the 80s, rather than when the person is 60. As a group their life-expectancy is much reduced, but the total time course is extremely variable. Personality changes do sometimes occur and the person may become disinhibited; others maintain an excellent social facade and are able to engage in small talk despite severe deterioration.

Demented people are often said to lack insight into what is happening to them as it is the very organ of insight that is dysfunctional. Certainly some patients deny any problems sometimes to the extent of, for example, accusing neighbours of stealing a purse when in reality they have mislaid it. Others, however, do seem to have some awareness of disintegration, and may complain of loss of memory. It is not unusual for such a person to show signs of anxiety and depression, perhaps in response to the repeated failures being experienced.

As Miller (1977a) points out, the diagnosis of dementia can be made with reasonable accuracy, following careful evaluation and exclusion of other possible causes of the presenting picture. This is particularly so of course where the patient is seen over a length of time and when the disorder is well advanced. In the earlier stages diagnostic problems do arise. Most people would probably have to admit to episodes of forgetfulness and a few of these alone do not constitute a diagnosis of dementia! A progressive deterioration is a key feature, however.

Some elderly depressed people show memory problems and some intellectual impairment. This has been described as 'depressive pseudo-dementia' (Post 1965). In most cases some improvement is noted after appropriate treatment of the depression. However a diagnosis made before antidepressant therapy is likely to be unreliable. Although certain psychological tests are claimed to discriminate well between groups of depressed and demented patients (Kendrick et al 1979), particularly when the assessment is repeated after six weeks or so, there are still patients who remain diagnostic puzzles over a period of months or even years. Diagnostic tests are usually standardised on groups of people with clear-cut depression and dementia, who rarely need to be assessed in this way in practice.

The nature and cause of cognitive impairment in depression remain unclear although studies like that of Miller & Lewis (1977) suggest it may be qualitatively different from that found in dementia. The diagnosis of dementia is not then completely straightforward. Marsden (1978), for example, reports data showing that 21 per cent of patients with dementia referred for neurological evaluation proved not to be demented, and most of those had a depressive illness. Most of the patients were under 70, as were those in a follow-up study of patients diagnosed as having pre-senile dementia, carried out by Ron et al (1979). They rejected this diagnosis (5–15 years after it had been made) in 31 per cent of their sample. Even patients who have retained the diagnosis of dementia over a lengthy period may prove to have no pathological changes in their brains at post-mortem. Conversely some senile plaques are often found in the brains of normal elderly people. Using computed tomography, atrophy of the brain and ventricular enlargement has been shown not to be confined to patients with dementia, and seems to occur more often in depressed patients than in normals (Jacoby & Levy 1980).

To emphasise that the patterns of dysfunction that have been outlined briefly above are *not* the normal expectation for all elderly people, figures for the prevalence of dementia in the elderly will be mentioned. Kay et al (1964) assessed a representative sample of over-65s in Newcastle-upon-Tyne. Five per cent were judged to have severe to moderate mental deterioration; a further five per cent had a mild degree of dementia. The prevalence rises rapidly for elderly people over the age of 80; nearly a quarter of these were found to have some degree of dementia. This is particularly relevant as it is in these older age groups that a large rise in the number of elderly people is anticipated in years to come.

Whilst people with dementia form a minority of elderly people, they are a large (estimated 700 000 in the UK) visible group. They make great demands upon health and social services. Although many are accommodated in institutions, in the UK something like three-quarters of people with dementia will be in the community – living alone, with relatives or friends. Families play a large part in supporting them (Bergmann et al 1978) and the strain on them can be considerable. Kay et al (1964) indicated that institutional placement is not simply determined by severity of dementia, with many severely demented people being supported by families and social services.

Psycho-social factors have not been proved to cause dementia (Garside et al 1965). In some cases a bereavement, change of house or other upheaval brings the dementia to the attention of doctors, social workers, etc. Usually close examination reveals, for example, that the spouse who died was doing a great deal to compensate for the person's deficits that were developing before the bereavement; the change of house removes a number of environmental props that were helping to sustain the person's failing functions, and so on.

Dementia is then a progressive deterioration of intellectual functions, affecting a large minority of elderly people. Diagnosis needs to be made carefully and is not without problems, particularly with respect to depression; depression and dementia not only can have similar manifestations, but also can occur together. It is a condition for which currently no medical treatments are available, and which places great strain on families, hospitals, residential care and community services. It is the problem of elderly people that has the most distressing impact for all concerned, and its study has been hampered by the general lack of positive interest in the elderly, their needs and problems.

A POSITIVE APPROACH

Attitudes towards the elderly in Western society have often in the past been discriminatory, rejecting and negative. Those attributes that elderly people do have have been discounted in a society where speed, innovation and physical attributes are placed on a pedestal. Wisdom, experience and a sense of perspective are not valued as much as in certain other cultures, where to be an elder is an aspiration – rather than a fear – of the young.

If healthy elderly people have received a raw deal, how much more have mentally and physically disabled elderly suffered? In terms of facilities medical geriatric and psychogeriatric units have often been housed in the oldest buildings, quite unsuitable for the purpose. Such hospitals may be in splendid isolation, many miles from relatives, friends and familiar surroundings. The surroundings may be glorious, but few go out and enjoy them. Visitors – often equally elderly – find that the journey restricts visits severely.

The role of the staff has been seen as custodial rather than restorative or treatment-orientated. Morale, typically, has been low; recruitment of staff difficult. Extra payments for working on geriatric wards in the UK have been considered necessary. Nurses would be deliberately moved from geriatric wards after a certain time. The expectation was that the work must be unpleasant, tiresome and depressing. Anyone expressing a desire to work in this field was viewed with surprise and bewilderment, as if no one in possession of their senses would choose to do so.

In recent years the growth in the elderly population that has been and is taking place has grasped the attention of those at every level of health, social and voluntary services. Fresh approaches are being pursued, more resources directed towards the ageing population. Custodial care concepts have been replaced by 'community care' as the sheer number of disabled elderly people being supported by relatives, friends and other social supports outside institutions has been realised. More positive approaches are filtering through some institutions catering for the elderly; there is more readiness to review traditional practices.

Attitudes have by no means changed completely. Often there is resistance to change. New ideas often need more resources that are not forthcoming. The elderly are still perceived generally as an unattractive group with whom to work; problems of recruitment in this field occur in a variety of professions – doctors, psychiatrists, nurses, social workers, psychologists etc. Our own profession of clinical psychology has shown an enormous increase in the last five years of the number working at least part of the time with the elderly. Yet this area remains the least attractive area of work for most trainees in clinical psychology.

In this book a particular positive approach to the confused elderly is discussed. This approach is at an early stage of development and many questions remain about it. However by stating the current position we hope that this approach can be used appropriately and usefully. Positive approaches can be misdirected, of course. A current approach, for example, is to give elderly people a great many tangible gifts at Christmas and other special occasions, when many elderly people would prefer companionship throughout the year, rather than being the recipients of seasonal handouts. The development in the UK of a 'hotel' model for residential care to replace the previous work-house system was another well-intentioned positive attempt to improve the lot of the elderly. It can now be seen however, to have resulted in old people's homes where by and large residents have no active role, where interaction is minimal, and where elderly people sit day after day, as if waiting to die. The approach discussed here – Reality Orientation (RO) – does seek to meet elderly confused people's psychological needs. It may be seen as a welcome complement to the provision of physical needs, which of course, in many ways, is much easier.

In the second half of the book, practical guidance is given as to how to put the approach into practice. The importance of seeing each elderly person as a 'whole person' with psychological, social and emotional as well as physical needs cannot be over-emphasised. RO is not a cure-all or a magical formula to solve all the problems of old people. It is certainly the most intensively researched of the psychological approaches to confusion available and is widely applicable. It has been likened to an 'aspirin': it may help some problems considerably, others less so, but sufficiently to aid other intervention. If used flexibly and in the context of the basic attitudes described in Chapter 6, it probably has fewer negative side-effects than aspirin! Indeed many of the side-effects may be positive, perhaps including increased morale among those using it.

Finally Reality Orientation may well mean different things to different workers. It varies in its application according to the special needs of any specific group in any particular area. The methodology which we outline is based on the inspiration of the work of James Folsom and colleagues in the United States, but has been developed and modified in the light of our own experience and research as well as that of other workers in the field.

2

An overview of psychological approaches to the treatment of dementia

INTRODUCTION

RO is not the only psychological treatment approach that has been used in treating the problems of confused elderly people. Barns et al (1973) review a number of treatment modalities, as have Miller (1977b), Woods & Britton (1977) and Shaw (1979). As will become evident, any categorization of these various approaches is inevitably somewhat superficial. There is a considerable overlap and much common ground, which is discussed by Woods & Britton (1977); a similar grouping of approaches will be employed here.

It is impossible to state with any certainty that all studies under review have included patients with senile dementia, who by virtue of the frequency and severity of their problems form the largest target population for RO. We have, however, sought to include only those approaches which seem applicable to such patients, recognising the range of impairment that they present. Thus some approaches may not be applicable to severely demented patients but only to those with more moderate difficulties and vice versa. Attempts will be made to identify the population used – unfortunately sufficient details regarding diagnoses are often not included in a study. The work of Copeland and his colleagues (Copeland 1978) should be noted. This indicates differences in diagnosis of organic brain syndromes between the UK and the USA. Organic brain syndromes are more frequently diagnosed in the USA, although there is no difference in the incidence of the disease in the two countries. Depression appears to be under-diagnosed in the USA, and thus a number of patients have a diagnosis of organic brain syndrome in the USA who would not be so diagnosed in the UK. Finally the methodology of many of the studies does not meet acceptable criteria for evaluation of therapeutic methods. This review then is intended to be indicative of the range and type of approach and suggestive of the kind of results obtained from them.

STIMULATION AND ACTIVITY PROGRAMMES

Sensory deprivation

Cameron (1941) demonstrated elegantly that the often observed increase in confusion and wandering at night in elderly people was related not to the effects of fatigue but simply to the effects of reduced sensory input, by showing that such confusion occurred in a darkened room during daytime. Elderly people may have reduced sensory input by virtue of normal deterioration in sensory acuity. Sight can show loss, as can sensitivity of hearing and touch. Some of the environments in which elderly people live – in institutional care or isolated in the community – can be monotonous and lacking in sensory stimulation. There are instances of voluntary deprivation when a person will choose withdrawal and reject stimulation, refuse to respond to the environment or react to it. In some cases this may be a means of coping with a large, unfamiliar institution.

These considerations suggest that, firstly, sensory deprivation can increase confusion in elderly people, and secondly, that many elderly people are deprived of sensory stimulation. Inglis (1962) drew a parallel with experiments on sensory deprivation in younger people. Briefly these experiments (reviewed by Corso 1967) removed all avenues of sensory stimulation. Some of the methods used included total immersion in a tank of water, bandaging, special helmets and incarceration in a polio life-support. It should be noted that sensory deprivation results as much from the provision of sensory monotony as from the removal of stimulation.

The point to be stressed is that it is *change* in sensory input that is stimulating. In general, such sensory deprivation on young, normal, volunteer subjects produced behaviour similar to that observed in psychotic patients. Such responses included difficulties in thought and concentration, perceptual distortions, thought disorder, hallucinations, deterioration in reasoning, logic and word finding which all occurred after a period of deprivation.

Inglis (1962) argued that elderly patients with memory deficits would be much more vulnerable to the effects of sensory deprivation, because when sensory input is curtailed the person must fall back on his recent memory in order to maintain orientation and clarity of thought. With an impairment of recent memory confusion will occur very quickly indeed as the person has nothing to provide support in the absence of continued input from the environment. So sensory deprivation is seen as interacting with and exacerbating (but not necessarily causing) the memory disorder and underlying cerebral pathology. The weakness of the comparison is that sensory deprivation in elderly patients is presumably long standing, chronic, and partial, whereas for the young volunteers it was acute and probably more extensive. However, several studies which have sought to increase the elderly person's level of sensory stimulation may provide practical evidence for the role of this factor in increasing confusion in elderly people.

Stimulation programmes

Early studies by Pappas et al (1958) and Cosin et al (1958) showed some positive changes compared with control groups. The former study included occupational and recreational therapies plus personalised attention from the nursing staff. The patients had a variety of diagnoses, with approximately half of the 250 – plus patients having a diagnosis of 'chronic brain syndrome'. All diagnostic groups improved with the intensive treatment provided, whereas control patients having a diagnosis of senile brain disease tended to deteriorate. Neither age nor length of hospitalisation affected response to treatment, although older control patients became significantly worse. The changes produced were thought to be in the areas of 'orientation, ideation, and emotional tone', with overt behaviour apparently not improving.

Cosin et al (1958) did find changes in behaviour following the increased stimulation of full occupational therapy, social and domestic activities. Purposive, appropriate types of behaviour increased in their experimental group of patients with senile

dementia. Gains tended to be made in the early part of the programme and were lost when, after four weeks of treatment, the
increased level of stimulation was halted for two weeks.

In Australia, Bower (1967) used a similar programme of stimulation with 25 female patients having senile dementia, working
specifically from the theory outlined above that the effects of
organic change and sensory deprivation interact to produce the
behavioural deficits of dementia. Structured stimulation was programmed for four and a half hours a day five days a week over a six
month period. Significant improvements were noted on independently carried out psychiatric, occupational therapy and nursing
assessments. A control group which could only be rated by the
psychiatrist showed a significant deterioration. However, the rating
of changes by staff directly involved in the stimulation programme
introduced the possibility of some improvement being attributable
to staff expectation of change, rather than to objective observation.
Also, the control group was different in important ways from the
experimental group and so the results, whilst encouraging, are not
conclusive.

The study of Loew & Silverstone (1971) included a more directly
comparable control group. 14 much older (mean 87.5 years) male
patients were exposed to physical, social and psychological stimulation. The diagnostic details, unfortunately, are vague, but apparently the patients were deteriorated physically and/or mentally.
Quantitative and qualitative increases in general energy level following stimulation over a six month period were found. The
experimental group showed a tendency towards improved cognitive functioning. A 10 month follow-up suggested that these
changes had been maintained. The patients in the experimental
group were rated as being more 'critical, demanding and challenging'. It is arguable whether this should be treated as a negative
finding as to some extent these attitudes may be seen as healthy
for an elderly person in this situation, compared with the previous
apathy and inactivity.

Finally, three uncontrolled American studies, which have in fact
included RO as part of a broader multimodal stimulation programme, will be mentioned. Salter & Salter (1975) used RO
together with retraining of daily living activities, recreational
activity, and environmental stimulation. Patients were relatively
young (mean age 68 years) and long-stay (mean 15.9 years) and
many did not have an organic brain syndrome. The proportion of

patients motivated enough to participate in educational and recreational activities increased dramatically over a four month period, and a number of specific improvements were noted in individual patients. Improvements in adjustment to long-term care in a home for the aged are reported by Rodstein (1975) who attempted to encourage participation in democratic self-government as well as using activity and exercise programmes and RO. Finally, Katz (1976) reports results of a study in which 108 nursing home residents received 'a combination of modified Reality Orientation, Remotivation and Milieu and Activity therapies'. Eighty patients were diagnosed as having chronic brain syndrome or senile dementia; 44 per cent of these improved and only 14 per cent became worse over an 18 month period, judged by detailed retrospective ratings.

These studies illustrate that RO can co-exist with other approaches; unfortunately they do not provide any indication regarding the relative importance of the various elements of the total treatment package. The other studies appear to suggest that activity and stimulation may be beneficial. No direct link, however, has been established with the sensory deprivation theory. Many of the reported changes might be seen as the results of staff encouraging and reinforcing more active patterns of behaviour rather than simply additional sensory stimulation leading directly to changes in behaviour. For example Loew & Silverstone's (1971) programme included toilet re-training, encouragement of self-dressing, having meals together, keeping a daily calendar and joining off-ward events. There was even a sheltered workshop available. Undoubtedly, all this is stimulating, but it is surely simplistic to view this varied, wide-ranging programme only in such terms. A more tightly controlled experimental situation would be required to test the sensory deprivation hypothesis further and to evaluate to what extent alleviation of sensory deprivation per se is sufficient to produce changes in the elderly.

Readers interested in the kinds of stimulating activities used are referred to Richman (1969) who describes 'Sensory Training', a group method in which all the senses of quite deteriorated patients are stimulated, as well as to the various studies mentioned above.

Physical exercise

Many of the above studies have deliberately or incidentally

included a fair amount of basic physical exercise (e.g. Rodstein 1975, Loew & Silverstone 1971). In this section further research will be described in which this component of activity and stimulation programmes has been isolated.

There is a fair amount of evidence that, in general, exercise is beneficial for elderly people (e.g. Barry et al 1966). Powell (1974) examined the effects of an hour of mild exercise five times a week over a 12 week period on elderly psychiatric hospital patients (mean age 69.3 years). Average length of stay in hospital was 24.3 years, so clearly many had chronic disorders. The 30 patients involved were in three groups – no treatment, exercise therapy, and a 'social therapy' group to control for the effects of increased attention. The 'social therapy' group had no physical activity, but did take part in arts and crafts work, games and so forth, for the same length of time and with the same amount of staff involvement as the exercise group. Changes in cognitive functioning, as measured by the Wechsler Memory Scale and the Progressive Matrices tests – favouring the exercise group – were found. Corresponding improvements in the patients' behaviour as rated by the nursing staff were not apparent – indeed there was a slight non-significant trend for the exercise group to deteriorate compared with the other groups on these measures. Powell offers the interpretation that this may arise from increased self-sufficiency, following on from cognitive improvement, awakening antagonism towards hospitalisation and its enforced routine, which again may be seen as an improvement over apathy. The lack of improvement in the 'social therapy' group is seen as related to the possibility of 'shutting off' these therapeutic activities through lack of interest, whereas the physical exercise is much more difficult to avoid covertly.

Further support for the effectiveness of physical therapy, on cognitive functioning at least, is provided by Diesfeldt & Diesfeldt-Groenendijk (1977). Their 40 patients were an older group (mean age 82 years) and all were thought to have an organic brain syndrome, with an average duration of hospitalization of 19 months. Two cognitive assessments were made with a one month interval. Half the patients took part in a 40 minute mild exercise session shortly before the retest, the other half did not. Patients who took part in the exercise session did better on a memory task than the control group, both on recall and recognition measures. General behavioural changes were not examined in this study.

There is, thus, a little evidence that physical exercise, by itself, can produce positive changes, specifically in cognitive functioning, but further studies are needed to elucidate the nature of the changes and how they are brought about. Physical activity in these two studies has been highly structured – light bending and stretching exercises whilst sitting in a chair, throwing a ball, knocking down skittles, brisk walking, rhythmical movements etc., all demanding task attention. The fact that the most active group of psychogeriatric patients – the so-called 'wanderers' who often appear to be walking around the ward or home from morning to night – do not treat themselves by their continual activity (Cornbleth 1977) suggests that it is the structured aspect of the exercise that is important. Physical exercise may be important in that it is one of the simplest forms of activity for this population.

CHANGES IN THE ENVIRONMENT

Introduction

This group of approaches is based on the underlying idea that the elderly person will respond to his or her environment, which can be manipulated to produce and maintain positive changes in the person's functioning.

Clearly there is an overlap with the previous section, where a stimulating environment was the therapeutic tool, and the next section where behavioural methods largely based on environmental manipulation will be discussed. RO also has effects on the person's overall environment through 24 hour RO. In this section those studies will be discussed that seem not to fall within these other approaches in any obvious way. This overlap may extend, however, to the processes by which these studies actually have produced changes in more subtle ways. In fact very few studies have examined in any detail exactly how changes come about at a finer level of analysis.

Physical changes in the environment

This includes attempts to bring about changes by structural alteration or by rearrangement in some way of the physical environment.

The classic report is that of Sommer & Ross (1958). They noted that a ward for geriatric patients – predominant diagnosis being arteriosclerosis and mean age 74 years – despite cheerful renovation and up-grading showed little sign of any human interaction! Chairs for instance were arranged mainly around the room and unsociably side by side, making interaction very difficult. Sommer & Ross sum up the position in this way:

'It seemed we had made strangers of our patients. They became observers; silent individuals sitting eternally in a waiting room for a train that never comes'.

Social interaction was recorded to establish a baseline. Then chairs were arranged in small groups around coffee tables, so that the patients sat facing one another to allow conversation to flow more freely if desired. The tables were useful resting places for magazines, flowers and other materials. Social interaction almost doubled after this re-arrangement.

However, the implementation of such an apparently simple change was not without problems. The patients themselves continually moved the chairs back to the walls and the staff found it hard to adjust to a less tidy and organised arrangement which impeded cleaning and transit.

This endeavour has probably been duplicated many many times over the past few years and Peterson et al (1977) have published a study replicating Sommer & Ross's work. They showed that talking increased with the arrangement of a few chairs around a table, but if the group was enlarged somewhat there was no improvement in comparison with the around-the-walls arrangement. Once again these authors found the patients persistently returning the chairs to the walls! In our experience if patients do not do this the domestic staff will in order to facilitate their work. Sommer & Ross suggest that people usually prefer to have their backs to something solid. This may be to increase security or to satisfy curiosity and ensure that all visitors and ward activities remain within their scrutiny! A sense of territory and the sanctity of the status quo in the institution may also be important factors in accounting for the patient's resistance to change. For example, Lipman (1968) has documented the extraordinary discomfort old people's homes residents will accept rather than move from 'their' particular seat. It may be necessary to place obstruction – partitions, pieces of furniture and so on – behind the chairs in the new arrangement for it to become permanent (Marston & Gupta 1977).

On a wider scale there has been some interest in the effects of the design of residential homes on the pattern of activity, interactions and functioning of the residents. Cluff & Campbell (1975) have related in an old people's home the configuration of the corridors on which the residents' rooms are placed to residents' satisfaction, social relationships, frequency of activity etc. For instance residents placed in a room at the end of a corridor spend more time in their own rooms. Harris et al (1977) arrived at a similar conclusion regarding the tendency of lengthy corridors to discourage residents' mobility in an observational study of eight purpose-built homes of widely varying design. Among other interesting findings they suggested that if residents were grouped in areas easily accessible to staff then the latter behaved in such a way as to encourage dependency.

A major aim of this particular study was to examine the extent to which residents who were 'confused' related and interacted with residents who were 'rational'. All the homes included had a mixture of 'confused' and 'rational' residents: there has been some controversy as to whether this mixing is the most appropriate way to meet the needs of the two groups. The case for integration includes the idea that the confused residents will benefit from the stimulation of being with rational people who are able to help their confused companions. Against integration is the notion that the rational ones will ostracise and exclude confused residents and that far from helping them may in fact refuse to have anything to do with them. In the UK both mixed and segregated homes have been built in different areas. Harris et al's careful observational research showed clearly that in fact mixed homes are not integrated in practice. Confused residents are segregated – in different sitting areas in a different wing or floor, with little if any interaction occurring between the two groups. This effective segregation seemed to occur despite the different designs of building. However, Harris et al feel that the design of a home that would make segregation and unnecessary dependence on staff more difficult than integration and independence would have more chance of success in combating staff and resident attitudes that appear often to be in the opposite direction. These design ideas are amplified by Lipman & Slater (1977) and include the notion of a small home built with a vertical (rather than the conventional horizontal 'corridor' arrangement) grouping of 'family units' in which about eight rational and confused residents would be mixed, with residents having a flatlet that could be used as more than a bedroom and in which they could prepare some meals if they so wished. Staff areas would be designed to be well away from these 'family units' to encourage independence, although some small communal facilities for use by any resident, closer to staff access, would be provided. These ideas have yet to be put to the test and as Lipman & Slater admit, changes in staff attitude are needed together with changes in design if their aims of integration and independence are to be achieved. The physical and attitudinal changes needed for 'family units' to be established within an old people's home or hospital will be discussed in the section on group living below.

Finally Matthews & Kemp (1979) report a study in which the day room of a psychogeriatric ward, housing 'severely mentally infirm' patients, in a large mental hospital was divided into four areas each decorated and furnished in different period 'styles' – Victorian/Edwardian; 1920s/1930s; 1950s; and also a normal modern hospital upgraded style. Direct observations of patients' behaviour were carried out before and after the change took place. Overall there were improvements in activity levels – both purposive and non-purposive – and a reduction in passivity. However, social interaction did not improve. As regards the particular rooms the oldest type was less used whereas the 1950s and modern rooms were quite popular. This was a surprising result in view of the hypothesis that older people would react better to surroundings reminiscent of their youth when they were perhaps happy and more active. The authors note that the rooms less used were also farthest from the toilet and this, in view of proneness to incontinence, is probably a significant observation. The nursing staff also commented that these rooms were probably too 'posh' to be other than admired and the objects on display fit only to be polished and carefully replaced. The chairs too may have been less comfortable. This part of the study suggests important variables which need to be adequately controlled and matched in future projects of this nature. The overall changes in activity levels noted earlier clearly cannot be attributed to any specific environmental changes and may be a response to non-specific aspects of the investigation. An important finding that may be of general significance however, was a dramatic reduction in the number of accidents; there was now much more solid furniture around to be clung on to and carpets had replaced linoleum obviating the risk of slippery floors.

There is then some evidence for physical environment having an influence on the behaviour of confused patients and although efforts to improve function by changing the physical environment can only be said to have shown limited success, in other sections it will be seen that these physical changes are often an important part of other approaches.

Prosthetic environments

For a variety of physical disabilities aids, or prostheses are available to help in the restoration of a competent performance, e.g. dentures, glasses, hearing aids. Lindsley (1964) advanced the notion of creating a prosthetic environment for geriatric patients in which their disabilities are compensated for by special features of that environment. Miller (1977a, p 133) expands on this theme, relating it specifically to confused and demented patients.

The elderly person is not exactly retrained – although some prostheses may require the person to learn how to use them before they can be effective. Thus for a patient who has difficulty in finding the toilet, and because of this is incontinent, a coloured line leading to the toilet marked on the floor could be part of the prosthetic environment (Pollock & Liberman 1974). This would presuppose that the patient could learn the new piece of information – the blue line leads to the toilet.

Other examples of prosthetic aids for this population are the special implements devised by occupational therapists and others to assist those with poor eating and dressing skills – nonslip mats for plates, thick handles for utensils to assist grip, Velcro fastening to replace buttons etc. Signs and memory aids which will be discussed later are also prosthetic. Jones & Adam (1979) have suggested that microprocessor technology could lead to the use of much more complex memory aids. A cassette recorder for instance, could provide the person with information and also store information for later use. In order for such a system to prove valuable to those living in the community a great deal of development will be necessary. It is interesting to reflect that technology has advanced sufficiently to aid the shopkeeper by signalling when unpaid-for goods are removed from his shop whereas wards may have to lock their doors to prevent a wandering patient from getting lost or hurt on the busy streets outside.

Lindsley makes a number of suggestions as to how input to the elderly can be more effective – the use of more than one sense (e.g. both a gong and a flashing light to indicate lunchtime) and how to facilitate their responses (larger switches, and less susceptible to being triggered off inadvertently).

Fine (1972) in a discussion of 'geriatric ergonomics' describes how the physical environment can effect mobility and micturition – two essentials for the survival of the elderly person. Urinary incontinence may result from losing the 'race between bladder and legs' and in this context high hospital beds and excessive distances to the ward toilet are undoubtedly unhelpful. As was shown above, more stable furniture on a ward can assist mobility. The vast empty space on many wards must seem like an eternity of space to a frail old person faced with the prospect of finding her way to the toilet. Observations have shown difficulty in negotiating even the new 'highly polished' non-slip vinyl flooring. To old eyes it appears dangerous and it is walked upon as though it was a sheet of ice – the assurances of the designers are not enough to promote confidence!

At this stage there has been little attempt to evaluate prosthetic or ergonomic approaches. The ideas are promising, but as yet there is little hard evidence to support them.

Milieu approaches

These seek to bring about changes in the functioning of the aged by modifying, not so much the physical environment, but more the social and interpersonal atmosphere of the ward, and the expectations of staff and patients. Thus Gottesman (1969, 1973) describes Milieu Therapy as counteracting 'social death'. Patients are provided with normal social roles to enable continued participation in areas of society where they are still able to make a contribution of some sort. In many ways it seeks to prevent or remedy the effects of institutionalisation, where in the past the institution itself has in effect encouraged patients to be dependent and apathetic by providing a purposeless existence.

Early accounts of this kind of approach (e.g. Donahue 1962) reported promising results with elderly patients who had been hospitalised for many years. A considerable number were eventually discharged – albeit with continued support – to the community. In Gottesman's own research the emphasis was on gradually increasing the demands being made of the patient and in encouraging greater responsibility for self-care and management. The provision of a sheltered workshop was seen as crucial. The patient was able to produce something useful and of good quality, and with the remuneration received was able to be a consumer as well as a worker. This approach led to greater social cohesion and some decrease of symptoms on interview. More participants worked and shaved themselves than those on the control ward. No differential improvements were seen in intellectual functioning or in observable 'odd' behaviours. Although the diagnosis of 'chronic brain syndrome' was applied to many of them, Bok (1971) indicated that they were ambulant, continent and not physically or psychologically deteriorated.

This group, who have been described as 'graduates', remain in fairly large numbers in many psychiatric hospitals and related institutions – despite attempts to prevent new long-term admissions over the past few years. They do seem to show some evidence of being helped by this change in milieu, which might be characterised by a change in staff attitudes from custodial to rehabilitative. However, is there any evidence that more clearly demented patients can benefit from such a change in milieu? Clearly, this may be possible if a custodial environment led to a demented person underfunctioning; the change of environment may then lead to the person functioning as well as possible within the context of any existing organic brain disease.

In a recent study of interaction between staff and residents in eight old people's homes in the UK, Lipman et al (1979) conclude that staff-resident interactions do not differ in quality for residents rated 'rational' or 'confused'. Most concern physical care, rather than being supportive to the person's psychological needs. Staff are dominant in deciding 'When, how and with whom residents eat, sleep, sit, bath and go to the toilet.'

Obviously even in relatively small, recently established community settings for the elderly, custodial care flourishes, whether the residents are confused or not. In a nursing home in the USA, where presumably some proportion of the residents are suffering from dementia (no details supplied in the study), Langer & Rodin (1976) showed that a very brief, simple environmental manipulation could be effective. One group of residents had stressed to them that they had a great deal of control and choice over their lives in the home; another group were merely told that the staff wished them to be happy. The first group improved significantly over the latter control group, on measures of alertness, active participation and general sense of well being.

There is, unfortunately, little documentation of programmes emphasising choice for confused patients or encouragement for self-responsibility. Savage & Widdowson (1974) report an attempt to do this on a psychogeriatric ward where virtually all patients were diagnosed as dementing. The nursing team enterprisingly looked at their own activities in relation to the routine of the ward and with regard to the individual's needs and abilities. They felt that the rigid routine of the ward was encouraging dependency, as it demanded a pressure to ensure that dressing, washing, eating etc. were performed by a certain time. This had resulted in staff completing the tasks instead of allowing the patient to care for herself. Patients were given much more responsibility for their own care and events were rearranged to meet this aim. Breakfast was available, for example, whenever the patients were ready rather than at a set time. Formal results are not available but the staff reported that there was less incontinence and more responsiveness generally.

Gustafsson (1976) does report an evaluation of such changes. Twenty-one patients in a Swedish hospital, mostly diagnosed as senile dementia cases with a high level of behavioural disability – poor self care, disorientation etc., were split into an experimental and a control group. The milieu changes were introduced sequentially, allowing a multiple baseline design for the experimental group. Changes in social interaction, eating skills and level of activity were monitored by direct observation of time-sampled behaviour.

The first change was to afternoon coffee. Previously this had been brought to the patients on a tray, sugar and cream had already been added, and a piece of cake provided. It was made unnecessary for them to move from the chair in which they were sitting. The experimental group now went to another room where coffee, cups, and all the necessary ingredients were placed on two tables. Staff were not present, and they were left to fend for themselves. They were left to choose what they wanted and where they were to sit. In short, a single environmental manipulation allowed more independence and choice and created a social situation. Meal times were also changed for this group. The previous routine based on time, when patients would be fed if they were too slow was eliminated, and free choice and unlimited time were offered instead.

The final change was to provide activity material on the ward – games, books, jig-saws etc. For one week this was left to patients' initiative to use and was available to both experimental and control groups. Then for one week the experimental group was encouraged by staff to use the material, then for another week the patients were again left to their own devices.

The results of the study are clear-cut and dramatic. Social interaction during afternoon coffee increased greatly in the experimental group and eating skills improved following the meal-time changes. Their level of activity increased when compared to the control group in the final week of the study after they had been encouraged to use the materials. The results provide strong support for the use of such an approach, encouraging independence and choice, particularly where the existing milieu may have led to under-functioning and patients not using all their skills and abilities to the full.

However, the whole milieu approach is dependent on staff changes of attitudes (Gottesman 1973). Bok (1971) and Bayne (1971) point out how difficult it can be in some situations for staff to accept patients taking responsibility for themselves and being more independent. We know of hospitals and old people's homes where efforts have been made to, for example, increase the social impact of meal-times, much as Gustafsson was able to do. After a few months the old pattern had returned, even though as Gustafsson points out the new regime may involve less burden for the staff (e.g. in not feeding patients unnecessarily). The lesson to be learned is that staff attitudes can be extremely resistant to change, and that sources of reinforcement may be complex and subtle. They may for example involve a desire to care for someone physically, which becomes difficult to satisfy with this sort of change of milieu. Practical aspects of staff attitudes will be discussed in Chapter 9, but suffice to say here that in many ways they are the key to implementing this approach (and others) which clearly has some limited empirical support.

Sheltered workshops

As mentioned above these are an important part of the milieu approach. Nathanson & Reingold (1969) have demonstrated their feasibility with patients having moderate to severe chronic brain syndrome. These patients were able to maintain their participation in the workshop for periods of well over three months. MacDonald & Settin (1978) showed that participation in a workshop was related to improvement in life satisfaction and social interest for nursing home residents (no diagnostic details given) compared with no treatment controls and a basic RO group. No changes in ward behaviour as rated by the nursing staff were apparent, however. Workshop sessions were held three times a week for 50 minutes over a five week period. The activity was making gifts for a children's home. The last session involved going to the children's home and actually giving them the gifts. The activity was purposeful with a clear end result. This is probably preferable to an activity which is repetitive but seems to have little intrinsic purpose or value. However, with severely deteriorated patients the problem will be to find an activity simple enough for the patient to be able to manage. The sheltered workshop is worthy of further exploration and may be of particular value with 'mild' to 'moderately' demented patients attending a day centre.

Group living

The group living concept combines aspects of milieu therapy with some changes to the physical environment. It is currently attracting much interest in the UK and is being implemented in many old people's homes. Regrettably there is as yet no evaluation of its effectiveness; only anecdotal information is available.

Although not involved in the first group living homes, Marston & Gupta (1977) and Gupta (1979) have done much to develop the concept in theory and in practice. They point out that a group of 40 or 50 – quite common in the lounge of many homes – is so large as to inhibit personal interaction. A study of homes in Cheshire by Townsend & Kimbell (1975) showed a positive correlation between the intensity of large group activity and the degree of confusion amongst the residents. On the evidence of this and other investigations Marston & Gupta suggest that groups are at their most effective when there are eight to 12 members. One might speculate that confused residents in particular would be adversely effected by larger groups, in view of their greater difficulty in remembering who people are and in forming relationships. For a group to work it requires a shared interest, activity or purpose – manifestly lacking in many homes. The rationale for having groups at all is the often reported loneliness and apathy experienced in many homes. If effective groups can be established then resident-to-resident interaction will increase. Together with this aim, choice and involvement of individuals in their own self-care were identified as objectives in raising 'quality of life' for residents. In many ways this group-living is a small group milieu approach.

A home with 40 residents would then be split into four or five groups. Each would have its own lounge/diner, with tea-making facilities, TV etc. Each group shares the range of self-care activities. They can get up in the morning at any time and help themselves to a light breakfast. At lunch and evening meal the group members set the table, serve themselves and afterwards wash up. They make their own drinks and have a choice of food, and are even consulted regarding menus! They are encouraged to participate in the choice of furniture and decorations for their rooms. They may make their own beds and clean their rooms. It has proved possible to adapt older homes at very little cost to this system which certainly does not need to be confined to purpose-built homes. Confused residents are integrated into the groups and are helped by their fitter peers, whilst carrying out what tasks they can. Rejection of the less able seems to occur less frequently in smaller groups.

Implementation of this approach requires consultation with residents, relatives and staff. Training in the new methods is needed for the latter and considerable support for all concerned in the first few weeks (described as 'utter confusion' in one home!) as the transition takes place and all concerned adjust to the new pattern.

The results – anecdotally – seem promising and exciting. Residents who were thought to be confused now play leading roles in the life of some homes. The dormant abilities of some residents have been revealed. They became more vocal and active, with activity centred around the domestic tasks rather than craft work etc. Staff now have more time to spend with residents and know them much more closely, and 'the number of so-called very confused people has been dramatically reduced'. Incontinence is also less. Relatives, volunteers and neighbours come into the home more and are entertained to tea by the groups who are now in a position to offer hospitality.

That this type of approach is also feasible in hospital settings is shown by an experimental placing of geriatric patients in a group living bungalow ward while their traditional ward was being upgraded. An anecdotal report on this was made by Adams et al

(1979). Marked changes in activity and interaction were apparent with the change in environment, which allowed the patients to do more for themselves. Incontinence and confusion, once again, seemed to improve and a number of patients improved enough to be discharged home.

A controlled evaluation of group living would be of immense value and it would be of interest to take as a comparison a large group situation where choice and independence in self-care were systematically encouraged. The problems group living has to contend with are firstly, elderly people who are 'loners' and do not wish to integrate into a group, who may even feel threatened by such unaccustomed intimacy. Some arrangements would have to be incorporated to allow such people to be apart as they wished. Secondly, there is the inevitable problem of staff attitudes. Marston & Gupta (1977) report that senior staff felt threatened by the proposed change and Adams et al (1979) also report that some staff felt unable to adjust to the idea of independent patients. Residential care in the UK is largely based on a hotel model with all services being provided for residents, perhaps as a reaction to the old work-house system and its abuses. The model accepting that care is *provided* is so well-established that a new model to encourage independence is quite contrary to the old rule and as such is bound to encounter resistance. If group living can gain empirical support for its effects on confusion it will be in a strong position to overcome this resistance, and to replace a model that has encouraged apathy, withdrawal, loneliness and a neglect of psychological needs in far too many residential settings for the elderly.

BEHAVIOURAL APPROACHES

Introduction

Behaviour modification has been extremely important in a number of areas of therapeutic endeavour in recent years – mental handicap, chronic schizophrenia, various problems of children etc. It is a rapidly expanding and developing field based on an empirically derived body of knowledge and related to psychological models of how new behaviour is learned and maintained–such as operant conditioning. A behavioural approach for the aged will be described more fully in Chapter 10. In essence, behaviour is broken down into specific, clearly defined components – this makes programme targets easier to establish. The conditions under which the behaviour will occur are ascertained (the discriminative stimuli) and the consequences of the behaviour are examined. If the result is something the person wants or desires then the behaviour has been positively reinforced and is more likely to occur again. If following the behaviour something unpleasant is removed then this is described as negative reinforcement so the probability of the behaviour recurring is also increased. On the other hand if something pleasant is removed, or something unpleasant added, then the behaviour is punished. For details of the complex relationships between frequency of behaviour, reinforcements and punishment readers are referred to a text-book on behaviour modification such as Kazdin (1975), or Kanfer & Goldstein (1975).

A number of authors have advocated using behaviour modification with the elderly e.g. Lindsley (1964), Cautela (1966, 1969), Pincus (1968), Labouvie (1973), Hoyer (1973), Hoyer et al (1975), Harris S L et al (1977), Baltes & Barton (1977). They have all written encouragingly, if speculatively, about the possibilities of a behavioural approach to the elderly and their problems. Although biological processes do occur in ageing and dementia, the elderly person's actual performance is always a result of interaction with the environment. If any learning is possible for the dementing person then the behavioural approach will facilitate the learning process. It will indicate the environmental conditions needed for new behaviour to be learned, or for existing behaviour to be maintained. – which is just as important. The environmental changes here are very finely regulated and individualised. They relate to the antecedent conditions and consequences which the environment – in its broadest sense – provides for the behaviour in question.

Although Woods & Britton (1977) have argued that many of the other approaches reviewed in this chapter can be usefully conceptualised in behavioural terms, there is disappointingly little research on the use of behaviour modification per se with patients clearly diagnosed as having dementia. Before reviewing relevant literature, it is important to clarify the learning potential of the dementing person if the approach is to be seen as at all viable with this population.

Can elderly people with dementia learn?

Studies have already been described showing the responses of elderly people to environmental conditions and so demonstrating that all learning ability has not been lost. The characteristic of dementia – a deficit in learning new material – is easily observed for example by providing a patient with a fictitious name and address and asking for a recall in five minutes. Such tests reveal the existence of a learning deficit and are not designed to provide evidence of any retained ability. What is of interest is to examine what conditions are most favourable for learning to take place.

Miller (1975) showed that patients with pre-senile dementia did badly in comparison with normal controls in learning lists of words when the amount of learning was assessed by recall or recognition. However, if recall was aided by giving the patient the initial letters of the word to be recalled then near-normal retention was apparent. If this finding could be replicated with old dementing people then this would provide at least one indication that learning can occur under certain conditions. This technique has, of course, immediate practical application in the giving of clues and prompts.

Elderly brain-damaged subjects were included in a study of conditioning of verbal responses carried out by Halberstam & Zaretsky (1969). The task looked at the increase in responses of a particular verbal class that were reinforced simply by the experimenter saying 'very good'. The brain-damaged group learned as well as the control group although they were generally slower in performance. A further study by Halberstam et al (1971) focussed on avoidance learning. In a laboratory situation subjects learned to make a motor response when a sound or light was switched on to indicate that a mild electric shock would follow. Again brain-damaged subjects showed clear learning of the required responses, although they were slower in making the response. An overlearning procedure, in which a large number of additional conditioning sessions were given, proved of benefit in improving the speed and quality of the responses. In both these studies brain-damaged subjects seem to have had focal impairments from cerebrovascular accidents rather than the diffuse impairments associated with dementia.

Demented patients with memory disorder were required to pull a lever to obtain a reward in a laboratory task of operant conditioning carried out by Ankus & Quarrington (1972). Forty-eight patients (aged 55–86 years) were included in the trial, and it appeared that the appropriateness of the particular reinforcer used for particular patients was of importance. Female patients preferred monetary rewards, and the male patients fluids – beer etc. Apparently this could be related to the opportunities females had to spend money in the setting involved. When the appropriate reinforcer was used relatively normal learning took place of the relationship between lever pulling and reward operative at any particular time, particularly if only gradual increases in the ratio of pulls to reward were made.

So there is some evidence to show the possibilities of new learning taking place in patients with pre-senile dementia, elderly patients with brain damage following cerebrovascular accident and, finally, elderly patients with dementia and severe memory disorder. It would appear that behaviour modification does have some learning potential on which to work, but clearly particular attention to maximising the possibilities of learning taking place will have to be given in this population.

Applied studies of behaviour modification

Behaviour modification has been applied extensively and imaginatively to the problems and needs of elderly people. A number of studies reviewed by Baltes & Barton (1977) have attempted (usually successfully) to modify intellectual behaviours in apparently normal older people. Thus Hoyer et al (1973) were able to show increases in response speed, following appropriate training, in elderly women. Other studies have sought such varied aims as increasing recruitment at a 'community-based nutritious meals programme for senior citizens' (Bunck & Iwata 1978) and increasing the amount of personal mail received by nursing home residents (Goldstein & Baer 1976). Disappointingly few studies have however been directed at the problems posed by dementia. In many of the studies that have taken place in old age institutions it is extremely difficult to ascertain the nature of the patients involved. In the following sections, on particular areas of application of behaviour modification, some attempts will be made to delineate the kinds of subjects taking part.

Eating

Several workers have reported one or more single-case studies. Geiger & Johnson (1974) increased the proportion of meals that six 'geriatric patients' ate correctly, in the sense that they consumed at least a specified portion of the meal. Prompting and reinforcement were used to bring about the changes. When these were withdrawn the amount eaten dropped again until they were reintroduced. Baltes & Zerbe (1976 a, b) report two cases where nursing home residents who were fed by care staff were helped by a careful training procedure, including graduated prompts and social reinforcement, to be much more independent in their eating. One of the subjects was 79 years old and had suffered a stroke, but the other subject was not reported to be cognitively impaired in any way. Finally, Burton & Spall (1981) report a case of an 80 year old depressed lady who was not feeding herself, and causing much concern. A programme of prompting, manual graduated guidance and reinforcement was successful in reinstating normal eating habits, maintained at a four month follow-up. Results for this area are encouraging but it is worth noting that only nine subjects are reviewed here – none reported to have dementia.

Mobility

Here again several case reports are available. Libb & Clements (1969) were successful in increasing exercise rate (on an exercise bicycle!) in three out of four subjects. They received tokens as reinforcers which were exchanged at the end of the session for something more tangible. These patients were not described in detail, other than 'regressed' with a diagnosis of chronic brain syndrome. Sachs (1975) includes two case reports of residents with mobility restrictions following a hip fracture some time previously. One had a chronic brain syndrome with Parkinson's disease. The walking of both improved when walking was systematically and specifically reinforced. Two further residents – one aged 92 years with a mild memory defect – who were confined to wheel-chairs for no clear physical reason were shown to increase their frequency of independent walking when, and only when, this was reinforced and prompted (MacDonald & Butler 1974). Although still only a few studies have been performed, a fair degree of improvement has been noted and there is an indication that some cognitively impaired residents were included.

Social and verbal interaction

Lack of social interaction is a commonplace observation in institutions for the elderly, and a few studies have attempted to use behaviour modification to increase the amount of social interaction. Most studies have, however, taken the patients away from the ward setting and placed them in a specially formed small group rather than modifying the behaviour in the natural setting directly.

Mueller & Atlas (1972) used token reinforcement together with conversation-facilitating activities to increase social interaction in a small group of five isolated patients described as being 'in reasonable touch with reality' (and therefore not likely to be dementing). Male chronic schizophrenics were the target population in Hoyer et al's (1974) attempts to increase verbal responses. Token and material reinforcers were used here and some prompting with two groups of four patients each. Verbal responses did increase – both for those receiving reinforcements and for those who simply saw the others receiving tokens etc. for increased verbalisation. Hoyer et al attribute this result to modelling effects.

A group activity was also the focus for intervention by Linsk et al (1975). Here 15 or so residents were involved who were 'a cross-section of the alert and confused residents'. This study probably included some subjects with dementia. Evidence is presented that the group's verbal behaviour increased during treatment phases; it was much less in the baseline and return to baseline phases of the reversal design employed. Related changes in the group leader's behaviour were noted. Increases in the number of questions asked (prompts to talk) and the amount of the leader's listening behaviour (a reinforcement for talking) were recorded. Throughout these studies it is apparent that arranging favourable conditions for talking (games, questions etc) can be of great importance in eliciting this behaviour in socially withdrawn elderly people, thus providing appropriate behaviour to be reinforced.

A single case study included in Sach's (1975) series showed increased social interaction in the natural setting for a 91 year old 'socially inactive' nursing home resident. Social praise was used to reinforce him for initiating conversation and responding to others. His rate of interaction decreased when this reinforcement was withdrawn, and increased when it was reinstated. Finally premealtime interaction in three 'chronically socially isolated' (but lucid) residents was increased, contingent on verbal prompting and social reinforcement by MacDonald (1978). The results for social interaction are then generally positive but most studies have not included dementia, and few have taken place in the natural setting of a lounge, living room or day room.

To some extent the assumption has been made so far that the elderly patients involved, if reinforced for social interaction and placed in a situation which prompts and is conducive to such interaction, do have the necessary skills to interact successfully. However an alternative model might emphasise that admission to a residential facility, as Berger & Rose (1977) argue, is a dramatic change to the patient's social environment. This necessitates an adjustment to a range of new situations and may require the development of new skills previously not in the patient's repertoire. Berger & Rose taught such residents social interaction skills with limited success, using behavioural methods of social skills training used widely with younger patients. The residents involved were selected to exclude disorientation. A more recent study by Lopez et al (1980) also excluded those with severe organic impairment, but nevertheless simple cognitive testing indicated a 'moderate level of confusion'. Structured Learning Therapy (SLT) (Goldstein 1973) was the interpersonal skills training package used to teach 56 elderly in-patients the skill of 'starting a conversation'. Positive results were obtained, with some evidence of generalization from the learning situation to new situations especially when 'over-learning' – repeated practice – was used. In a further study Hoyer et al (1980) sought to identify patient characteristics related to the skills of 'expressing a complaint', using SLT with a similar group of patients. Mental status – i.e. current information, orientation etc. – was the best predictor of outcome. This suggests that more demented patients would benefit least from this approach, although the fact that the mean length of hospitalisation in both studies was around 20 years suggests that poor performance on Mental Status may have been related to other factors (apathy, withdrawal etc.) than memory disorder related to dementia.

In some ways it seems rather unreasonable to necessitate elderly patients learning the new skills needed to interact in current residential care facilities. Perhaps more important as a priority is establishing conditions in residential care where normal social behaviour is encouraged and elicited, and the social skills that most elderly have before admission could then be maintained and enjoyed by all concerned. Some patients may still have difficulties in social skills, but to concentrate on training adjustment to unsatisfactory conditions is misguided. It is preferable to attempt to change the environment itself.

Participation in activities

Lack of activity is another often-described feature of institutions, and goes hand in hand with lack of social interaction. Quilitch (1974) used token reinforcement to increase the numbers of elderly persons undertaking purposeful activity, but did not test whether it was simply the provision of the activity (a Bingo game) that led to the increased activity. On this occasion tokens were exchanged for refreshment at the end of the Bingo session. The increase in activity occurred despite many residents being 'disabled, regressed and incontinent'.

Two studies by McClannahan & Risley (1974, 1975) increased participation in activities in a 100-bedded nursing home, where half the residents were diagnosed as having 'arteriosclerosis and other heart and vascular diseases'. The first study employed a somewhat artificial activity – residents went to a designated area, had a brief conversation with the experimenter and received a little spending money. The number of residents taking part was shown to be influenced by whether or not the activity was previously announced and whether or not spending money was given. Thus the least number of residents took part when there was no announcement and no money and most when there were three types of announcement and money. The second study involved puzzles and games being available on some days for an hour a day. Results indicated that when encouragement to use the equipment was given an average of three-quarters of the residents were engaged in activities; on days when no equipment was available only 20 per cent were active in some way or other; and when equipment was available, but no prompting given, only a slightly higher proportion were active (25 per cent) than when the equipment was not there. Prompting and encouragement then have a big role in the usefulness of recreational equipment. Similarly Jenkins et al (1977) in the UK increased the number of residents engaged in activity by providing material for 45 minutes a day in two old people's homes. Again considerable prompting was used, and also continued praise and encouragement throughout the session. Of particular importance here is that one home was specifically for the 'elderly mentally infirm' where all had a diagnosis of dementia. Further studies by this research team have explored other activities (e.g. Powell et al 1979, on indoor gardening) and how – given the considerable encouragement required to obtain participation from residents – these programmes can prove feasible in homes where staff resources are limited.

Finally an intervention aiming to increase both participation in an activity and social interaction was attempted by Blackman et al (1976). They increased attendance at a social area of a home for the aged, by providing reinforcements and prompts to attend. Social interaction was not specifically prompted or reinforced, other than by the social setting and by enjoyment of the interaction. The increased social interaction was entirely between residents. Staff-resident interaction levels were not altered. Two-thirds of the residents were described as 'confused and disoriented' by nursing staff and so probably included a fair number with dementia.

Continence

In our experience incontinence is one of the most difficult and disturbing problems facing those caring for the aged. It need hardly be said that the problem is deeply disturbing for the elderly patient. In an unpublished study carried out by Woods & Britton (1975) over a third of elderly patients in a large psychiatric hospital were incontinent of urine by day more than once a week. Over half of these patients were in fact incontinent several times daily.

Incontinence in the elderly is not confined to dementia – although there is a strong relationship. In this survey a quarter of the elderly chronic schizophrenic patients were incontinent but generally less frequently – usually once a week or so. In this study a 67 year old mute schizophrenic who had been in hospital for more than 40 years reduced his frequency of wetting at night markedly, following the introduction of a behavioural programme similar to that devised by Foxx & Azrin (1973) for use with mentally handicapped people. The programme included prompted toileting, reinforcement for remaining dry and for using the toilet appropriately.

Atthowe (1972) reports complete elimination of nocturnal incontinence in 12 chronic schizophrenic patients (five of whom were over 65 and six of whom were lobotomised). A combination of aversive procedures (tending to emphasise the discomfort and anti-social nature of incontinence) and token reinforcement for remaining dry were used. Tokens were exchanged for more comfortable living conditions. It should be noted that the positive reinforcement was particularly important for those most frequently incontinent initially, some of whom needed seven to eight months of treatment. Follow-up nearly two years later showed that the gains had been maintained. Also as part of a ward-wide token economy scheme in the UK Hartie & Black (1975) report a 50 per cent reduction in nocturnal incontinence in five elderly patients (one head injury, four chronic schizophrenics) following the introduction of rewards for dry nights and ensuring that patients urinated before retiring.

Studies involving patients who seem more likely to have a diagnosis of dementia have generally produced less encouraging results. Twenty-one patients with 'organic dysfunction' were split into control and experimental groups (on separate wards) by Grosicki (1968). Both groups were checked hourly. On the experimental ward if the patient was found to be dry he was given three minutes attention by the staff member, if not he was changed with minimal interaction. Nursing staff followed the 'usual procedure' with control patients. Subsequently material reinforcers were introduced to reward the experimental group for using the toilet. The results appeared to favour the control group, who showed a marked reduction in incontinence which was not maintained at follow-up. These negative findings are puzzling. It is difficult to envisage that the effect of hourly checking per se could continue beyond the two week baseline period, as it seems to have done. Grosicki interprets his results as inconclusive and points to various problems encountered in carrying out the study. Probably the use of two different wards may have introduced variables of patient management other than those intended.

However, Pollock & Liberman's (1974) study of six male patients, all diagnosed as having dementia, also showed no significant reduction in incontinence following social and material reinforcement for being dry when checked during the day. For nocturnal incontinence the 'bell and pad' method so familiar and generally so successful in treating enuretic children has been applied to 19 elderly residents (two-thirds judged to be seriously impaired in awareness of their surroundings and others) by Collins & Plaska (1975). A control group was used where patients were paired with experimental subjects and both were awoken and toiletted whenever the experimental subject set off the alarm as he began to urinate in bed. Thus any effect of the bell and pad could not be related to the increased amount of nocturnal toiletting but rather to the pairing of desire to urinate and getting up and going to the toilet. Results over an eight week treatment period were by no means dramatic, but there was a significant, although small, reduction in bed wetting in the experimental group. Conditioning seemed most useful when the buzzer was activated immediately the resident began to urinate, without delay. There was some evidence that the buzzer did halt the urination and encourage urinary control. The authors suggest using the bell and pad together with operant techniques (e.g. rewarding dry beds, rewarding using the toilet etc.) over a longer period in order to increase the method's effectiveness.

To summarise these results – it seems that behavioural methods have demonstrated applicability to chronic schizophrenic nocturnal incontinence, but results for patients who possibly had dementia have been much less encouraging. In view of the importance of incontinence we will discuss some factors that may contribute to these poor results and offer some hope for the future.

Firstly, incontinence is the most difficult, practically, of the target problems so far reviewed. All the previous interventions could possibly be confined to an hour or two a day, and intensive work carried out then. By its very nature incontinence has to be modified throughout the day and throughout the night and so limited intervention is more difficult. This is turn means much greater committment and cooperation from care staff on the ward, as Turner (1980), in a useful review of the behavioural approach to incontinence in the elderly, indicates.

Secondly, correct toiletting requires a number of skills – dressing, mobility, ability to find the toilet, ability to recognise it, to control urination until the toilet is reached etc. This chain of behaviours can break down at any point and so an individual analysis of problems will be required in order to identify the problem in each case. Thus the poor results of patients with dementia do not indicate that the incontinence is necessarily 'organic' and therefore untreatable. For example in Woods & Brittons' project (1975), already mentioned, eight female incontinent senile dementia patients were studied intensively and comprehensive data on their toiletting collected. Five of the eight had problems in finding and getting to the toilet at the appropriate time and seemed to have little difficulty in using it correctly once there. Thus with these patients a strictly 'organic' incontinence seemed unlikely in that the micturition response still functioned normally.

Thirdly, goals of treatment need consideration. An ideal goal might be complete continence and independent toileting. With severely demented patients a more attainable goal might be remaining dry with regular prompting. If the individual's micturition pattern guides the toileting programme it will be more efficient and rewarding for all concerned.

Certainly, as in King's (1980) highly successful, multi-modal approach to the treatment of incontinence there is a need in this area for both medical and psychological intervention to maximise the chances of success with such a complex problem.

Miscellaneous target behaviour

Single case studies have been reported showing following behavioural intervention, successful decrease in screaming (Baltes & Lascomb 1975); increase in safe smoking behaviour in a 74 year old patient with a diagnosis of Korsakoff's syndrome with dementia (Seidel & Hodgkinson 1979); and a decrease in complaints of feeling hungry (which occurred even after a full meal) in a 58 year old man with pre-senile dementia (Burton & Spall 1981). Three case studies of attempts to improve oral hygiene in brain-damaged nursing home residents showed mixed results – with one patient not responding to the intervention at all (Sachs 1975).

General programmes

A few workers have attempted to apply behavioural techniques to a wide range of target problems, on a particular home or ward, rather than focussing on one particular area. For example Filer & O'Connell (1964) gave feedback to two groups of elderly chronic patients as to whether they were meeting expected levels of functioning. One group in addition received rewards for satisfactory performance. Although both groups improved on constructive work, self-care and punctuality the group receiving contingent rewards improved much more. A re-educational, broadly behavioural, approach is described by Parker (1974), Lodge & Parker (1977) which was implemented at Carlton Hayes Hospital, Narborough. The parallel was drawn between the learning difficulties of the elderly and the mentally handicapped. Methods used with mentally handicapped children were applied to six patients with moderately severe senile dementia. The innovative methods used were varied, but included encouragement of independence and of normal social behaviour; provision of activities, environmental cues, emphasis on conversation, changes in staff attitudes and expectations. Anecdotally results were dramatic; in six months mobility improved, previously chair-bound patients moved about voluntarily; all the patients were continent (none were previously) and greater recall was evident. Even occupations were established where before patients had been 'unresponsive, apathetic . . . . and vacant'.

A token economy programme has been evaluated with elderly psychiatric patients by Mishara & Kastenbaum (1973). This is essentially a ward-wide operant programme in which desirable behaviours are rewarded by tokens, which can be exchanged for privileges and items like cigarettes, extra food etc. Which behaviours should be rewarded and the exchange rates for various rewards are clearly laid out and can be varied to meet the needs of particular patients. The use of tokens enables a reward to be given immediately – when it is most effective – which would be impossible for most other reinforcers. Forty patients were on such a token economy ward; another 40 were on a 'free enrichment' ward where the same reinforcers were available – regardless of the patient's behaviour. A test was thus made of the importance of the enrichment being contingent upon appropriate behaviour for changes to take place. Results suggested some improvements on both wards, with the token economy ward having most effect, particularly in decreasing the amount of staff help patients required in performing self-care tasks.

As part of this project the effects of wine as an enrichment or reinforcer were evaluated (Mishara & Kastenbaum 1974). On both wards the availability of wine reduced the amount of sleep-inducing night-time medication and on the token economy ward it proved an effective reinforcer, although not as powerful as cigarettes. Its reinforcing qualities seemed to vary from patient to patient – some found it aided reminiscence, some simply enjoyed its help in bringing sleep, some used it as a stimulus to social interaction.

Similarly Chien (1971) introduced 'beer therapy' on a male geriatric ward. Forty patients (average age 73 years), diagnosed as either suffering from functional psychosis (30 per cent) or chronic brain syndrome (70 per cent) were randomly placed in four groups. The beer and social therapy group had one hour a day on five days a week in the hospital pub. No drugs were used, but beer and choice of activity were supplied. The fruit punch and social therapy group were given the same conditions, apart from alcohol, and acted as a control for the former group. The drug and social therapy group also had the same conditions, no alcohol, and were served fruit punch and concentrated thioridazine. The drug group stayed on the ward, only received thioridazine and acted as a control for the punch and drug group. The study lasted nine weeks. Rating scales were used – the Brief Psychiatric Rating Scale (BPRS), the Nurses' Observation Scale for Inpatient Evaluation (NOSIE) and a five point social activity scale. The most significant changes were shown by the beer group (though one patient died it was not ascertained if the beer had been an influence!). The drug group did better than the punch group, which could indicate that the pub setting was not a reinforcer of social change. However, the greatest social improvement was made by the drinkers, who were never known to refuse a beer! Refusal to drink the punch was quite common – perhaps the idea that punch replaced the normal pub drink caused sufficient disappointment to reduce social activity as this group also frequently absented themselves! Chien discounted the nutritional value of beer and concluded that such social drinking was beneficial and improved his patients' quality of life.

The study by Mishara & Kastenbaum also examines what this research team have defined as 'self-injurious behaviour' (Mishara et al 1973). This covers a wide spectrum of 'observable behaviour which could possibly contribute to bringing about a premature end to one's life'. Examples vary from choking due to improper eating, through careless cigarrette use and bumping into objects. Both token economy and free enrichment wards were found to have lower frequencies of self-injurious behaviour than comparable custodial care wards, when allowance had been made for half the patients on one of the latter wards being tied to their chairs by the nursing staff – thus effectively reducing behaviour of this nature as well as any other!

Diagnostic details of the patients are included. Forty-eight of the 80 had a diagnosis of chronic brain syndrome. Mean age was 69 years and average length of hospitalization was 21 years, so once more, although clearly behaviourally deteriorated, it appears obvious that these patients had grown old within an institution.

Excess disabilities

In the early 1970s a series of publications emanating from a research team at the Philadelphia Geriatric Centre highlighted the subject of individualised treatment of excess disabilities of mentally impaired elderly people. Excess disabilities (EDs) are those functional incapacities that are greater than expected in view of the patient's level of impairment; in other words the discrepancy between the potential and actual level of function. In this study such excess deficits were isolated by a consensus of opinion from a multi-disciplinary team following extensive assessment of the patient. Two groups of matched female patients were involved (mean age 82 years), living in identical accommodation; one group received individualised therapy for the EDs and the other did not. Treatment continued for a period of one year, when the baseline assessments were repeated and external raters evaluated progress in each excess disability, blind to whether the patient had received treatment or not (Brody et al 1971). The results indicated that the treatment of EDs had been successful, with the experimental groups showing more improvement; changes in areas not directly treated were not found. Both groups showed a deterioration in general health over the year. EDs in the areas of family relationships and activities responded most to treatment.

At follow-up nine months later (Brody et al 1974) EDs in the experimental group had deteriorated, and it seemed that continued treatment input was required to maintain improvement. It should be noted that the institution involved has relatively good resources and a reputation for sophisticated care; however, it is clear that in some areas this was insufficient to produce and maintain maximum functioning without an additional individualised treatment programme.

The treatment programmes derived from multi-disciplinary assessments covered a wide range – activities of daily living, behavioural, interpersonal, environmental and social disabilities, occupational and recreational activities, physical, emotional and psychiatric problems were all covered. Specific goals of treatment were set, with the components of the therapeutic plan clearly set out, together with the responsibilities of each team member for carrying them out. Treatment plans apparently included modification of environmental factors such as furnishings, decorations, staff attitudes etc. where necessary (Brody et al 1973). Others involved consultation with medical specialists e.g. for visual problems. Two case illustrations are provided by Brody et al (1973), but unfortunately it is still extremely difficult to ascertain the exact form of the treatment methods used.

This study is included in the behaviour modification section not because operant behavioural procedures were employed, for if they were this is not made explicit, but because the study is in the behavioural tradition in its specification of clear, graded treatment goals, in its recognition of individual differences in needs for treatment and in its explicit treatment plans, leading to a consistent approach across disciplines. This type of approach may be particularly appropriate where a number of disciplines are involved, in enabling an overall view of the patient to be obtained, without the unfortunate compartmentalization that can occur so often.

Conclusions on behaviour modification

It is difficult to escape the conclusion that in relation to dementia at least, behaviour modification is an extremely promising approach, but as yet there remains a lack of convincing evidence for its effectiveness. The same cannot be said of people grown old in institutions, chronic schizophrenics or whatever; here there is abundant evidence for the effectiveness of such intervention.

Some might argue that it is against the spirit of a behavioural approach to continually distinguish these groups of patients. If their behaviour is the same, which might well appear to be the case in some instances, then it is that behaviour which is to be modified, not some postulated underlying disease process. However, there are differences in prognoses, life – experience and, at finer levels of analysis, actual behaviour. These make it very important that methods which are effective on patients who have been hospitalised for 20 years or more are not assumed to apply to the far greater number of elderly people who have functioned well into their 60s, 70s or 80s and then begun the progressive deterioration of dementia.

A further problem in evaluating the behavioural approach has been a tendency for studies so far to introduce a number of simultaneous changes, rendering it impossible to sort out what has or has not been effective. This is understandable in an applied situation, but must be more carefully controlled if an evaluation is to have any validity.

GROUP WORK

Several approaches have been devised that have been based on group meetings once, twice or more a week. Remotivation is claimed by Birkett & Boltuch (1973) to be the most common form of psychotherapy used in mental hospitals in the USA. It consists of a series of 12 or so meetings, once or twice a week, lasting from 30–60 minutes for 10–15 patients under the leadership of care staff who have received a few hours of training. The discussion is highly structured and makes use of objective topics of conversation and visual aids with sensitive areas such as religion, politics and sex being excluded. At each session only one chosen topic is discussed.

A study by Bowers et al (1967) suggested that changes did occur in remotivation groups in a nursing home, both with respect to the residents' behaviour in the group and their social functioning. The pre-group ratings were carried out retrospectively, however, which tends to weaken these findings. It was claimed that even patients with organic brain syndrome improved. Birkett & Boltuch's (1973) evaluation compared remotivation groups with a placebo group therapy (as far as possible on analytic lines). Most patients in both groups had a diagnosis of senile dementia. The results showed a non-significant trend in favour of the remotivation group in terms of improved interest, awareness etc. The authors had little doubt following the trial that remotivation is much more suited to demented patients than traditional group therapy, as a much more active therapist is required with this population. Toepfer et al (1974) speculate that similarities exist between remotivation and behaviour therapy and suggest that this should be made more explicit. Desired behaviour in the group should be operationally defined and reinforced, for instance.

In a recent report Gray & Stevenson (1980) seem to have done this. They have extended the remotivation format slightly, with positive feedback for accurate statements being made explicit. The desired outcome was to increase social interactions between group members in these resocialization groups. Over a four month period of once-weekly meetings, highly significant increases were obtained in three groups of five to six members, all of whom appear to have been confused and disorientated. Indeed the most desocialised group (who initially fought over refreshments and ignored one another) showed most improvement. Qualitative changes in the nature of interactions was also observed, as members became more socially aware and supportive of each other.

Kiernat (1979) describes a group approach which emphasises more discussion of past life experiences, a life review activity. Twenty-three residents in a nursing home – all 'confused' – met twice a week for an hour in three groups for 10 weeks. Materials were brought in to stimulate discussion of the past, with attempts being made to use items to stimulate all the senses; obtaining these materials required a fair amount of preparation. Life-events were discussed in chronological order, up to the present time. It is not clear whether this refers to one session or to the whole period. Evaluation of the results is difficult, but it seems that residents who attended sessions most frequently showed the greatest improvement in their behaviour.

This type of approach is clearly akin to the idea that reminiscence is a desirable and useful activity for elderly people. Langley & Corder (1978) describe Reminiscence Therapy which aims to encourage elderly people to reminisce so that 'they will thereafter be less depressed, less intellectually disabled and therefore able to cope both personally and socially'. Reminiscence can be encouraged as in Kiernat's study by a variety of items, pictures and so forth from the past, by period settings (as by Matthews & Kemp 1979), or by the use of live theatre providing reminiscence entertainment e.g. music, re-enacting a scene from the past with the active advice and correction of the elderly audience, etc. (Langley & Corder 1978).

A three month controlled study by Harvey & Kinsman (1981) investigated the value of Audio-visual Reminiscence Aids (slide and tape presentation of material dating back to 1890). The subjects were 30 elderly, mentally frail residents in an old people's home – mean age for experimental subjects was 82 years, and for the controls 87 years. Reminiscence sessions were held in a social atmosphere, once weekly, for about an hour. No significant changes were found – perhaps as sessions were rather infrequent. Trends towards decreases in apathy and undesirable social behaviour favoured the experimental groups. An important observation was that reminiscence seemed to facilitate staff-resident interaction.

As yet the effects of such structured reminiscence with senile dementia patients remains unclear, but is certainly a promising avenue for investigation. It could possibly increase interest and attention by using the store of knowledge and experience of old people as a resource.

In concluding this section the reader's attention is drawn to the work of Irene Burnside whose sensitive and innovative approach to group work with the aged, whilst not formally evaluated, is an inspiration to those working with this population (Burnside 1971).

REALITY ORIENTATION

Origins

Reality Orientation can be traced back to 1958 when an 'aide-centred activity programme for elderly patients' was set up at a Veterans Administration Hospital in Topeka, Kansas, USA, where Dr James Folsom was then working. Almost certainly RO existed before then, but at this time a structure and a name began to be applied. The programme went with Dr Folsom to the VA Hospital at Tuscaloosa, Alabama via Mount Pleasant, Iowa, and was further developed and refined. By the mid-1960s published descriptions began to appear (e.g. Taulbee & Folsom 1966) and the methods were beginning to crystallize. In 1969, the American Psychiatric Association published a short booklet, outlining the methods of RO together with the comments of a psychologist and a physician, entitled 'Reality Orientation: a technique to rehabilitate elderly and brain-damaged patients with a moderate to severe degree of disorientation' (edited by Louise Stephens). An RO training programme has been in existence at Tuscaloosa for ten years or more, and nurses and others working with the elderly from all over the USA and from other countries have participated in short training courses there. In 1978 the training team there published a practical guide to RO (Drummond et al 1978).

RO is of course now used in many countries. The first published account of its use in the UK was by Brook et al (1975). This was the first controlled study reported, and was carried out at Warley Hospital in Brentwood, Essex. It is likely that the methods were being used elsewhere in the UK before this. The growth of interest in the UK has been rapid; some adaptations and developments of the methods have been attempted. Workshops and courses on RO attract a great deal of interest and in a variety of settings throughout the country RO is being implemented in one form or another. Accounts of the methods used in the UK have been provided by Degun (1976), Conroy (1977), Holden & Sinebruchow (1978) and Holden (1979 a, b) among others. Further useful descriptions of the methods from the USA include Hefferin & Hunter (1977), Cornbleth & Cornbleth (1977) – a very detailed and specific guide to RO – and Hahn (1980).

Varieties of RO

Three major components of RO are usually identified. The first is 24 hour RO (sometimes called 'informal RO' or the 'Basic approach'). This is a continual process whereby staff present current information to the person in every interaction, reminding the patient of time, place, and person and providing a commentary on events. Confused and rambling speech is not reinforced. The environment is structured with signs and cues to help the person remain aware of the surroundings. RO classes, or intensive sessions, are a supplement to 24 hour RO but in some centres have been used in isolation. These sessions are also variously called 'Intensive RO', 'Formal RO', 'RO Groups'. Sessions are held daily for half an hour to an hour with three to six patients depending on the level of confusion. Group leaders do not require particular professional expertise, and qualities such as enthusiasm, a positive, flexible and creative approach are more important. Specific training in the procedures is needed however. Sessions may be divided into different levels according to the degree of deterioration, often basic, standard and advanced levels are described. In Basic group sessions ('classes') the emphasis is on presentation and repetition of current information and orientation material related to simple information on day, weather, names and months. The Standard group uses sensorial stimulation and past/present discussion to develop interpersonal relationship and learning. In the Advanced group there is less emphasis needed on basic orientation so activities are wider ranging. In some hospitals 'graduation' ceremonies have been arranged when patients have benefited as much as possible from RO or are being promoted to an Advanced group. A diploma is presented to a group member by a senior staff member. In the UK the emphasis has been more on a social setting than a classroom, with, for example, the use in Leeds of simulated pubs. Possibly the creation of a social environment helps the patient to feel less pressured, more comfortable and less likely to withdraw than in a possibly threatening classroom situation. However, this factor may well be closely related to cultural aspects. In the USA there is greater social implication for graduation and connotations of increased self-esteem which are not operable in UK or in other countries which have their own situations associated with social pleasure, esteem and relaxation. The final traditional component of RO is the use of prescribed attitudes (Attitude Therapy) to be used by all care staff with a particular patient. These include kind firmness, active friendliness, passive friendliness, matter of fact and no demand, which are chosen according to the patient's personality and needs. Their use is thought to facilitate staff consistency in approach to each patient. However, their actual use has been little documented and with some patients different attitudes may be required by different situations, thus complicating their use considerably (Ginsberg 1953).

Application of RO and relationship to other approaches

Obviously much more will be said about the effectiveness of RO in Chapter 3 and about the actual methods involved in Part II. In this chapter we have sought to describe other approaches so that RO can be seen in a wider context.

At this point we should stress that RO is specifically designed for disorientated, confused patients and is therefore appropriate for use with senile dementia, although by no means confined to that diagnostic group. It is a flexible approach. Different levels of groups are described and it is appropriate for different degrees of confusion. It is based on interaction between staff and patient, both in the 24 hour RO and RO sessions, and provides, of course, many opportunities for prompting and social reinforcement of desired behaviour (usually correct verbal orientation). It also involves environmental changes through the use of memory aids, signs etc. Above all it is a communication approach that enables care staff to make contact with confused people, giving the staff member some principles to apply to a situation that is often fraught with difficulties and where crossed wires are more common than true communication.

RO involves staff and institutional attitudes; it involves positive attitudes which indicate that talking and explaining things to a dementing person is worthwhile even if it seems to be forgotten immediately. It also involves a respect for the elderly person. Communication implies listening as well as talking, and listening applies to what is unspoken as well as what is verbalised. Without this respect no communication takes place and RO becomes a pointless exercise.

RO can operate in some ways as a prosthetic environment. In the group or outside the person is enabled to succeed. Clues and prompts are given, he or she is shown where to find the answer to the question. He is asked questions that he is still able to answer. The effects of any memory problems are minimised rather than emphasised, as it is so easy to do. Perhaps by succeeding in this way the person will in fact function better as he gains confidence; certainly it will be a refreshing enjoyable change from the repeated failures which characterise the process of dementia.

There is much common ground with resocialisation, remotivation and reminiscence approaches: the major difference is that this is a continuous process and is not intended to be only apparent in a group setting. When past events are used in RO they are always brought up-to-date so that the person is able to integrate past and present. The similarity with activity and stimulation approaches will become clearer when the methods are described in more detail, but certainly in RO sessions it is activity and stimulation that are often as apparent as the continuous orientation to current surroundings. Given the success (limited but clearly apparent) of these other approaches we would emphasise that they are not mutually exclusive, and we favour the strategy of using the most effective parts of each in any overall programme for a particular group of patients.

3

The effectiveness of RO

This chapter will consider what many would believe to be the fundamental issue about RO: does it work? The evidence that is available will be reviewed and discussed and related questions will be examined – such as under what conditions and with which elderly people it may be most effective – before identifying as yet unanswered questions that future research might profitably investigate. Most of the research that has been carried out on RO will be reviewed here; some of the implications of this research for theories about how RO might work will be extracted and discussed in the next chapter. A fair proportion of the studies unfortunately are as yet unpublished; they 'are included so that the up-to-date position at the time of writing can be discussed.

The evaluation of the efficacy of any treatment method is fraught with difficulties. Debates continue about the effectiveness of many well-established therapeutic methods with other client groups. In some ways the task is more difficult with elderly populations; patients fluctuate a great deal more, have more risk of becoming physically ill and even dying, perhaps quite independently of the treatment procedures being used. Other difficulties will become clear as the literature is reviewed but these general considerations do emphasise that the present review is tentative and by no means the final word on the subject! Hopefully it will clarify some of the issues involved in answering 'does RO work?

Finally, by way of introduction the importance of this question should be considered. It could be argued (as Hanley 1980 has done) that RO represents an approach to the patients that is to be valued on humanitarian grounds in that it gives emphasis to interactions based on respect, concern and recognition of individual identities. In this light RO may be a 'good' thing whether or not it changes the patients. What may be important is that staff and others concerned treat patients in a genuinely caring fashion. The question of 'does RO work?' remains. However, the emphasis is shifted from changes in the elderly person to changes in the caring person.

DOES RO WORK?

The final point above indicates the need for amplification of this apparently straightforward inquiry. Additionally it should be asked on whom it works, and also what is meant by 'work' in this context. Thus the issue must be raised of exactly how to tell if RO is working or not and what criteria might be applied. Taulbee & Folsom (1966), pioneers of RO, noticed that with some of their patients 'their look of hopelessness changed to hopefulness' when they began RO. If changes are occurring then it is necessary to define along what dimensions these changes are taking place, whether it be facial expression, memory for current events, self-care skills or whatever. As far as staff are concerned the changes might be in attitudes to their patients, changes in the way interactions are made with patients and so on.

A further complication with elderly people in particular arises over our concepts of change. Suppose measures of some attribute of the patient are made and then one month after they have begun RO that attribute is re-assessed. If it is exactly the same as before this could be thought of as indicating no change; but suppose that if that person had not had RO he or she would have deteriorated – as over a period of time patients with dementia are usually considered to do – then absence of change may still indicate a positive effect of treatment. Thus even a deterioration could still be consistent with a positive effect of treatment, as long as the deterioration is less than it would have been without treatment.

So changes are being sought – in patients or staff – that are more positive than they would have been without RO. 'Positive' can be difficult to define more precisely; it is straightforward enough if memory is being assessed – improved memory is a positive change. However 'amount of complaining' is another matter; some might see it as a good thing if the person becomes more complaining and asserts himself more; others might see it as an unnecessary nuisance. Value judgements may then come into play here; generally changes in the direction of more independence on the part of the patient and more recognition of the elderly person as an adult individual by the staff are viewed as positive, but there will of course be grey areas, open to debate and interpretation.

DOES RO CHANGE THOSE EMPLOYING IT?

The effects of using RO on care-staff have been relatively little explored. Effects on relatives using it have not been examined in any systematic way as yet, but are at present under investigation (Holden). Taulbee & Folsom (1966) described how RO could involve nursing assistants, who spend much more time in contact with the patients than any of the other professionals, becoming members of the rehabilitation team. Through RO they become more than agents of physical care, they become in effect therapists; clearly in some instances this could lead to greater job satisfaction and morale. Holden & Sinebruchow (1978) actually had as an objective of their study of RO the development of 'an approach which would attract the interest of nursing staff' and reported, anecdotally, that providing the nursing staff with their own therapeutic approach had given them a sense of achievement. In contrast, Woods (1979) reported that care-attendants in his study of RO reported a preference for leading a social conversation group rather than an RO group. The extra resources of imagination, creativity and planning needed to prevent RO sessions from being boringly repetitive were seen as being important here. It may be that staff in different settings and of different backgrounds react differently to carrying out RO – and may well use quite distinct methods. The whole question of staff-attitudes will be discussed in more practical detail in Chapter 9. However there is one study in which staff attitudes to elderly people were actually assessed, before and after an intensive five day training programme in the RO approach. Smith & Barker (1972) report a marked increase in positive attitudes to the elderly in a group of 94 trainees, which was maintained after a six month interval. A variety of occupational groups were included, but generally did not differ in their amount of attitudinal change. This is an encouraging result – especially as attitudes are often extremely difficult to modify so quickly. It should be noted, however, that it is in response to training in RO and that the trainees were not necessarily involved in RO over the succeeding six month period. What we are considering here is more an attitude change in response to *involvement* in RO over a period of time – the appropriate studies of this have not yet been carried out. Doubt must exist however, particularly as far as 24 hour RO is concerned, as to what extent in even the best-conceived programme RO is actually carried out. Clearly if long-term beneficial effects in attitude and morale are to be attributed to involvement in RO there must be some indication that RO is actually in operation. Change in a person's behaviour is often a precursor to attitude change, and change in the care-worker's behaviour from non-RO behaviour to RO behaviour may well be seen as a desirable aim, if the RO approach to the person is seen as incorporating humanitarian values. The doubts mentioned above arise from the often reported infrequency of staff-patient contact in many institutions for the elderly (e.g. Galliard 1978). Presumably this lessens the amount of 24 hour RO that is possible and is reflected in the continued occurrence of patently *un*-reality orientated statements observed in RO groups. If they occur there, they are almost certain to occur in the broader environment of the ward.

Woods et al (1980) attempted to measure changes in RO behaviour in care-staff after a training session, consisting of a talk illustrated with slides, discussion, a handout, some demonstration and role play. RO sessions were recorded on audio tape before and after the training had taken place. The tapes were then analysed to assess changes in RO behaviour. A critical issue here was to define precisely the nature of RO behaviour – in this case of course only verbal behaviour could be considered. This proved to be a difficult task. Different workers view RO in slightly different ways, and it is probably fair to say that it is a dynamic, developing concept. However an operational definition was finally arrived at (Table 3.1) and each staff statement on the tapes carefully categorized accordingly. Table 3.2 shows the findings with a significant increase in the proportion of RO behaviour occurring after training. The proportion of negative RO statements showed little

Table 3.1 Operational definitions of verbal RO

These are guidelines for placing remarks made by leaders in RO sessions into the following three categories:

1. *RO* – remarks and comments in line with the methods of RO and so aiding the RO process.
2. *Negative RO* – remarks and comments clearly in direct contradiction to the methods of RO giving person incorrect information, encouraging incorrect response etc.
3. *Neutral* – these are things said that do not fall into either of the above categories; they neither aid nor hinder RO; they neither orientate nor disorientate the person.

For making this decision the following general definition of verbal RO is used:
staff verbal behaviour that orientates residents to reality
orient – to acquaint with the existing situation
reality – that which has actual existence and is not merely an idea or imaginary

Thus statements giving the person correct, current information are clearly RO. However, when displaced reality is being discussed for RO to be coded the displacement must be made clear in the statement e.g. 'You *used* to work as a tailor, Mrs Smith'.

When a question is asked it is coded RO if:
a. it gives the person information also, e.g. 'Have you seen the rain outside, Mr Jones?'
b. it is about a point of fact and the staff member has the information available to check the person's response
c. it relates to feelings or opinions *and* provides some information e.g. 'Did you like your dinner of *fish and chips* today, Mr Brown?'

Other comments are coded as RO if they reinforce the person's previous reality-orientated behaviour e.g. praise, repetition, encouragement, agreement may all be RO responses.

change; training seemed to help these staff be more efficient RO leaders, with less remarks being 'wasted' (from an RO viewpoint) following training.

Some of the post-training recordings were made some one to two months after training so this effect is probably not merely transitory although its duration is of course uncertain. In the same study it proved impossible to carry out a similar exercise outside

Table 3.2 Mean proportions of staff statements consistent with RO, inconsistent with RO and neutral in RO sessions carried out by five staff members before and after training

	Before training	After training
RO statements	77.4%	89.4% *
Neutral statements	21.1%	9.4% *
Negative RO statements	1.5%	1.2%

* Before-after difference significant at 5% level (correlated t-test, 1 tailed).

the RO group room and to evaluate the effects of training on the amount of 24 hour RO carried out. A high proportion of the staff-resident interaction occurred in relation to bathing, dressing, toiletting etc., and not in the 'public' areas of the Home where interactions might be observed relatively unobtrusively. However, Hanley (1980) has been able to attempt such an investigation, and reports considerable difficulty in implementing 24 hour RO in a hospital setting. He devised a system in order to assess both the quantity and *quality* of 24 hour RO being carried out, before and after the implementation of 24 hour RO.

He found no change in the number of interactions staff had with patients (approximately nine interactions per patient in an eight hour period), and even more disappointingly no change in the *quality* of the interactions, measured by the mean number of the following seven features of 24 hour RO present per interaction.

QUALITY FEATURES OF 24 HOUR RO (as used by Hanley 1980)

Staff member: engages patient verbally
names patient
names self
refers to time or place
explains procedure
refers to prop
speaks properly.

Most discouraging of all was that when staff rated their own interactions with patients they indicated that they thought they were carrying out many of these procedures, when the direct observation of interactions indicated clearly that they were not. For example all 15 nursing staff involved said that most of the time they called the patient by name, whereas in fact this only occurred in 48 per cent of the interactions. All staff said that most of the time they explained procedures to the patients, but this only occurred in 14 per cent of the interactions and finally 13 of the 15 nurses stated that they named themselyes and the same number said they referred to props at least once in a while. Neither of these interactions occurred in *any* interactions observed. Hanley's work then confirms the doubts raised as to the extent to which 24 hour RO actually occurs. Clearly replication is needed in other institutions, but we must bear in mind that 24 hour RO is not implemented in a vacuum. In different institutions 24 hour RO will already be applied to differing degrees, there will be different types of staff, different attitudes, different institutional goals. The effects of different institutions on the implementation of 24 hour RO is of great practical importance, but it is extremely difficult even to research. The extent to which the institution values staff-patient interaction, patient independence, is patient- rather than staff-centred, and is rehabilitative rather than custodial, will all have an impact on 24 hour RO.

Work on evaluating changes in staff is at an extremely early stage. Some positive changes in attitudes have been reported and also some increase in behaviour consistent with RO in RO groups has now been found following training. Little is known of the long-term effects on staff carrying out RO, whether positive attitudes are maintained, or whether the RO itself is maintained, without additional training and support. These areas are worth exploring, together with the effects on relatives of being asked to carry out RO – whether they can use it, what factors make it difficult for them to carry it out and how their attitudes to their elderly relative change through using RO.

DOES RO CHANGE THE PATIENT?

Anecdotal reports

A great deal of the early work on evaluation of RO consisted of anecdotal material, case reports, uncontrolled data and so on. Although carefully controlled data is needed to answer the question, the anecdotal material gives some indication of the dimensions along which change may take place and the possibilities that might exist. However, it must be borne in mind that stability or less rapid deterioration are in certain circumstances acceptable goals, so that a control group is needed to provide an estimate of what would have happened without RO.

The Taulbee & Folsom (1966) 'hopelessness to hopefulness' transformation has already been commented upon and certainly one area in which change might be seen as desirable is in the person's report of feelings of happiness, self-esteem and the behaviours that accompany such feelings. Folsom (1968) in describing the earliest RO project, at Topeka, Kansas, talks of an air of liveliness' being evident on the unit as rehabilitative measures began to be applied. In addition to greater involvement of patients in a variety of activities, social activity increased considerably as 'patients began conversing and making friends'. Dr Folsom reported that RO programmes were developed whilst he was at Mount Pleasant, Iowa. In a pilot study taking place over one year 57 per cent of patients admitted improved sufficiently to return to their pre-hospital adjustment; previously only 3 per cent of the geriatric patients had shown sufficient improvement to do this. Discharge rates may thus be another variable effected by the implementation of RO. Data for a further one year at the Veteran's Administration Hospital at Tuscaloosa, where RO has now firmly established its roots, is reported by Taulbee & Folsom (1966) and Folsom (1968). From January 1965 to January 1966, 64 patients began RO. Twelve did not continue through physical illness or death; two patients were completely unable to cooperate, but only four patients showed deterioration over the year. Seventeen patients completed basic and advanced RO courses and five of these patients were discharged, and others showed improvements. By July 1969, 227 patients had been placed in RO classes (Stephens 1969) and 20 per cent had been discharged or were on trial visits to home or community facilities. This type of data is of course particularly difficult to evaluate as it is impossible to estimate what discharge rates might have been without RO. What is important at this stage is the impression these workers convey that RO in some way can improve patients enough to enable discharges to take place where previously they might not have done.

Further anecdotal data is supplied in brief case histories of seven men undergoing RO presented by Folsom (1967, 1968) and Taulbee & Folsom (1966). Four of these had been hospitalized for more than 15 years and had clearly grown old in the institution and presented as chronic rehabilitation problems. These patients showed considerable progress. Two were mute before starting RO, and a third would not converse; following RO all were talking more, and one was described as outgoing. One patient became generally more responsive and was transferred to a nursing home; another ceased to use a wheelchair and became much less incontinent and violent; the other two began to attend off-ward activities. Two of the three more recent admissions worked well in RO eventually and one was discharged, his confusion having lifted; the other became more cooperative and talked more freely. The third patient's progress was minimal, but he had only been attending RO a short time.

These case studies then suggest that changes in sociability, mobility, incontinence, aggression and cooperation may all be related to RO. It should be noted, however, that if the case studies are representative, RO was developed as much with elderly chronic psychiatric patients with years of institutionalisation, as with the type of patient who is admitted from the community suffering from acute or progressive confusion.

Finally in this section on the anecdotal evidence – which of course gave RO its impetus and prevented it from being abandoned at an early stage of development – Folsom (1968) presents nursing staff opinions about changes in patients following RO. Increased socialization, improved self-care (feeding, washing etc.), more interest in TV, food, surroundings etc., more cooperation, more family contacts are all mentioned. Generally the impression is given that patients had more pride in themselves and their accomplishments, more self-confidence and dignity. In looking at quantitative data on change following RO it will be seen that it is this latter area of self-esteem that is hardly explored at all – amost certainly partly because of the difficulties of assessing it 'objectively' with this population. This is unfortunate, as whatever other changes RO might bring to patients, there is no doubt that improved self-esteem would be of tremendous intrinsic value.

Uncontrolled studies

Both Taulbee & Folsom (1966) and Stephens (1969) refer to a controlled evaluation of RO being commenced at Tuscaloosa. Unfortunately nothing seems to have come of this and it was not until 1974 that a detailed report appeared providing some quantitative data on changes in a large number of patients undergoing RO at Tuscaloosa. Letcher et al (1974) report data on 125 male patients, being all those taking part in RO there from 1965 to 1970, with the exception of 81 patients who had been transferred or who had only been rated once so that no before and after comparison was possible. Ratings were made according to level of nursing care needed, four levels being specified. Average age of the patients was 82.8 (range mid-40s-90s). The results of this retrospective

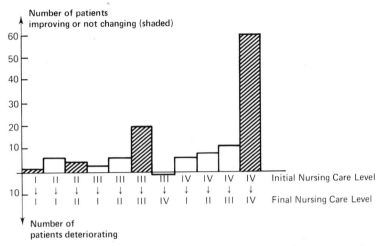

Fig. 3.1 Reality orientation: nursing care levels before and after the programme for 125 male patients, mean age 82.8 years on admission. Level I minimal nursing care; Level IV intensive nursing care. Derived from Letcher et al 1974. Reproduced, with permission, from Age and Ageing (1977) 6: 106

survey are shown in Figure 3.1. Only one patient is reported to have deteriorated; 32 per cent improved and 68 per cent remained the same.

The results appear encouraging, especially if the expectation is that the patients would have declined, so remaining stationary is a good outcome. This is particularly apposite as 80 per cent of the men were reported as having 'organic brain syndrome due to cerebral arteriosclerosis'. However there are some limitations to the study. Firstly nearly half the men began and ended the study at the lowest level, level IV where the patient is completely dependent on staff members for physical care. There is no way in which any deterioration in these men could have been recorded, and so the large proportion of men remaining the same is grossly inflated by those patients. Secondly, there was a wide range in the amount of time patients spent in the programme (ranging from 2 to 56 months). The rate of improvement was found to be much higher for those who remained in the programme for at least 18 months. Thirdly, there is no control group, so we have no indication as to what extent the observed changes are related to RO as opposed to the other activity and rehabilitation programmes operational at the time. However the study is important in indicating that a rehabilitation programme, of which RO was seen as an important part, can be related to positive changes in self-care in a sizeable proportion of these elderly patients.

'An individualized activity programme' is the description Salter & Salter (1975) apply to their evaluation of RO, recreational activities, environmental stimulation and self-care activities, for long-stay patients in a state psychiatric hospital. Participation in educational and recreational activities increased from 14 to 76 per cent in four months. Patients who previously did not talk began to do so; there were improvements in mobility, continence and dressing. Reinforcement techniques were used in order to aid motivation and it is not clear to what extent RO was responsible for the changes observed.

A similar study of RO as part of an overall active rehabilitation/ stimulation scheme is reported by Katz (1976). This study extended over 18 months and involved 108 selected residents in a nursing home, 80 of whom had a diagnosis of chronic brain syndrome (of varying severity) or senile dementia. Of these residents 44 per cent were thought to be improved, 20 per cent unchanged and 18 per cent became worse (18 per cent could not be rated). Changes were assessed retrospectively but documented reports were used to aid objectivity, as well as the views of the different members of the staff team. Changes had to be specifically stated in objective, concrete terms. The treatment given varied greatly in different wings of the Home, but formal RO meetings seemed to have a maximum frequency of three times per week. There was a trend for greater improvement to be associated with attendance at a greater number of RO sessions, but it is impossible to say what the effects of RO per se were, or what would have happened in the absence of the active stimulation, as no control group was used. Again, despite the limitations of the study, the results offer some encouragement in documenting positive improvement in this population. Indeed improvement was the most frequent outcome in all diagnostic groups, except mild chronic brain syndrome, where slightly more were unchanged.

Whilst Katz (1976) is unclear as to whether 24 hour RO was used in addition to RO sessions, Barnes (1974) makes it plain that his study looked specifically at the effects of the RO classroom in isolation from 24 hour RO or any other therapeutic programme. Several other studies have since followed this example and it is interesting to consider the possible reasons for this. The classroom sessions have always been seen as a supplement to 24 hour RO, an addition to reinforce the continuous orientation process. However, it is the classroom that seems to attract most attention as Hahn (1980) points out – in descriptions of the technique, and in photographs etc. This may be because in the first place the classroom is a more tangible feature of RO. Secondly, it is of intrinsic interest to know the respective contributions of these two fundamental aspects of RO to its overall effectiveness. Thirdly, it is much more feasible to implement RO sessions and be sure that they are taking place, perhaps bringing specially trained researchers to lead the sessions. Teaching existing staff to carry out 24 hour RO, as has been previously mentioned, can be extremely difficult especially where levels of staff-patient interaction are relatively low. Fourthly, it is often believed that to encourage interest it is advisable to demonstrate success – a basic form of salesmanship. In many cases the use of the 'dramatic' introduction of RO sessions can be seen as a method to convince dubious staff of the efficacy of a programme so that the 24 hour system has a better chance of being implemented. These are the attractions of carrying out studies on RO sessions alone, and clearly as we look at a number of studies we have to bear in mind the presence or absence of 24 hour RO, although there have, as noted above, been few attempts to show that 24 hour RO has actually been implemented in practice.

Barnes (1974) planned to carry out RO classes with 12 geriatric patients in a nursing home for a six week period, but unfortunately only six were able to attend all the classes and so results are only available on these patients. The patients – who are described in exceptional detail by Barnes – all had a diagnosis of senile dementia. Assessment of progress was made with a questionnaire covering basic information which was given four months before RO started and at the beginning and end of a six week period of six days per week RO classes. Additionally the questionnaire was given one week after the end of therapy.

Observations were also recorded by the Nursing Director of certain aspects of the resident's behaviour during the study period. No significant changes were found in the resident's knowledge of basic information, with the exception that there was a fall-off after treatment had been stopped. Similarly there were no changes in the Nursing Director's formal assessment of behaviour, but a number of changes in other aspects of behaviour were reported anecdotally; two residents appeared much calmer, and in fact there was a positive observation for each of the six residents. Three residents were thought to deteriorate in the week after the RO sessions ended.

Again there is little 'hard' evidence for efficacy of RO in improving either knowledge of basic information or behaviour. Again there is no control group as such, but the four month baseline does allow some estimate of the natural rate of deterioration to be made. However, once more there are hints that RO may be achieving something – although it is difficult to measure directly what this is. There is some suggestion though that once RO is stopped deterioration may occur very quickly indeed, and Barnes argues that this indicates the need for RO to be a continuing process. He speculates that a longer treatment period might have produced greater changes. It is certainly the case in this study – as in others to be reveiwed below – that the short treatment time and small number of subjects make it increasingly difficult to obtain statistically significant results, especially where the effects of treatment are expected to be relatively small.

The hard-headed experimenter will by now be losing patience! No control groups, hardly a significant result to be seen! We wish to emphasise, however, how extraordinarily difficult evaluation of any therapeutic programme may be, particularly with an elderly population in hospital or home settings where there are many many variables that are difficult, if not impossible, for the researcher to control. For example, in Barnes' study, half the subjects were lost through death, physical ill-health, not wanting to attend sessions and so forth, and there were even some changes in medication – for physical reasons – all beyond the researcher's power to influence. What is important as a first step is to gather evidence that a programme has some effects and what these effects appear to be, and then to enter into the process of studying the results more closely in a controlled fashion. There is a danger of continuing with programmes that are ineffective because they *appear* to work and never making a careful evaluation of the effects. The danger lies not just in wasting staff time, raising false expectations and so on, but also in never refining the treatment procedures and improving them as aspects which are particularly useful with particular kinds of patients are discovered. There is then a time for anecdotal reports, uncontrolled studies and so on, as procedures are developed, but there must also be a time when the programme is put to a more stringent test.

Controlled trials of RO

The first controlled trial of RO was carried out by Brook et al (1975) at Warley Hospital, England. Eighteen patients were assigned either to daily RO sessions or to control groups. The control patients went to a specially equipped RO room for half-an-hour a day but simply sat in a circle and, unlike the RO group, received no encouragement from the therapists to use the RO materials; their questions were answered as briefly as possible. Ratings of the patients' self-care, orientation, socialisation etc. were made fortnightly by nursing staff who were not aware to which group particular patients belonged and so could not have been inadvertently biased in favour of RO. Results were presented for three levels of initial functioning, high, medium and low, so that any differential effects of RO at different levels of patient functioning might be seen. The results are shown in Figure 3.2; all groups seemed to improve in the first two weeks. After this the control groups deteriorated while the RO groups either maintained progress or continued to improve. The most deteriorated patients showed the least improvement in RO.

This first controlled study clearly favours RO with this group of elderly psychiatric patients (all but one having a diagnosis of dementia) whose mean length of stay in hospital was just under

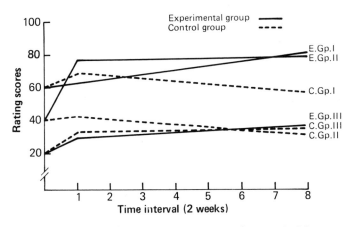

Fig. 3.2 Ratings of intellectual and social functioning of patients in RO (experimental) and control groups by nursing staff unaware of group membership over the 16-week experimental period. Reproduced, with permission, from Brook et al 1975, British Journal of Psychiatry 127: 42–45

two years. Note that changes in observed behaviour were found, and these were backed up by anecdotal reports (Degun 1976) of improvements in incontinence and table-manners, reductions in withdrawn social behaviour and so on. Two patients at least were discharged, where continued hospital care might have been the expectation. Again patients initially more demented showed less improvements generally. Although only one or two patients were thought to regress after the end of the study period, no systematic follow-up seems to have been carried out. It is stated that a watch was kept for signs of depression, but there are no indications given of mood changes in the patients. These changes were found using RO sessions in isolation from 24 hour RO, but add weight to the possible effectiveness of the total programme. It can be argued that if improvements are possible with just three hours or so therapy a week, the potential of 24 hour RO could be very great indeed. However this study in common with the others already reviewed does not in fact *prove* that RO produced the changes observed. In the previously mentioned studies there were other treatment modalities coexisting with RO, or the novelty of doing something quite out of the ordinary nursing home routine, i.e. attending a daily class, or the extra attention that RO groups bring. In Brook et al's study other treatment approaches may be assumed to be equivalent for RO and control groups; both groups did something new and out of the ordinary, by leaving the ward and entering a stimulating environment for a short time each day; but only the RO group received additional staff attention and encouragement, and this extra staff attention, given in the form of RO, may have been responsible for the improvements, rather than RO itself. This is an important issue for RO to face; how it has been explored more fully will be discussed later. Since Brook et al's study a number of other reports have appeared in the literature and these are tabulated in Table 3.3. In order to draw conclusions from these studies it is important to notice the many differences between them – in target population, in setting where the project was carried out, in intensity of RO used, in the experimental period, in the methods of assessment used etc. Some of these important variables are listed in Table 3.3, together with information from the above studies for easy reference. Their results will be reviewed in approximately chronological order. The cross-national diagnostic differences mentioned in Chapter 2 are again of relevance here in interpreting results obtained.

A state mental hospital in Florida, USA, was the setting for Harris & Ivory's (1976) study. They evaluated the effects of RO (including 24 hour RO) introduced in one ward and used a similar ward where traditional treatment was given as a comparison group. A number of significant changes in verbal orientation were found over the five month treatment period, and improvements in the psychiatric aides general ratings of the RO patients' orientation, 'crazy talk' and social interaction were also evident. Attempts to assess behavioural change in other areas – dressing, self-care etc., were largely unsuccessful, apparently due to pre-treatment group differences, which the authors attribute to different expectations of the staff on the two wards. On face-washing and bathing where comparisons were made – no improvements were noted. Harris & Ivory point out some of the methodological difficulties with their study; the RO ward received much more external attention than the control ward, it acquired the status of a 'special' ward and thus staff morale there was probably higher. By carrying out RO the staff gave the patients much more attention than they normally received. The aides who carried out RO also carried out the various assessments and so may have been expecting improvements more than their control counterparts, although as the two assessment periods were separated by five months this probably had little effect. There is, however, reinforcement for the hypothesis that RO – through attention, innovation or of itself – is related to more change than is no treatment, in this case with large groups of relatively young long-stay (and therefore presumably generally chronic – although diagnoses are vaguely defined here) patients.

Similar results were obtained by Citrin & Dixon (1977) with a much older group of nursing home residents who were all moderately disorientated. Following two months of the total RO programme significant differences were demonstrated on a test of basic information and verbal orientation in favour of patients receiving RO in contrast with untreated controls. The Geriatric Rating Scale was used to explore changes in more general aspects of behaviour, less directly related to the content of RO. Here the authors conclude that 'it is questionable whether RO had any effects on the behavioural functioning of the residents involved'. Some doubt must apply to this statement as the RO group showed a significantly better level of behaviour after treatment than the controls, where before treatment there had been no significant differ-

Table 3.3 Group studies of RO

Authors	Location	Setting	Mean age	Mean length of stay	24-hour RO	No. of RO sessions per week	Number and sex of subjects	Control groups	Duration	Assessment methods
Letcher, Peterson & Scarbrough 1974	Tuscaloosa USA	VA Hospital OBS (80%) CVA (15%)	82.8	—	X	Daily	125 M	None	2–56 months	4 point overall need for nursing care rating
Salter & Salter 1975	Mount Vernon USA	State Psychiatric Hospital. OBS Schizophrenia. Mental retardation	68	15.9 years	X	Daily	21 M	None	4 months	Proportion motivated to participate in recreational and educational activities provided
Katz 1976	New York USA	Nursing home. CBS Senile dementia etc.	84	—	?	1–3	108 90F 18M	None	18 months	Retrospective–specific behavioural descriptions from records
Barnes 1974	Georgia USA	Nursing home Senile dementia	81	Less than 3 years	No	6	6 2M 4F	None	6 weeks	Information questionnaire. Nursing director's observations
Brook, Degun & Mather 1975	Warley Essex UK	Psychiatric hospital. Dementia (1 head injury)	73.3	1.9 years	No	Daily	18 10F 8M 9 RO 9 Control	Group taken daily to RO room No active therapy	16 weeks	Behaviour Rating Scale

Author & year	Location	Setting	Mean age	Length of stay		Sessions/week	N & groups	Control	Duration	Measures
Harris & Ivory 1976	Florida USA	State Hospital CBS, OBS, others	66.6	24.6 years	X	Daily	29 RO 28 Control all F	NT	5 months	Florida State Hospital Behaviour Rating Scale (i) Ward behaviour (ii) Verbal orientation (iii) Aides' impressions
Citrin & Dixon 1977	Nebraska USA	Nursing home Moderately disorientated	84	—	X	Daily	12 RO 13 Control	NT	2 months	RO information sheet Geriatric rating scale (GRS)
MacDonald & Settin 1978	New York USA	Nursing home	64.4	—	No	3	10 RO 10 SW 10 NT 21F 9M	SW NT	5 weeks	Life Satisfaction Index NOSIE (nurses' rating) Behavioural Mapping Index
Voelkel 1978	Ohio USA	Nursing home/ Moderate/ severely mentally impaired	80+	2.67 years	No	3	10 RO 10 RS 19F 1M	RS	6 weeks	Mental status Questionnaire. PSMS Physical self-maintenance scale
Holden & Sinebruchow 1978	Leeds UK	Geriatric Hospital CVA, dementia, others	77	1.43 years	X	5–6	46 13M 33F 30 RO 16 NT	NT	3 months	Stockton Geriatric Rating Scale Clifton Assessment Schedule
Cornbleth & Cornbleth 1979	Pittsburgh USA	VA Nursing home OBS	75.18	5.34 years	No	5	22M	None	3 months	RO Questionnaire Geriatric Resident Goals Scale

Table 3.3 (cont.)

Authors	Location	Setting	Mean age	Mean length of stay	24-hour RO	No. of RO sessions per week	Number and sex of subjects	Control groups	Duration	Assessment methods
Woods 1979	Newcastle-upon-Tyne UK	EMI Homes Dementia	76.6	Less than 3 years	No	5	14 12F 2M 5 RO 4NT 5 SA	SA NT	5 months	Wechsler Memory Scale, Concentration test, Information and Orientation test, Gibson Spiral Maze, Crichton Geriatric rating Scale
Johnson 1979	Dundee UK	Psychiatric hospital Dementia	80.1	—	No	5	61F 33 RO 11 SA 12 NT	SA NT	1 month	Direct observation Test of RO in geriatric patients
Holden & Sinebruchow 1979	Leeds UK	Geriatric hospital CVA, dementia, others	80.3	0.9 years	X	5–6	16 6M 10F	NT	3 months	Crichton Geriatric Rating Scale Holden Communication Scale
Woodward 1979	Tooting London UK	Psychiatric hospital Dementia (9) Depression (1) Paraphrenia (3)	80.5	3.75 years	No	4	13F	None	3 months	Geriatric Rating Scale, Orientation Test
Lockyer 1979	Wakefield UK	Psychiatric hospital	67.77	24.23 years	X	5	16F 4, 24	OT NT	8 weeks	Crichton Geriatric

	Location	Setting / Diagnosis	Age	Duration	Control	Frequency	hr RO sessions		Duration	Scales
		Dementia, Schizophrenia					hr RO 4, 24 hr + RO sessions 4 NT 4 OT			Scale Holden Communication Scale
Hanley McGuire & Boyd 1981	Edinburgh UK	Psychogeriatric hospital Old peoples' Home Dementia	79 81	—	No	4	57 53F 4M 28 RO 29 NT	NT	3 months	Geriatric Rating Scale Koskela Test (includes verbal orientation) Orientation Test
Riegler 1980	New Orleans USA	Nursing home. moderate/severe degree of confusion.	79.6	—	No	2	8 2M 6F 4 RO 4 RO + music	—	8 weeks	Geriatric Rating Scale Philadelphia Geriatric Centre Mental Status Questionnaire.
Merchant & Saxby 1981	Plymouth UK	Geriatric hospital Dementia, CVA	83	3 years	No	Daily	10 4M 6F	NT	8 weeks	Clifton Assessment Procedure Crichton Geriatric Rating Scale Holden Communication Scale Slater and Lipman Confusion Scales

Key:
OT = Occupational Therapy
NT = No Treatment Control
OBS = Organic Brain Syndrome
CBS = Chronic Brain Syndrome
CVA = Cerebrovascular Accident
SW = Sheltered Workshop
RS = Resocialisation
EMI = Elderly Mentally Infirm
SA = Social Attention

ence between the groups. This seems to be overruled by the authors as the RO group were (non-significantly) better before treatment. Perhaps a statistical analysis allowing for this could have led to more conclusive results. So there were definite cognitive improvements, but more general changes remained doubtful.

The problems mentioned above in relation to Harris & Ivory's study concerning use of an untreated control group on a separate ward also apply here. They can be overcome by using a group of patients receiving an amount of staff attention comparable to the RO group; if the alternative therapy is seen as relevant and as likely to succeed as RO then staff expectancy effects may also be brought into line. In attempting to control for quantity of staff attention inevitably RO sessions are the prime focus, as it is much more practical to have alternative therapies for a fixed time period than to have a continuous therapy parallel with 24 hour RO. MacDonald & Settin (1978) and Voelkel (1978) compared three times weekly RO classes with other therapies – a sheltered workshop and resocialisation groups respectively. In neither study were behavioural changes shown in the nursing home populations used. Voelkel's resocialisation group improved more on an information and orientation test than the RO group – but the RO group before treatment were generally at a lower level, so the resocialisation group, Voelkel suggests, may have had more capacity for relearning and responding to their group. MacDonald & Settin's assessment of changes was more wide-ranging than any previous study and included an index of life-satisfaction (LSI) in self-report form. On this scale, and on nurses' ratings of the resident's social interest, the sheltered workshop group improved; the RO group in fact tended to deteriorate on the LSI, whereas untreated controls showed little change.

These two studies, both tending to favour alternative approaches challenge the efficacy of RO. Were they however a fair test of RO? Scarbrough et al (1978) certainly argued that MacDonald & Settin's interpretation of RO was erroneous. Voelkel's description of her resocialisation group resembles closely activities other workers have used in RO. MacDonald & Settin's sheltered workshop group would certainly be beyond the capabilities of many patients included in other RO programmes. They comment that their RO residents mentioned to staff 'that the sessions seem boring and useless'. Similarly Voelkel states that most of her RO participants read the RO board without any difficulties and several were irritated at having to read the information, the approach thus appearing child-like. It seems clear that in both studies the RO technique may not have been pitched at the appropriate level for the residents concerned and the alternative therapies may have been much more rewarding and satisfying for the residents. There is an indication here that RO must be adjusted appropriately for the residents involved, and that techniques appropriate for severely disorientated patients may need to be withdrawn with patients who are more in touch with reality. This highlights the difficulties of defining exactly what RO is or is not.

Other attempts have since been made to control for the effects of staff attention. Woods (1979) carried out such a study in a Home for the Elderly Mentally Infirm. Residents with a severe degree of memory disorder either attended RO sessions or a conversation group each held on five days a week for 30 minutes, over a five month period. A similar group of residents in another Home received no additional treatment but were assessed at the same intervals as those in the experimental groups. The care attendants in the conversation (or 'social therapy') group were instructed to encourage the residents to talk about anything at all and to praise them for participating. RO materials were not used in this group (although it was held in the RO room) and residents were not corrected if they began to ramble. In addition to the often-used information/orientation test and a behaviour rating scale, other cognitive measures were used including the Wechsler Memory Scale (the WMS assesses a number of different aspects of memory and learning) and a concentration test. The results of the various cognitive assessments were clearly in favour of the RO group. Significant differences were found on the concentration test, information/orientation test and on the Wechsler Memory Scale (Figs. 3.3, 3.4 and 3.5). On the concentration test the 'social therapy' group seemed to fare worse than even the untreated group. Further unpublished analysis of results from this study suggests that the WMS improvement was not simply related to its information/orientation and concentration components. Although these are two of the three factors consistently found in factor analysis of the WMS (Kear Colwell 1973) in fact it is on the other factor (Kear Colwell's Factor I), which is interpreted as a measure of new learning, that the RO group improved significantly more than the two control groups after nine weeks of treatment. (Mann Whitney U test, $U = 4$, $n_1 = 5$, $n_2 = 9$; $p < 0.025$, 1 tailed). Thus

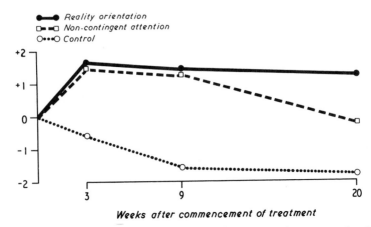

Fig. 3.3 Mean changes in total score on composite concentration test over time in Woods' (1979) study. Non-contingent attention group significantly less improved than RO throughout, and relative to untreated control group at 3 and 9 weeks.

more general cognitive improvements seemed to be occurring here. Despite these encouraging findings in the cognitive sphere no behavioural changes could be demonstrated on the Crichton Geriatric Rating Scale, modified to facilitate comparisons with Brook et al's (1975) results. Possible reasons for this will be discussed later, but certainly the RO sessions were successful in chang-

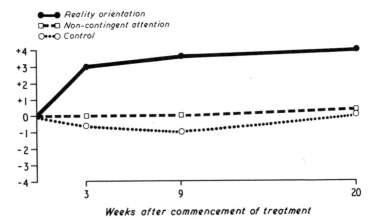

Fig. 3.4 Mean change in total score on composite information and orientation test over time in Woods' (1979) study. RO significantly more improved throughout than combined control groups (which do not differ).

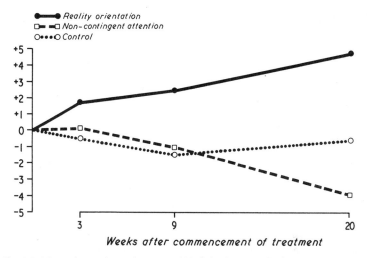

Fig. 3.5 Mean change in total score on Wechsler Memory Scale over time in Woods' (1979) study. RO significantly more improved at 9 and 20 weeks than control groups combined, which do not differ throughout.

ing the cognitive area of functioning on which they directly focussed. That the conversation group was a viable alternative therapy as far as care staff were concerned was demonstrated by their previously mentioned preference for this group over the RO group, which they found more taxing to lead.

These cognitive improvements were confirmed in a larger study conducted in a psychiatric hospital by Johnson (1979). Again RO patients improved significantly on an information/orientation test whereas social attention and no-treatment groups did not, and these differences were apparent after only one month of treatment. An innovative attempt to monitor behaviour change by the time-consuming method of direct observation and time-sampling procedures was discontinued when no changes in behaviour or social interaction were apparent.

In a large-scale study conducted by Hanley et al (1981) in both long-stay psychogeriatric wards and an old people's home, 28 subjects received four times weekly RO classes and 29 control subjects received no treatment over a 12 week period. Some small but significant changes in verbal orientation were found but again no differences on a behaviour rating scale between RO and control groups were established.

Does general behavioural change occur?

Leaving aside for the moment the two studies in which RO compared unfavourably with 'alternative' therapies a clear trend is apparent in the remaining six controlled trials that have been reviewed. All six have found clear improvements favouring RO over non-treatment or social attention controls but all except Brook et al's study have only been able to demonstrate these changes convincingly in the area of cognitive functioning i.e. verbal orientation, knowledge of basic information and so on. Only Brook et al (1975) provided evidence supporting general changes in functioning in the ward or home setting, despite the previously mentioned frequent anecdotal reports of behavioural change in the literature.

The question of whether general behavioural changes occur or not is of great importance as a clearer definition of the ways in which RO is effective or not is sought. Changes in verbal orientation are interesting and potentially have some usefulness but there is no doubt that it is improvements in self-care, in finding the toilet, in dressing and in social interaction and so on that workers and relatives would prefer to see, and one might hypothesise that these general changes would do more to increase the person's dignity and self-respect.

It might be argued that behavioural changes are not found in some studies as 24 hour RO is not utilized and so the potential for reinforcing appropriate behaviour outside the actual RO room is not utilized. This is untenable however as the one study that did show general changes in functioning used only the RO room and two studies using 24 hour RO found no changes. Of course, as commented previously, the intensity of the 24 hour RO received might be questioned as it is difficult to establish to what extent it actually occurs and perhaps future work might relate degrees of behavioural change to actual intensity of 24 hour RO. It might be argued that RO cannot be expected to bring about general changes in functioning, as its focus on reorientation is so distinctly cognitive. However the 24 hour approach is intended to be used during activities of daily living (e.g. Drummond et al 1978) and there are the anecdotal results and Brook et al's findings to be accounted for.

Possibly, as Woods (1979) suggested concerning the results of his study, the measures of behaviour used are too insensitive, but in the various investigations a variety of measures have been used. Perhaps, as Lockyer (1979) in a thoughtful account implies, the emphasis on group changes may obscure changes in the individual's behaviour and Woods (1979) for example pointed out that the variation in behaviour rating scores increased greatly over the course of his study, indicating that individuals were changing in different ways. In a later section the limited amount of research looking at individuals in-depth rather than at groups of patients will be reviewed. Rating scales can be problematic however and Lockyer (1979) showed clearly how different raters use the same scale in quite different ways, and it may be that more attention is needed to training raters in the consistent use of the scale or in developing other more reliable methods of assessing behaviour – although Johnson's negative results using direct observation are not encouraging here.

To confirm however that in some settings behavioural change can be demonstrated even with rating scales, a recently completed study by Holden & Sinebruchow (1979) is presented. Holden & Sinebruchow (1978) had previously been unable to demonstrate any differences between RO groups and no-treatment controls over a 12 week period using the Stockton Geriatric Rating Scale and the Clifton Assessment Schedule but found differences in outcome nonetheless (see Fig. 3.6) which led them to conclude that these particular assessment techniques were unsatisfactory in this context. It should be noted here that discharge as an outcome should be treated with some caution as it is greatly influenced by the patient's social circumstances and hospital policy. In the subsequent study two other rating scales were utilized – the Crichton

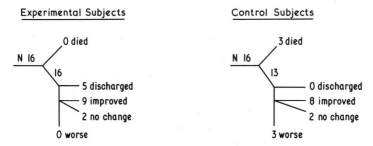

Fig. 3.6 Tree table. Outcome of controlled study based on CAS and Stockton ratings, plus discharge records. Holden & Sinebruchow 1978. Reproduced, with permission, from Age and Ageing 7: 83–90

Geriatric Rating Scale (as used by Woods 1979) and Holden's five point Communication Scale, (see Chapter 5 and Appendix 3) covering particularly conversation, awareness, knowledge and communication. The setting was once more a geriatric ward and diagnoses included dementia, depression, Parkinson's disease, strokes etc. The patients were split into two groups who received formal RO sessions alternately for one month each over a three month period. Following their month as an RO group the group would remain together on the ward whilst the other group went to a special room, fitted out in the style of a pub. The nursing staff had considerable experience of RO and certainly to some extent used it on the ward as in 24 hour RO.

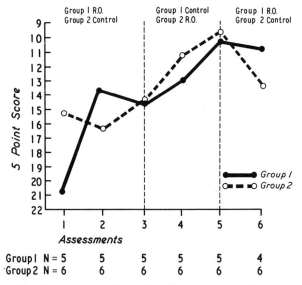

Fig. 3.7 Holden Communication Scale. The difference between improvement rates of Group I and Group II up to assessment 2 were significant (P< 0.05). Holden & Sinebruchow 1979.

The results of the study are shown in Figures 3.7 and 3.8. On the Holden Communication Scale Group 1 improved markedly in its first RO session period and continued to improve during the control period – perhaps underlining the ward nurses' continuation of the RO. Group 2 really began to improve after the cross-over; some of their gains were lost when they became controls again. The scale may be sensitive to the effects of illness (a

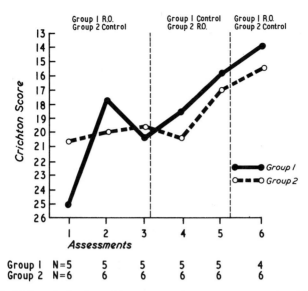

Fig. 3.8 Crichton Scale. Group I improvement between assessment 1 and 6 was significant (P < 0.05). The difference between improvement rate of Group I and Group II up to assessment 2 was significant (P < 0.05). Holden & Sinebruchow 1979.

viral infection) which affected many patients on the ward at points 3 and 6. The results of the Crichton Scale are similar, again documenting behavioural changes commencing during the group's first period of formal RO sessions and to some extent being maintained and improved on during subsequent control periods. Group 1 showed a significant improvement on this scale between the beginning and end of the study and on both scales the rate of change was significantly different between the two groups in the first two weeks of the first period of formal RO sessions.

There are some drawbacks to the study: the raters were not completely 'blind' to group membership; the control condition may well not have been a pure 'no-treatment' condition after the first month; diagnostic criteria in geriatric wards may differ from other settings and the relationship of the results to diagnosis is in any case unclear. However, behavioural changes have been shown and so the question of whether behavioural changes occur remains wide open.

Most recently a preliminary controlled study by Merchant & Saxby (1981) has also found behavioural as well as cognitive changes. There were significant improvements in the RO patients compared with controls on the three factors – orientation, communication and socially acceptable behaviour – that the authors derived from factor analysis of the battery of measures listed in Table 3.3. These changes were achieved with daily RO sessions for eight weeks. As in Holden & Sinebruchow's (1978 1979) studies the emphasis was on a social atmosphere, and the study was also conducted in a geriatric setting with patients with mixed diagnoses.

In addition Cornbleth & Cornbleth (1979) and Woodward (1979) using before and after designs without control groups have shown significant general behavioural improvements related to the introduction of RO classes over three month periods. Clearly then the issue is not yet resolved and there may be many factors involved in the apparent discrepancies between studies. One factor may be the degree to which the RO session is a formal classroom teaching session rather than a social setting where learning is encouraged (as in Holden's pub) and where it is possible to capitalise on previously learned social responses. Another may be the subject population and the degree to which the institution has in the past ' encouraged' dependent behaviour. Thus for example if the particular group has been under-functioning in self-care then RO may tip the balance, whereas if the institution is already encouraging independence there may be less scope for improvement. Initial levels of dependence are important here; for example Woods' (1979) residents functioned initially on the Crichton Rating Scale much better than Holden & Sinebruchow's (1979) patients on the same scale. The extent to which staff carry over into 24 hour RO reinforcement of appropriate functioning is probably also important, and again may be related to differences in attitudes and practices between institutions.

Woods (1979) and Woods & Britton (1977) have suggested that direct training of a particular skill might be needed if more general changes are to occur. Hanley et al (1981) have applied this approach to ward orientation i.e. the patient finding her way from one place to another on the ward. Patients received either no treatment, RO classroom or RO classroom plus some sessions of ward orientation training. This latter procedure involved the staff member taking the patient individually round the ward, asking them to locate different areas and giving clues and directions when the person was unable to do so. This latter group did much better than the RO classes alone or no-treatment on a behavioural test of ward orientation. The groups did not differ on amount of verbal orientation assessed in the usual way. This type of training, it might be argued, should be part of 24 hour RO, and the importance of studies such as this are that the specific components needed for a useful RO programme may be defined more clearly.

Further studies will be needed before even a tentative answer can emerge from the conflicting data as to whether group changes do occur in general functioning, and – very importantly – under what conditions these changes are most likely to occur. In conclusion it can be said that whatever changes occur are relatively small and variable, but this is not to say that ultimately they will not prove to be valuable.

Other research findings

There are a few group studies that additionally have looked specifically at various parameters relevant to RO and these preliminary results are presented here in order, if nothing else, to delineate further issues surrounding the effectiveness of RO other than the central issues discussed above.

1. The relative contributions of 24-hour RO and RO classroom sessions

The relative contributions of these two aspects of RO have been hardly compared at all, the crux of the problem being the difficulty in demonstrating that 24 hour RO is effectively taking place. Hanley et al's (1981) study in which ward orientation training was shown to be effective clearly adds credence to the possible superiority of 24 hour RO in bringing about generalized change. Lockyer (1979) compared 24 hour RO with 24 hour RO plus classroom sessions in a long-stay psychiatric hospital and reported that the latter group generally improved more. Woods et al (1980), in a very different setting, were unable to demonstrate differential changes in cognitive or behavioural functioning between groups of residents in a home for the elderly mentally infirm, one of which had RO sessions in addition to the 24 hour RO planned for both groups. This does not prove of course that either is effective, but certainly any differences were too small to show up in a study using small groups of residents. In both studies questions are raised as to what extent 24 hour RO was occurring and research is needed in which this is directly monitored before conclusions are reached.

2. *The use of memory aids in the environment*

One aspect of 24 hour RO is the provision of visual aids in the environment giving items of information. Hanley (1980) has additionally shown that with respect to ward orientation, large signposts identifying different ward locations were not sufficient to improve patients' orientation. But behavioural change was evident when the signposts were used as part of the ward orientation training procedures outlined above. Similarly, Bergert & Jacobsson (1976), in a Swedish study, concluded that environmental cues were useful in re-orienting the person to time and place but that the person had to be taught to use the cues provided; they suggested that when the cues were not present, orientation decreased again. These findings emphasise the need for 24 hour RO to be an active process in which environmental cues and memory aids are pointed out to the patients, as they may well not make use of them of their own initiative.

3. *Intensity of RO sessions*

As can be seen from Table 3.3 the frequency of RO sessions used in various studies has ranged from once per week to seven times per week. The ideal frequency must depend to some extent on the subject population used, with, presumably, the frequency of sessions being related to the degree of disorientation. However as yet there is no empirical evidence on this. This is unfortunate, as it would be important to its application in day centres etc. if two or three times a week sessions were useful. In virtually every study, sessions have been given once only on any particular day. Johnson (1979) raised the possibility of whether additional RO sessions each day would be of benefit, particularly in situations where 24 hour RO could not be implemented. She compared a group of patients receiving RO sessions once a day with a group receiving twice a day sessions, but found the same range of improvements on verbal orientation with both procedures and no apparent benefit from doubling the number of RO sessions each day. The least confused patients seemed to do worse with two RO sessions per day than one; where there is little memory loss and little variety between sessions, boredom may set in, for patients as well as staff!

4. Group v. individual sessions

In certain circumstances a person cannot be included in group RO, perhaps because of severe deafness, restlessness or double incontinence. In these situations individual RO sessions are often recommended. Johnson (1979) has compared the efficacy of group RO sessions with 10 minute individual RO sessions, and has shown that it is equally as effective as group RO, in improving verbal orientation, but it does not appear to be more effective. There were some indications of it being most effective with the severely deteriorated patients. It may be that these patients have least to gain from the social influence of other patients in a group, and most to lose from being distracted by others and from losing concentration when another patient is the focus of attention. Even these extremely brief individual sessions have then been shown to be of some use.

5. Maintenance of effects of RO

How long-lasting are the effects of RO? Does it have to be continuously applied in perpetuity or is a brief intensive period of RO sufficient to produce lasting change? Barnes (1974) showed a significant deterioration in verbal orientation only one week after RO classes ceased and reported some corresponding anecdotal deterioration in behaviour. Holden & Sinebruchow (1979) followed up their patients six months after RO sessions finished. They reported significant behavioural deterioration on both the Crichton Geriatric Rating Scale and the Holden Communication Scale. Hanley (1980) reports a rapid fall-off of verbal orientation in residents in an old people's home when the frequency of RO sessions was reduced, but there is some suggestion of maintenance with part-time groups with his patients in a hospital setting. His ward orientation procedure effects certainly lasted for five weeks after training – when the post-treatment assessment was made – but after five months ward orientation had returned to baseline levels.

The available evidence seems to suggest an absence of maintenance of treatment effects, with gains often being lost very quickly, and certainly being lost over a period of months. The effects of a reduced intensity of RO following on more intensive training are as yet unclear. If gains could be maintained in this way it would be of great practical use in day-centres where relatively infrequent 'maintenance RO' could be given. The whole question of maintaining improvements in patients discharged from hospital merits urgent exploration.

6. *Components of reality orientation*

To some extent research on different aspects of RO has been covered in the comparison of the effects of 24 hour RO and RO sessions above. However there is generally a dearth of research breaking RO down into its components and evaluating their relative effectiveness. Johnson's previously mentioned comparisons of group and individual RO removed many of the social factors operative in RO sessions, and shows these may not be necessary for cognitive improvement to occur in some populations at least. Riegler (1980) has carried out a fascinating study comparing the effects of RO sessions with and without music on a small number of nursing home residents, and found a clear superiority for the music group in terms of improvement on a basic orientation and information test. The use of music included 'singing and playing rhythm instruments to accompany songs and jingles dealing with names, members, day, date and year'. Other activities included listening to and discussing music concerning particular times and places. It may be the music helped group members participate more, relax more and enjoy the sessions more, making them less serious, classroom-like and formal. Riegler points out some difficulties with her study – relatively infrequent group sessions (only twice per week) in particular, but has illustrated well the usefulness of looking at different aspects of the total RO treatment package, as in this way it is possible to rationally and empirically develop and refine the methods used.

7. *Patients benefiting most from RO*

As Table 3.3 shows, RO has been applied in a wide range of settings, nursing homes, residential homes, geriatric hospitals, psychiatric hospitals etc., and with patients with a wide range of diagnoses. There are no clear emergent trends from the various studies as to particular settings or diagnostic groups where it is most useful. Care needs to be taken that the form of RO is adapted for the particular population according to degree of disorientation, or the problems outlined by MacDonald & Settin (1978) and Voel-kel (1978) of boredom with basic RO groups in higher function-ing patients may be encountered. Certainly other therapies should be considered where patients are at a level to participate in them, with RO perhaps being at its most useful where the patient is too confused for other types of therapy. However these issues need more empirical investigation before hard and fast rules are estab-lished. Within the senile dementia diagnostic category, Brook et al's (1975) results suggested that the lowest functioning group showed least change and Woodward (1979) similarly found larger changes in her less deteriorated patients. Contrary results are pro-vided by Johnson (1979) however who found changes in verbal orientation of comparable size at each of three levels of function-ing in her long-stay psychogeriatric population. Hanley et al (1981) similarly report that degree of dementia did not appear to be a significant determinant of change. As Johnson's results on frequency of sessions and on the utility of individual sessions imply, it may be that RO has to be adapted to the needs of the more deteriorated patient, but there is evidence to suggest that in some circumstances severely demented patients – as defined by these authors – can benefit from RO sessions, and presumably therefore from 24 hour RO also. Differences between the studies mentioned here may reflect differences in patient populations and selection criteria used.

8. Use of RO in day-centres and day-hospitals

Increasingly day-hospitals and day-centres are becoming impor-tant in the assessment, treatment and support of elderly confused people, allowing them to remain in their own homes longer and providing much-needed relief for relations and friends. There has been little study as yet of groups of day-patients receiving RO. A study has been carried out in Edinburgh; the results were disap-pointing with little behavioural change apparent as assessed by the Crichton Geriatric Rating Scale (Hodge 1980, personal communi-cation). Patients were however rated as more cooperative follow-ing RO sessions.

One of us (R. Woods) has used RO in a day-hospital setting, where patients attended at most twice a week, and so sessions were thereby limited to twice a week also. Data for six female patients (all with a diagnosis of dementia) before and after RO are available. Results on a memory and information test showed that four patients made improvements after RO sessions commenced, a fifth scored at the level she had been at seven months previously and the last patient showed a transitory halt and improvement in what had been a downhill trend, before deteriorating very rapidly indeed. The rapid deterioration seemed to coincide with physical ill-health. One of the improved patients returned to a level recorded for her three years previously, having also been showing evidence of a gradual deterioration in memory. The most improved patient had a mixed diagnosis of dementia and depression, but had been receiving antidepressant medication for some time before RO started. Behaviour ratings showed relatively little change; there was a clear improvement for the patient who had also been depressed and the patient who ultimately deteriorated rapidly showed an improvement in her behavioural functioning concomitant with her improvement in cognitive ability.

It is of interest that the most severely demented patient in this series did show improvement and so RO in a day setting may not be appropriate *only* for patients with a memory loss of a mild to moderate degree, who formed the majority of this sample.

Finally, Greene et al (1980) have reported the preliminary results of a study of RO sessions in a Glasgow day-hospital. This followed some moderately successful individual interventions (reviewed in the next section). Groups of four to six patients met twice a day on the two days per week that they attended. Patients had a mild to moderate degree of dementia. All were living with a relative who could monitor any changes in their behaviour in their own home or had a relative who lived close by. The relatives completed rating scales on the patient's mood and behaviour at home, and also on their own degree of stress and their own mood. The 13 patients involved were also cognitively and behaviourally assessed at the hospital. Assessments were carried out at the beginning and end of a four week baseline period, after six weeks of RO sessions and finally after a further six weeks where RO sessions were not held.

Results showed a dramatic significant improvement in verbal orientation, following RO. The gain was lost at the six week follow-up assessment. Changes in relatives' ratings of the patient's behaviour and in their degree of stress were not significant, but relatives' mood did improve significantly with RO, and deteriorated again at follow-up. This was despite the relatives being unaware of the procedures being followed in the project. These findings then hold some encouragement for the use of RO in day-settings. A longer period of treatment and an untreated control group would be useful in future studies; there is a need to go on to evaluate the effects of teaching relatives to use RO in addition.

The individual case

The many studies reviewed so far have, without exception, been looking at group changes, group differences, group effects. Even when changes have proved to be significant the size of the improvement has often been small over the group as a whole. Group studies have their place, but if the extent to which RO works and its attendant limitations are to be really understood individual cases need to be examined, preferably where objective measures have been taken over a period of time. In the behavioural literature particularly single-case design experiments are used a great deal and can be extremely powerful in comparing and contrasting different aspects and phases of a treatment approach.

The first published case studies of this type were carried out by Greene et al (1979). These studies as well as illustrating the responses of three individuals to RO also serve to show its utility in a day-hospital setting, where the studies were carried out, and to demonstrate the effects of simply providing information about time, place and person alone without the other activities and socialisation that usually accompanies RO.

Three cases are reported, all females showing severe to moderate impairment in all areas of cognition and having a diagnosis of organic dementia. RO sessions were highly structured in that they consisted of a standard list of questions of general and personal orientation given in conversational manner over a 30 minute period. Each patient was seen individually twice on each attendance at the day-hospital. In baseline phases correct answers were not supplied when there was no response or it was incorrect. In RO phases correct answers were given where necessary. In both phases the patient was told when correct answers had been given.

Patient 1 was seen four times a week. Week 1 was a baseline phase, weeks 2–3 and 6–7 were RO phases and in weeks 4–5 a return to baseline conditions took place. Finally the patient was seen once a week in weeks 8–12 under the baseline conditions. Improvements in orientation score were apparent in the RO periods. These were lost in the return to baseline phase and gradually returned to initial levels five weeks after the end of the RO sessions. General changes in the patient's behaviour during RO phases were suggested by anecdotal reports; for example her husband temporarily stopped demanding her admission.

The second case study attempted to systematise the more general effects by including ratings made by the unit OT of the patient's performance and social functioning in OT sessions. The patient was 52 years old and had pre-senile dementia. She was seen on three days per week, and a similar design was followed as with Patient 1, except that in the final phase of once-a-week sessions RO was included. The results showed a clear improvement in orientation in RO phases. This was maintained in the return to baseline phase, and orientation remained at a high level during once-a-week RO sessions. The OT ratings were made without knowledge of the experimental phase, and showed that ratings of performance of activities parallelled the changes in orientation. The patient's social rating increased steadily in all phases. The authors speculate that this may be related to general stimulation effects whereas the changes in performance scores seem more likely to be related to changes in orientation.

The third patient was an older (72 years), more severely demented lady, seen three days a week. Results for this patient were similar with respect to orientation, with a decline in performance however at the return to baseline phase. Changes in OT ratings were not quite as marked, but did show some improvement. Generalisation to items not taught in the RO sessions was tested to ensure that the improvements noted were not simply from parrot-fashion learning. These items, which included differently worded questions, photographs of people included in the orientation test and new items, showed the same pattern of improvement in RO phases.

Nicol (1979, personal communication) provides anecdotal data that relatives of Patient 2 noted some change in her functioning at home, but Patient 3's ratings at home by relatives were not significantly correlated with her orientation scores. This patient's improvement in orientation still left her with large gaps in her repertoire whereas Patient 2 was approaching maximum orientation scores by the end of therapy. For Patient 3 the total of four weeks orientation may have been insufficient to produce orientation-related behavioural change at home.

Greene et al (1979) introduce the concept of a gradient of generalisation; the more a behaviour depends on orientation the more change will be apparent in it following RO. This is a hypothesis well worth pursuing further. Woods (1980) in an unpublished single-case study has explored further the issue of generalisation from items of orientation that are taught in RO sessions to ones that are not.

The patient was a 68 year old lady who had been an in-patient in a psychiatric hospital for three months with a diagnosis, supported by neurological investigation, of Korsakoff's psychosis. Twice daily structured RO sessions (with specified information *only* being taught) were conducted by nursing staff. If the patient did not know an answer a clue was given, followed by the correct answer if the patient could not make use of the prompt. The experimental design made use of a multiple baseline (Table 3.4) in which all information items were assessed regularly. The RO sessions covered only a proportion of these items at any time. Assessment sessions took place at the beginning, middle and end of each phase, each of which was 9–12 days long, except phase IV which lasted one month. The results are shown in Figure 3.9.

Generally items showed most improvement during the phase of treatment when they were specifically taught. Two exceptions should be noted. The patient's performance on list I items did improve markedly in phase I but continued to improve during phase II, before falling off during phase III, after three weeks of

Table 3.4 Multiple baseline design of case-study

Experimental phase	Treatment conditions
Baseline	No RO sessions
Phase I	List I taught
Phase II	List II taught
Phase III	List III taught
Phase IV	All unlearned items taught using a diary as a memory aid

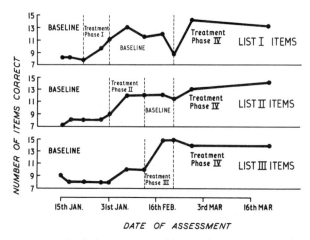

Fig. 3.9 Learning of verbal orientation and basic information in a single-case experimental study – see text for details of multiple base-line design and the phases of intervention.

other items being taught. The records that nurses kept of RO sessions suggested that the assessment at the end of phase I gave an underestimate of her near-perfect knowledge of list I items at that time; the 'improvement' in phase II was in fact probably maintenance of improvement already made. The other exception is the slight improvement of list III items in phase II; these gains were made on items in list III that had similar content to certain items in list II. An overall 60 item personalized memory and information test showed gradual improvement over the experimental period

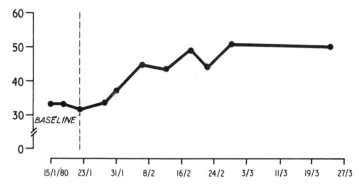

Fig. 3.10 Scores on a 60 item information and orientation test achieved by subject in the single-case experimental study shown in Fig. 3.9.

(see Fig. 3.10). The final phase, in which all lists reached near-maximum levels, was an attempt to help her learn to use her diary and to reorientate herself from that, and improvements seem to be well maintained in this phase.

This study emphasises that re-learning can take place and there can be little doubt that the changes in verbal orientation seen here were directly related to the RO sessions given and in particular to the items of information supplied in the RO sessions. Sessions were relatively brief (10 minutes or so) and deliberately limited in scope. This is not recommended as a way of carrying out RO of course, but should be seen as an attempt to look closely at one feature of it – that of giving information. Here there was relatively little generalisation from one orientation item to another, with the exception already noted. It is to be hoped that further single cases will be studied in detail, as so often in group studies there is a great deal of individual variation which is not explored. Individual studies could add greatly to our understanding of the results of group studies.

CONCLUSIONS

We have seen some evidence then that RO changes patients; in particular verbal orientation has most often been shown to be improved. The question of generalisation to other areas of functioning remains open; changes in behaviour have been less reliably demonstrated. The role of 24 hour RO in encouraging generalisation of changes has yet to be explored fully, although Hanley et al's (1981) study of ward orientation training is most encouraging in this respect. Many questions remain to be answered and many of the studies reviewed here are inadequate in one way or another (partly because of the methodological difficulties outlined previously). It is our hope that some directions and issues will have been raised here, and that future researchers will be able to shed light where at present so many issues are shrouded in cloud!

Institutional differences are almost certainly of importance in our consideration of at times conflicting results. Woods & Britton (1977) identified the need for researchers to give more details of their institutional settings.

By 'institutions' more than just simply large mental hospitals are included. Shepherd & Richardson (1979) have shown that even in small day-centres (for younger people) different institutional attitudes may apply and the same is likely to be so for any facility, large or small, residential or day-care only.

Little progress has been made in this direction as yet. In the long run it may be at an institutional level that RO makes its most important and far-reaching changes. In order for staff to change in ways consistent with RO the whole ethos of the institution may have to change, and in this light RO may be seen as a philosophy for a dramatic change from purely custodial care, to a care that firmly places the emphasis on the needs and potential of the individual. This will be developed further in Chapter 9 in the discussion of staff attitudes.

4

How does RO work?

Evidence has been presented in the previous chapter indicating some limited, but consistently found, efficacy of RO, particularly with respect to verbal orientation. Consideration will now be given to the manner in which these changes have arisen. Several possibilities that have been suggested will be outlined, and what evidence there is for them will be discussed. It should be borne in mind that although group changes are generally small the improvement in individuals can be dramatic – some explanation is needed for these impressive changes that do occur. Also in a population as heterogenous as the 'confused elderly' it is quite likely that different processes may be responsible for improvement in different individuals, and, furthermore, several mechanisms may be operating simultaneously.

'REACTIVATION OF NEURAL PATHWAYS'

In her introduction to Folsom's work on RO Stephens (1969) states: 'The process can reawaken unused neural pathways and stimulate the patients to develop new ways of functioning to compensate for organic brain damage that has resulted either from injury or progressive senility, or from deterioration through misuse'.

The issues arising from this statement are:

a. Can parts of the brain suffer from disuse? Muscles need to be exercised in order to remain efficient; do neural pathways require regular use for the same reasons?

b. If certain pathways in the brain are blocked, damaged or even dead can other connections be made in order to maintain function by using other routes or a by-pass system?

c. Can brain cells regenerate?

These are very profound and complex problems which have intrigued scientists for at least the past 150 years. The most controversial issue – which relates particularly to a and b above is the extent to which particular functions are under the control of specific localised parts of the brain. The work of Paul Broca and Carl Wernicke in relating particular speech deficits to specific areas of the dominant hemisphere would seem to support a localisation viewpoint. However, as Hughlings Jackson has indicated, localisation of a deficit is different from localisation of a function. In the light of recent evidence, whilst there is probably considerable localisation of certain major functions, total localisation appears illogical and a theory of large scale psychological processes working within functional systems is developing.

To what extent is recovery from brain damage possible?

Zangwill in his introduction to the classic work by Luria on 'Restoration of function after brain injury' (1963), states: 'In man, unfortunately, recovery from the effects of brain injury is apt to be a good deal less complete [than in animals] and residual defects are distressingly common'. However, despite quite extensive damage persons sustaining head injury and other brain damage can obtain restoration of function – to some degree and sometimes to an incredible degree. Paralysis, motor and sensory function can all return to near-normal. Even disorders of speech, gnosis and praxis can improve dramatically. Four mechanisms for this restoration of function will be considered. Note that actual damage, rather than the progressive deterioration of dementia, is being examined here.

Superficial or temporary injury

The injury could be superficial, like any external scratches and bruises, and the systems are only suffering from shock rather than permanent damage. In 1914 Von Monakow defined his concept of 'Functional Diachisis' – recovery is seen as being due to the re-establishment of temporarily impaired neural systems. He inferred a temporary state of shock, or disinhibition. The difference between initial and residual symptoms is then due to a specific lesion temporarily disrupting the neural tissues some distance from the actual site of the lesion spreading there by means of direct fibre pathways. As the shock effect subsides there is a gradual improvement. In 1958 Kempinsky found support for such an effect as his recordings from cortical areas distant from the cerebral lesion showed transient depression followed by normal functioning. Hoedt-Rasmussen et al (1964) showed that in strokes there is a marked transient decrement in metabolic rate in brain areas opposite a lesion.

Simple examples of such a recovery would include concussions, little strokes, or transient ischaemic attacks (TIA), and the remarkable recovery seen after several weeks or months from a more severe stroke. The extent of the original lesion determines the residual dysfunction.

Substitution

This theory is closely linked with the Classical Gestalt School of Psychology. It implies a dynamic unity, in which particular functions are not necessarily linked to set locations in the brain. According to Goldstein (1939), when a part of the brain is damaged the rest of it adapts in order to take over the function for which it was responsible, or in which it was involved. New strategies would be substituted and behavioural processes would assume responsibility for restoration. It is possible that redundant mechanisms, already present in the brain, could be employed. Several workers have found an indication that 'recovered' behaviours are not identical to those exhibited by normal animals used in their experiments. As explanation it is suggested that some neural structures failed to act as perfect substitutes for the original ones (Finger et al 1973). Gazzaniga (1974) suggests that diachisis is insufficient alone to account for recovery from massive brain damage. He states: "I believe recovery' in the adult, resulting from non-physiological improvement, is the result of pre-existing behavioural mechanisms not necessarily routinely involved in a particular act now covering for the mental activity under question".

In his opinion the restoration is due to 'other existing behavioural strategies that are capable of handling the job but have previously been involved in the other more supportive roles'.

This implies that a previously little-used system with the capacity for carrying out the specific function can take over when necessary.

Radical re-organisation

This theory holds that there is a radical re-organisation of the destroyed activity. The function is restored by means of different and unaffected neuronal structures assuming the role of the damaged one. If primary structures have been damaged then secondary areas can be brought into use. However, if a secondary area is destroyed the whole functional system will suffer. In order to restore function in the latter instance it may be necessary to employ new methods. These may 'lead to the creation of new functional systems, and almost any area of the cerebral cortex may be included in a particular functional system in order to reintegrate the disturbed activity of the brain' (Luria 1963).

The degree to which neural tissue is able to take up new function (neural plasticity) remains controversial. The extent to which new links can be formed rather than the preserved links being re-organised is still unclear. Readers are referred to Luria (1963), Blundell (1975), LeVere (1975), Finger et al (1973) and Hécaen & Albert (1978) for more information.

Regeneration

The recovery is seen as due to actual restitution of tissue. In the last decade research findings have shown, quite clearly, that various forms of regeneration do occur. Several accounts are valuable as reference (Finger et al 1973, LeVere 1975, Hécaen & Albert 1978, Bowen & Davison 1978, 1980). Axonal sprouting after ablation has been found in cortical and sub-cortical structures, but studies (mainly in animals) have shown that recovery is most effective in early youth. There are doubts as to whether regeneration occurs in mature, let alone ageing brains.

Hécaen & Albert (1978) express concern about the use of animal studies to form opinions about human brain function, and point out the highly complex system of human brains, cerebral assymetry and the probability of a more complicated process being involved, and Bowen & Davison (1978) indicate that the greatly differing life-spans of animals and men make comparisons more difficult.

Comments

This discussion of four possible mechanisms of 'reactivation' of neural pathways is necessarily inconclusive, and it is beyond the scope of this book to indicate a preference for any of them. They are presented as intriguing possibilities, rather than as well-established processes.

To return to the questions posed as a result of Stephens' statements about neural pathways, some can be answered and some remain tantalising problems yet to be solved. Cells *can* regenerate, certainly in extreme youth, but there remains doubt about the adult and ageing brain. There *are* suggestions in the literature that function can be maintained by using other routes or strategies, or by using by-pass systems. The possibility of parts of the brain suffering from disuse and 'wasting' as disused muscles do is fascinating and seems quite likely for highly localised functions; some theorists would argue that such little-used areas might be called upon to take over functions in damaged regions!

The theories that have been outlined may not be mutually exclusive. They point the way for intensive research evaluating the effects and mechanisms of rehabilitative techniques. Workers like Gazzaniga et al (1971, 1972) are having success in retraining after strokes and Luria demonstrated how function could be restored to the brains of war-wounded patients with head injury. Other improvements can occur without specific intervention. Thus where RO is successful in producing changes in stroke patients or elderly people who have suffered other actual brain injury, then the adaptive capacity of the brain should not be discounted as a possible reason. There is no evidence, however, that these changes do occur as a result of RO intervention – indeed this aspect does not seem to have been systematically investigated.

In the context of senile dementia and other progressive disorders it is conceivable that some of these mechanisms *could* occur. Diachisis might occur in multi-infarct dementia, for instance. Regeneration would be valuable in any disorder! Re-organisation and substitution are likely, however, to require more time and retained capacity than might be available once a deteriorating process is under way. Again no link has been established between

RO and restitution of neural structures as such in dementia. Whatever the form of brain injury Stephens' suggestions must remain speculative – although in the light of current theory not completely far-fetched with regard to actual brain injury.

INCREASED ATTENTION AND STIMULATION

Any form of research carried out in an attempt to change behavioural patterns should be questioned as to the effects of added attention. This has been called the Hawthorne Effect after the first researcher to be concerned about such a variable. All investigators need to be aware of the inevitability of some degree of change arising simply because the system is the focus for much more attention than usual. Attempts to allow for this variable include the use of control subjects who, while not receiving the actual therapy, receive all the other extra attentions which arise due to the experimental situation. Untreated control groups have been used in several studies, but they do not allow for these non-specific effects of any intervention. For instance, Harris & Ivory's (1976) comparison group was on a separate ward from the RO group. The RO ward had 'special' status; as well as the researchers' input there was interest from outside the hospital. Staff morale was reported to be raised by this increased interest in the ward. This could then have been a major factor in the changes reported. Given that elderly people are often in institutions that are characterised as unstimulating, with little attention or variety for the patients and low staff morale, any innovation of a therapeutic nature might produce positive changes regardless of actual form and content of the treatment.

Brook et al (1975) did control for these factors. As the control groups also went daily to the RO room both groups received added variety and exposure to a more stimulating environment than on the ward. Ward staff may well have felt involved in a 'special' project but this would have affected both groups equally as group membership was unknown to the nurses, and so could not have affected their ratings of ward behaviour. This study, therefore, gives support to more than innovation, or the provision of stimulation, being responsible for the greater changes produced by RO than the control procedure.

However, the extra attention given to the RO groups by the therapists might account for the improvement. The control group in marked contrast to the RO group received no encouragement or direction from the therapist – they simply sat in a circle. Efforts have been made to control for this additional staff attention by Woods (1979) and Johnson (1979) who both used 'social attention' comparison groups. These group sessions aimed at encouraging conversation in a group meeting held each day for the same time as the RO sessions. In Woods' study RO methods were not used in these groups and rambling or confused talk was not corrected. It will be recalled that both studies found RO to be superior in terms of cognitive change suggesting that the form of attention is of importance, and that generalised attention may not be as successful in providing improvement as attention that specifically encourages and reinforces orientated behaviour. These findings are not an artifact of staff realising that 'social attention' was a form of placebo. In Woods' study the same care staff led both groups and as previously mentioned, preferred the 'social attention' believing it to be more effective. These results cannot then be related to the fulfilment of expectations. Non-specific effects do not seem to be sufficient to account for all the changes produced by RO. Staff attention is almost certainly an important and effective therapeutic tool but it needs to be directly focussed on appropriate behaviour, rather than supplied in an indiscriminate manner.

In Chapter 2 a number of general and sensory stimulation programmes were outlined. These can be seen as attempts to ameliorate the sensory deprivation that some elderly people are said to undergo. In practice RO may involve both an increase in general stimulation and increases in sensory stimulation so it is possible that these are some of the factors which make RO effective. However, a firm conclusion cannot be drawn as to the extent of their contribution to RO. Only in the single-case studies of Greene et al (1979) and Woods (1980) have these effects been removed to any degree. The success of these interventions suggests that stimulation itself cannot be the only therapeutic factor leading to change, but it could certainly account for part of the changes noted in other studies. In the practical situation, for the present, the best strategy may be to use general stimulation and attention in the context of RO to maximise the gains produced.

GENERAL COGNITIVE EFFECTS

If RO produced a general increase in the person's cognitive functioning – in alertness, concentration, and new learning ability etc.,
as well as in verbal orientation – then performance in a number of
other areas could be facilitated. These general effects could also
result from practice at and reinforcement of being attentive and
concentrating on cognitive tasks as are usually carried out in RO
sessions. Remaining attentive, or vigilant, has a large motivational
component (Broadbent 1958) and variety of stimulation has
proved to be of importance (McGrath 1960, McGrath et al 1961).
In RO stimulation is varied and the sessions should be enjoyable and
rewarding in order to maintain motivation at a high level.

The evidence for general cognitive changes occurring is slight.
Most studies have only assessed verbal orientation. Two studies
that have looked at broader aspects of cognitive functioning have
produced contradictory results. Woods (1979) showed improvements in concentration and new learning ability in RO subjects
compared with social attention controls. Hanley (1980) in a much
larger study, found changes in verbal orientation, but not in other
aspects of cognitive functioning. The occurrence of general
improvement in the level of alertness and concentration of elderly
people is, as yet, open to question. If this could be established
there would be the fascinating task of relating it to possible
changes at a neural level, or to motivational aspects.

BEHAVIOURAL RE-EDUCATION

As discussed in Chapter 2, elderly patients with severe memory
disorders are capable of some new learning. RO may be seen as
providing good conditions for their limited learning to take place.
Appropriate behaviour is elicited and reinforced in RO which may
be viewed as a behaviour modification programme for orientation.

There is some evidence for this point of view. Hoyer et al
(1975), for instance, report an unpublished study by Hoyer &
Spitzberg which demonstrated reinforcement effects operating in
RO sessions. The single-case studies described in Chapter 3, carried out by Greene et al (1979) and Woods (1980), also demonstrate clear-cut learning of verbal orientation under appropriate
conditions. Hanley et al's (1981) ward orientation training also

demonstrates clear specific learning of information taught to the patient. The comparisons of Woods (1979) and Johnson (1979) of RO sessions with 'social attention' sessions have emphasised that attention has to be given to desired behaviour for improvements to be obtained.

All this strongly suggests that re-training and re-learning must almost certainly form part of any account of how RO operates. The approach is bound by the limited learning ability of the elderly person with dementia, and this may be a factor in the relatively small gains that are made with RO. Clearly where capacity is limited it is important that it is used as efficiently as possible – perhaps by learning to use memory aids as suggested by Bergert & Jacobsson (1976).

OVERCOMING DEPRESSIVE WITHDRAWAL

Seligman (1975) argues that repeated trauma can lead some people to adopt a position of 'learned helplessness'. The person then fails to carry out tasks of which he or she is capable. There is withdrawal from active participation and a belief that control over the environment is lost – that nothing can be done to make any difference to the situation. Self-esteem becomes lower as everything seems more and more hopeless and useless.

These considerations are relevant for at least two major groups of patients. Firstly, those with senile dementia or other organic damage will be faced with many failures at tasks that were previously extremely easy and straightforward; for some of these patients this failure will be distressing and perhaps traumatic. One way of dealing with this is to do less and less, and thus avoid failure by not attempting any sort of task. As a result they will function at a much lower level than their true degree of impairment necessitates.

The second group of patients are those who have also become depressed and withdrawn, but with only minimal, if any, cognitive impairment. They may have had a number of experiences of rejection, suffered losses, isolation or other trauma. They may even have been diagnosed as having dementia as diagnostic errors do occur (see Chapter 1). Studies indicate that such people may be placed in an institution for physical or social reasons.

RO by its repeated exposure to success may begin to combat the helplessness and assist the person to function at a level more in keeping with his or her full potential. Increased self-esteem could be a powerful mediator of generalised improvement.

If an elderly person has withdrawn because of shame, depression, feelings of inadequacy and lowered self-respect and is then placed in a situation where the aims are so simple that it is guaranteed that some response will receive praise, self-esteem will improve. When someone is faced with the realisation that memory is failing and that abilities and status are also suffering, self-doubt and depression seem almost inevitable. Failure is the factor which becomes the focus of attention, not only by the self but also by others. If instead of concentration on the many failures – inability to wash and dress, inability to move about freely – these are minimized and there is praise for simple things confidence can return. To praise a person for the positive things that he or she can do is an effective method of approach. To know what day or month it is is a simple memory task, to be able to tell a story about a past experience is always possible to some extent, to be able to recognise a smell, to know the name of a flower or a fruit, these are simple aims on which to build. It is easy to say 'That's right' with some enthusiasm. To an elderly person becoming used to being always wrong this is an achievement which will encourage further attempts towards self-expression and help.

However, evidence for this theory is limited. Only MacDonald & Settin (1978) have included any sort of 'adjustment' measure in a study of RO (they used the Life Satisfaction Index) and in fact found that RO patients tended to deteriorate on the LSI, whereas patients in a sheltered workshop reported increased life satisfaction. It has been suggested that RO was used rather inflexibly in this study, with the RO being set at too low a level for the elderly people involved. Clearly if hopelessness is to be overcome RO has to be used in such a way that the person experiences success rather than boredom!

Other evidence has to be anecdotal. Certainly a large number of patients with a diagnosis of early dementia may in fact have a depression or may have depression plus early dementia. Our impression is that such patients often do well on RO. Mrs B sat in her chair for some months, declaring that she was incapable of doing anything. She felt that she was useless, a nuisance and frequently wept with despair. She believed that she would not do anything right in RO, but, on the contrary, once there she found that she could do things she thought impossible. She required a great deal of reassurance and encouragement, but smiles began to appear as success after success occurred. Her self-care improved, and she was well enough to be discharged within a few weeks.

Clearly this possibility needs systematic exploration. The absence of general changes may be against it as being the overall mechanism of change, but it may be important in some cases. The difficulty in pursuing it further is the problem of assessing feelings, mood etc. in a memory-disordered person.

FINAL COMMENTS

There has been little in the way of satisfactory evidence in this chapter, and much speculation. This simply reflects the present state of theorising about RO. Most effort has been applied to establishing whether or not it works, and very little attention has been given to *how* it works. In many ways RO seems to have developed as a practical coming together of methods and ideas, rather than having from the start a firm, reliable conceptual base. On the available evidence, and from our experience of using RO, the behavioural retraining model and the combating of depressive withdrawal seem to be the most useful models for its operation. Indeed the former may largely account for the small changes usually found in group studies, and the latter for the more dramatic changes which also occur.

5

'We care what happens to people only in proportion as we know what people are'. *James Henry*

Assessment: some possibilities

WHY ASSESS?

There are a number of possible reasons for making an assessment, of some sort, of an elderly person. Diagnosis, prognosis and placement are three of the most common purposes of assessment as far as elderly people are concerned. In the context of RO four quite different assessment issues are involved:

1. Selection of patients for RO
2. Assessment of aspects of patient's functioning that may affect response to RO
3. Monitoring of change during the course of (or after) RO
4. Identification of target areas to be worked on in therapy.

These aims of assessment will be expanded below; what must be emphasised is that it is these aims that determine which assessment methods are appropriate. Measures that are excellent as diagnostic or prognostic aids will not necessarily be of use in this quite different context; this chapter is not then a complete coverage of assessing the elderly, but focusses on these aspects of assessment that are relevant to RO.

1. Selection

Although 24 hour RO does not involve any selection of patients, usually it would be too time-consuming for all patients to be involved in RO sessions. The aim then would be to pick those patients who would benefit most from RO sessions. Obvious criteria for excluding patients from group sessions would be severe deafness, blindness, and restlessness and agitation of such an extent that the person is unable to remain seated for 5 minutes, let alone the 30 minutes of the group session. Receptive dysphasia (see below) is a further indication for exclusion from group sessions. How then to pick those who will benefit most from those who remain? Experience gained in RO studies ought to be helpful here as to what type of patient benefits most? Unfortunately, as we saw in Chapter 3 the evidence is contradictory regarding which level of severity of dementia benefits most from RO sessions. However, there are some indications that will be detailed below.

A second aspect of selection is allocating the person to the appropriate level of RO group – basic, standard or advanced – so that they are not exposed either to being left behind because the level is set too high, or to boredom as it is set too low.

2. Aspects of functioning affecting response to RO

Here the aim is to identify factors that will either hinder – or facilitate – response to RO. Speech, reading, writing and visuo-motor difficulties are among the former, and enjoyment of social interaction might be among many factors that would be useful to the person in RO.

3. Monitoring of change

As discussed in Chapter 3 evaluation of RO may mean monitoring changes in staff as well as in patients. Generally assessment of patients is useful to identify what progress, if any, is being made for feed-back for the therapists. It is important to be clear about which areas of functioning are being monitored, and where change can be expected.

4. Identification of target areas

This aim of assessment comes into its own when therapeutic programmes are being individualised (see Chapter 10). However, in RO sessions it is useful to know what the person's areas of disorientation are, and what he does know usually, so that help can be given accordingly. In 24 hour RO if it is known that the person is particularly disorientated around the ward and cannot find his bed, particular attention and help can be given for this.

HOW TO ASSESS?

Staff – trained and untrained – are observing and assessing patients continually. These assessments are based on the staff's perception of the patient and are coloured by their reactions and their attitudes to the patient. Most often they are 'stored' in the staff-member's memory, to emerge in discussion and conversation. 'I'm sure Mrs Jones is more confused today' or 'Mr Smith didn't dress himself this morning – he usually does'. Problems arise when staff-members use the same words to mean different things 'I had to help Mrs Brown with her dinner' could mean anything from actually spoon-feeding Mrs Brown to helping her cook it, to take an extreme example.

Usually there is a system for recording observations, for instance in nursing notes, or in the resident's file. This has the advantage of providing a permanent record, remaining when staff have left the ward. A difficulty with these notes may be that different staff-members record different aspects of the person's functioning, so that comparisons with previous behaviour and with other patients may still be difficult.

More formal assessment methods have been devised to over-come some of these difficulties. They provide a structure for the observations; they make more explicit how the person functions; they involve less subjective and potentially biased opinion from the staff-member; they provide results easily compared over a period of time or with other patients. It is for these reasons that the use of formal assessment procedures is to be recommended. They do have their limitations and drawbacks, which will be pointed out, and they need to be used with common sense. They do not replace the care-staff's observations, but can enhance them by providing structure and the opportunity to highlight the problems of particular residents.

WHAT TO ASSESS?

From the various aims of assessment, important areas that will be considered in turn are:

1. The person's cognitive functioning – concentration, memory, orientation and so on

2. The person's specific neurological difficulties if any – speech problems, visuo-motor deficits etc.

3. The person's general functioning and behaviour – self-care, socialisation, activities and so on. What the person actually does

4. How the person feels – is he generally sad or happy, satisfied with life or depressed?

5. Staff attitudes and the kind of care provided in institutional settings.

COGNITIVE FUNCTIONING

The most frequently used cognitive tests with elderly confused patients are information and orientation tests. There are many forms of such tests; they consist of a number of items concerning:

Current orientation e.g. What day is it today?

Personal information e.g. How old are you now?

Current information e.g. Who is the Prime Minister? (President in U.S.A.)

Personal memory e.g. Where were you born?

Non-personal memory e.g. What were the dates of the First World War?

The questions are asked in a one-to-one situation; no assistance is given to the patient, but usually it is permissible to re-phrase or repeat the question. Scoring usually presents few problems – answers are easily checked and if anything other than one point for each correct answer applies the criteria for 2 or 3 point responses are laid down. In short these tests are intended to be objective and to produce a reliable score, regardless of the tester, which is indicative of the level of memory impairment.

The major difference between the tests available is in length. Kahn et al (1960) have ten items, whereas Fishback's (1977) Philadelphia Geriatric Center Mental State Questionnaire has 35 (although a few of these are rated by nurses). Choice of the appropriate test depends on the purpose of the assessment. For selection of patients a short questionnaire will probably be adequate to indicate the person's rough level of functioning. Holden & Sinebruchow (1978) found the Information/ Orientation sub-test of the Clifton Assessment Procedure for the Elderly (CAPE) of Pattie & Gilleard (1979) useful for predicting response to RO. This sub-test has only 12 items and is extremely quick and easy to administer. Pfeiffer's (1975) Short Portable Mental Status Questionnaire is another short test that would be appropriate in this context.

For monitoring of change and identification of particular gaps in knowledge longer tests are more appropriate, covering a wider range of items. Apart from Fishback's test these include the 20 item RO Information Sheet developed at Tuscaloosa and used by Citrin & Dixon (1977); the RO Questionnaire (30 items) published in Cornbleth & Cornbleth (1977) and used in their 1979 study; the 26 point Memory and Information Test of Blessed et al (1968); a composite test of 30 items used by Woods (1979); and many other variations on the same theme! The set of items used by Woods (1979) covers much the same areas as the CAPE and the Blessed et al test and is included as Appendix 1 as an example of the type of test used.

These tests are usually assumed to be very reliable, so that a re-test after a few days even by a different rater would produce a similar score. Evidence to support this is found in the re-test reliability of the Information/Orientation sub-test of the CAPE. This is 0.87 after three or four days for acute psychiatric admissions, 0.79–0.90 over two to six month periods for hospitalised elderly and for residents of Old People's Homes. As for the longer tests, Woods et al (1980) found a correlation of 0.98 between scores on the 30 item test obtained by ten residential home residents with dementia over a one week period, with different testers.

Although these tests are unsophisticated compared with some psychometric instruments they are singularly appropriate for the elderly people for which RO is intended, and have been shown in several studies to have strong relationships with other indices of dementia. The best example of this is probably Blessed et al's (1968) classic study which showed memory and information test scores to be related to the number of senile plaques (one of the pathological changes associated with senile dementia) found at post-mortem in the brains of elderly people.

For the purpose of monitoring changes there is no reason why a standard test should be used. There is much to be said for devising more personalised information tests, with questions relevant to the patient's family and circumstances, as was done by Greene et al (1979). Cornbleth & Cornbleth (1977) include items asking the person to show the way to various parts of the ward i.e. ward orientation, rather than just the usual verbal orientation. Ward orientation should certainly be assessed, and clearly this direct observational method is the way to do this. Whether it is wise to include the ward orientation and verbal orientation scores together is another matter, as the skills involved may be quite different.

Blessed et al's test includes memory for a name and address. An invented but plausible name and address is read to the patient, who then repeats it. Five minutes later he is asked for the name and address again. The person is given one point for each part he recalls up to a maximum of five points. Many elderly confused patients score zero on this item. Typically they respond 'what name and address?' If the person does recall even partially, then this is an encouraging sign of retained new learning ability.

Several of these tests are accompanied by items which are intended to assess concentration and attention. The CAPE has a 'Mental Ability' sub-test; Blessed et al have three items. These are items ranging in difficulty from counting from 1–20 to reciting the months of the year backwards. In the CAPE there are time limits, and bonus points are awarded for fast performance, so to some extent speed of response is important. Essentially these items measure – in this elderly population – ability to maintain concentration on a well-rehearsed and practised task. A composite concentration and attention test, used in Woods' (1979) study, is included as Appendix 2.

The CAPE includes additionally, as part of this 'mental abilities' sub-test, a reading test (14 words of increasing difficulty) and a writing test (the person is asked to write his own name). These items are extremely useful prior to RO, in giving some idea of whether these two channels of communication will be viable with the particular patient.

These attention/concentration tests are also intended to be objective, and have a high degree of re-test reliability. For the CAPE reliability is 0.89 over a re-test period of a few days and 0.61–0.74 over a period of two to six months.

These are then the two tried and tested objective measures of cognitive functioning in elderly confused people. For selection the shorter tests are recommended, and the CAPE with its reading and writing items is particularly useful in this regard. For monitoring change and for discovering particular areas of disorientation the longer versions, preferably personalised, are recommended.

Although other types of tests have been used in studies of RO there are not at present any other well-established cognitive tests that can be suggested. For example, Woods (1979) used the Wechsler Memory Scale (Wechsler 1945), which covers a number of aspects of memory, including information, orientation and concentration items (which correspond with some items in the composite in Appendices 1 and 2). However, the test as a whole is quite difficult to give to a severely deteriorated elderly person, and was used to give some indication of the level of memory impairment of the sample used. Other tests have similar difficulties of acceptability, perhaps as they are designed for diagnostic purposes rather than the monitoring of function in patients clearly having dementia. Undoubtedly efforts are being made to develop other forms of cognitive assessment suitable for more severely deteriorated patients that can detect small changes. These may well emphasise speed of information processing; microprocessor technology greatly facilitates the measurement of response latencies. This work is at an early stage as yet, however.

Finally, some practical points regarding cognitive assessment. If the aim is monitoring change then it is advisable to assess the person several times before RO commences. Preferably the assessment should be at the same time of day, and should continue until the result is consistent from day to day i.e. within two to three points at the most. If selection or identification of assets or deficits that will affect RO is the aim, then the reason for any failure on the test shown should be examined thoughtfully. A low score does not in every case indicate a severe dementia. Other factors that can lead to low scores are life-long low intelligence, deafness, poor eyesight (for the reading and writing tests), severe depression and/or anxiety leading to slowness of thought or distractibility, and speech difficulties – expressive or receptive. Thus test scores need to be evaluated in the light of other information about the person. Specialist help for sensory deficits, and any possible amelioration, is a necessity. Likewise depression and extreme anxiety – if reassurance does not help – need appropriate treatment. Speech difficulties and their assessment are discussed in the next section. Life-long low intellectual difficulty may be suspected from the person's educational or occupational history, and from a low reading level that is not part of a visual or dysphasic problem. Reading level is a good predictor of previous intelligence, and the New Adult Reading Test is a useful tool to clarify this issue (Nelson & McKenna 1975). Of course, these factors can occur in combination, adding further complications! It is important to realise then that there may be multiple explanations for poor performance on such tests. The converse occasionally happens also, and a person of superior intelligence, who has deteriorated from a previously very high level, scores so well that the true state is overlooked. Careful screening and retesting are advisable in such circumstances.

As was clear in evaluating the results of RO (Chapter 3) the person's cognitive functioning and performance in other areas are not completely correlated. Thus improvements on cognitive tests have no wider implication until changes in other areas are also found. Given the aims of RO however, this is certainly a direct means of examining whether it is having any effects at all, even if ideally more general changes are desired.

NEUROPSYCHOLOGICAL ASSESSMENTS

In order to understand what is happening in an elderly person's world other aspects of cognitive functioning require investigation. It is not always appreciated that older people can develop impairments which are often not global in nature and which lead to specific cognitive problems. When they are noted these are sometimes misinterpreted as indicating the presence of a progressive deterioration. If any form of rehabilitation is to succeed appropriate investigations should be initiated and the results explained to all concerned, including the apprehensive patient.

It is also important to appreciate that a generalised dementia can be made up of a number of particular dysfunctions. Specific impairments do occur in dementing processes as well as in trauma, stroke or physical disorders. In the early stages these impairments may be minor, but as the deterioration in function becomes more severe, obviously, the problems become more apparent. Awareness of their implications and presence – for whatever reason – can assist staff in planning management and treatment programmes in a realistic manner.

This is a complicated field which we will attempt to simplify as far as possible. Abilities and functions are not necessarily linked to a particular location in the brain. Although certain major functions – such as speech – may be associated with a specific location, other centres may also be involved in some way. These main centres will be mentioned, but it is the resulting behaviour which is of importance and which plays a vital role in management and treatment. Readers are recommended to consult Walsh (1978) for a more detailed account of neuropsychology.

Aphasia – speech disorders

Relatives and friends as well as a number of staff are often under the impression that speech disorders resulting from strokes indicate a progressive deterioration and assume that reasonable comprehension no longer exists. There are many forms of speech disorder which occur for many reasons. This is an outline of the fundamental divisions for general guidance.

Dysarthria

This is often confused with true language disorder. It is an impairment in the actual production of speech due to a lesion in the upper or lower motor neurones, the basal ganglia, or in the cerebellum which results in weakness, paralysis or incoordination of speech musculature. The usual definition in dictionaries describes dysarthria as imperfect articulation. Problems of oral communication can be due to impairments not only in articulation but in one or more of the following: respiration, phonation, resonance, volume, rate, voice quality, intonation or rhythm. The use of word or sentence construction may be correct, but, to the listener, speech may sound indistinct.

Receptive dysphasia

Receptive dysphasia occurs as a result of damage to the part of the brain concerned with comprehension – usually the Wernicke's area of the dominant hemisphere, where the left temporal lobe joins into the frontal and parietal lobes. This is called the posterior part of the superior temporal gyrus (see Fig. 5.1).

The patient fails to understand what is being said to him. He has difficulty with verbal communications. His speech, superficially, may sound normal, but often there is a 'press of speech' – using too many words, bits of words, or even made-up words; when this is put together speech is often unintelligible and is called jargon. Contact with others is difficult or impossible. Associated problems can include difficulty in naming objects and in

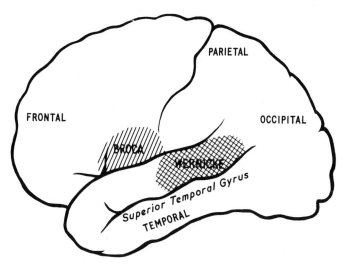

Fig. 5.1 Main areas of the brain including speech centres.

reading and writing. With such difficulties a person may even appear psychotic. However, the degree of impairment can vary from person to person, and because of apparently normal, though slow speech the situation can be overlooked. Any doubts with regard to hearing should also include questions about the possibility of a receptive dysphasia.

Expressive or Broca's aphasia

This takes various forms. The damaged area is the posterior part of the dominant frontal lobe called the inferior frontal convolution of the temporal lobe (see Fig. 5.1). A stroke patient who is right-handed can have damage which causes a paralysis or weakness of the right side and produces an expressive aphasia. This impairment of speech can vary from complete loss to mild word-finding problems, grammatical errors, hesitancy and shortened sentences. Usually understanding is preserved as are automatic phrases – 'one two three', or 'good morning'. Writing is affected, and reading and calculation may also suffer.

There are many other varieties of aphasia, including global aphasia which affects all forms of language. For those who require a more detailed account a textbook such as Benson (1979) would be appropriate. The two forms of aphasia mentioned (or dysphasia

– the two terms are often, if incorrectly, used interchangeably) do overlap in severe cases, and so may be predominantly expressive or receptive. Guidance from speech therapists can enable relatives, friends and volunteers to assist in practice and in the constant encouragement that is required to obtain improvement. Special forms of therapy, such as Melodic Intonation Therapy (a use of melody and rhythm), are being developed and proving successful in selected cases (Albert et al 1973, Sparks et al 1974).

Apraxia

This is an impairment of voluntary and purposive movements which cannot be attributed to muscle weakness or defect, nor can it be attributed to lack of comprehension. Quite simply, the person is able to perform movements, knows what he wants to do, but if consciously trying to make a gesture or a required movement cannot organise and co-ordinate both the thought and appropriate action. This disorder is fairly common, and is often misinterpreted as uncooperativeness. Clumsiness, 'He's all fingers and thumbs' and 'She doesn't remember what to do with her fork' are usually noted. There are several forms of apraxia the principal ones being Constructional, Ideomotor, Ideational and Dressing.

Constructional apraxia

First defined by Kleist in 1922 this form of apraxia has been particularly in the province of neuropsychology as it is difficult to elicit clinically. Special tests are required to isolate it. Although movements are possible the patient has difficulty in assembly, and the parts of an object cannot be put together correctly in order to achieve the whole. There is a defect in the transmission of information to the limbs concerned with the action. For example, a motor mechanic would develop problems in putting an engine back together. Arguments have arisen as to whether the difficulty results from a motor impairment for complex, sequential activities or a defect in visuo-spatial perception (how one sees spatial relationships). Studies have shown that right hemisphere damage (parietal and tempero-parietal lobes) causes visuo-spatial perceptual defects, so that even with a model to copy the patient cannot construct or draw a simple geometric figure (Warrington et al 1966, Gazzaniga 1970, Dimond 1972). Patients with known damage in the left hemisphere (parietal or tempero-parietal lobes), can perform the tasks once supplied with visual clues, and, furthermore, can improve with learning (Warrington et al 1966, Hécaen & Assal 1970). It is now accepted that left hemisphere lesions cause a motor defect – an inability to establish a programme for the required action, – and right hemisphere lesions show visuospatial disturbances which may even be aggravated by visual cues and learning situations (Hécaen & Albert 1978).

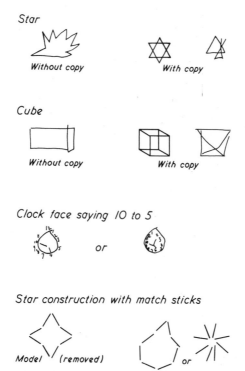

Fig. 5.2 Drawing showing spatial or apraxic disturbances.

Constructional apraxia can be demonstrated quite simply by asking a patient to draw a star, a cube and a clock face. Construction of a star with sticks or matchsticks is also useful (Fig. 5.2). Even with a hemiplegia it is possible to construct with the unimpaired hand. If the shapes produced are disoriented or inaccurate a model can be provided to copy. With elderly people it is rarely necessary to provide a complicated and undesirable test battery, but with younger and fitter over-60s it may be possible to introduce the Block Design Test – or Koh's Blocks – which provide more information.

Ideomotor apraxia

This condition is an inability to perform simple, single gestures. More complex gestures may be possible. Automatic or incidental gesture is performed perfectly. This may be thought of as a loss of memory for the pattern of the action – or engram. Although the pattern is preserved it is not under voluntary control. A Catholic can go to Mass, where he can make the sign of the cross without any difficulty. When asked to repeat it in the clinic he is totally unable to do so.

Simple gestures can be tested by asking the person to:

Wave goodbye. Pretend to stir the tea. Imitate a series of hand and arm poses (Christensen 1975).

Responses to imitation are usually better. Generally ideomotor apraxia results from bilateral brain damage.

Ideational apraxia

This is noticeable when a person attempts to carry out a complicated gesture or action. There is full understanding of what is to be done, the physical capacity to perform the action is preserved, but there is a disruption in the order and sequence of the total action and in the ability to plan properly.

In ideomotor apraxia the plan, or engram, is preserved, but the gesture is not. In ideational apraxia the single gesture is preserved but the overall plan is lost. The classical example is to ask the patient to take a match from a box, strike it and light a candle. The patient can repeat and understand the instructions, but when responding becomes very confused. The match may be struck upside down, or on the candle, or the candle may be struck on the box. The correct, logical sequence cannot be performed. Once again, well-established and automatic actions can be normal, as they do not require conscious thought. However, once the patient has to think about the response, or there is some stress, errors are multiplied. Imitation is usually more successful.

With such a complicated disability, explanations can become equally complicated! Both ideomotor and ideational apraxia are associated with lesions in the dominant parietal and temporal regions, but there is still controversy about instances of bilateral or even diffuse damage causing such impairments. Practically speaking the problem of location is irrelevant here. What is relevant is the need for an awareness of these disabilities as a sign of actual damage, so that suitable plans can be made for rehabilitation which will take the resultant behavioural problems into account. A detailed account of the apraxias can be found in Hécaen & Albert (1978).

Dressing apraxia

Lord Brain isolated this syndrome and named it in 1941 – though it was recognised before. Hécaen & Ajuriaguerra (1942–45) indicated that it results from lesions in the non-dominant parietal and occipital areas. It is a visuo-spatial defect and the degree of impairment varies. Inability to dress, slowness, confusion as to which piece of clothing goes where, and inability to fasten buttons are all common complaints which can be related to a number of physical problems as well as to a dementing process – dressing apraxia is one of the more frequent reasons. The patient just cannot find the right gesture to associate the clothes with his or her body. The mental plan for an almost automatic action has been lost. Sometimes, when a patient suffers from one side neglect (anosognosia) and actually ignores one side of the body (see below), there will be difficulty in dressing that side. This form of apraxia usually is associated with right parietal and occipital areas.

There are a number of other forms of apraxia; for instance buccofacial – the inability to perform voluntary movements such as sticking out the tongue; limb and gait disturbances and even whole-body apraxia can occur. Apraxia for speech is a common disability in the speech therapist's day. A patient may be able to eat and swallow correctly, or even produce involuntary speech, but there is an inability to make the correct movements of the tongue and lips in order to produce voluntary speech. Once again there is no physical reason for this and comprehension usually is normal. The patient may produce the same automatic phrase when trying to speak e.g. 'I don't know what to say, I don't know what to say' or 'Do, do, do, do.'

Treatment

Treatment of the apraxias varies. It is often based on using preserved function and adapting it to compensate for the loss, practice of a graded programme of related tasks or the use of rhythm.
For instance distraction can assist a patient to speak or complete
an action normally. Concentration on a rhythm instead of the
actual words can be enough to allow speech to come. Simple sentences like 'It's a ni – ce day' can be sung to a beat. The patient is
amused, distracted from the real problem and then delighted to
find that the words have been produced. Similarly with actions, by
distracting attention from the movements the required action can
be made. For instance, teeth brushing may be impossible until the
chant of 'up, down' is used or a beat is tapped out. Grasp reflexes
which will not release from a handshake can be resolved by distraction – stroking the back of the unwithdrawing hand. The
graded programme could be used in retraining, for example an
apraxic hand. A series of large, medium and small beakers are of
use. Aiding the person to grasp the largest beaker, aiding movement in order to place it in another large beaker would be the first
step. Encouragement to repeat this, then to try it alone would constitute the next phase. When this is successful the next size can be
introduced, until by practice, and with reinforcement by praise,
the actions are relearned. Tasks with meaning – helping with the
washing-up – are usually the most successful.

Agnosia

This is:
> An impairment in the accurate perception of objects which is
> not due to a defect in the sensory systems, ignorance of the
> nature of the object, defective intelligence or to confusion.

It is a condition which is generally unknown, almost impossible to
elicit by clinical methods and the subject of much neuropsychological investigation. The commonest and best-recognised
form is Visual Agnosia, but there are a number of others.

Visual agnosia or object agnosia

This is:
> An inability not only to name, or demonstrate the use of an

object, but an inability to appreciate its character and meaning, or to even remember ever having seen it before.

Obviously it is necessary to distinguish this from aphasia and visual memory loss. Other sensory input is required. Usually if another sense is used the clues lead to recognition. A characteristic smell, noise or feel provide these clues. A patient while recognising the colour, shape and size of a lipstick remained unable to name it. She stated that the object was a maroon and gold container, cylindrical in shape and about three inches in length. Only when encouraged to remove the lid, smell the perfume and rub the contents across the back of her hand was she able to identify it. The problem appears to be associated with damage around the lateral ventricles extending into the occipital lobes. The Popplereuter's test (included in the Luria investigations, Christensen 1975) is useful in identifying this impairment. It comprises of a set of pictures of mixed-up everyday objects – a jug apparently containing a paint brush, an axe, and a pair of scissors is one example. Another test from the Luria investigations comprises sets of photographs — an object is vague in the first picture and later becomes quite distinct.

Colour and Auditory Agnosia are other forms occasionally found which can cause problems in treatment and management. A patient with auditory agnosia has word deafness. He cannot grasp normal conversation and becomes very distressed. Usually slow, distinct speech helps the problem considerably. With colour agnosia colour not only cannot be named, but matching and association of colour are impaired.

Spatial agnosia

This disorder is fairly common and is a spatial disorientation, a defect in finding the way even in familiar surroundings. A young navigator who had a mild stroke was unable to understand maps that had been given to him as an amusement during recovery. This happens in older people too. There is loss of appreciation of right and left, incapacity for drawing simple maps of the house, or the ward. Recognition of individual objects in the environment is preserved though localisation of them is disordered. Under this heading there is the not uncommon phenomenon of autotopagnosia – a failure to recognise or localise parts of one's own body (related to parietal damage). Body agnosia is also associated with another, fairly common disorder – anosognosia. One side of the body is neglected or denied. The patient may say her left hand does not belong to her, or even that it belongs to someone else. It is not rare to hear that a patient believes that there is a strange hand in her bed, and she can require some persuasion to accept that hand as her own. Dressing the neglected part of the body is also a problem, and food on one side of the plate will not be touched. The affected side is almost invariably the left one. From a management viewpoint it is important to be aware of this state. Simple measures can be instigated. At mealtimes the plate can be turned around so that a full meal is obtained. The wanderers who get lost on the way to the toilet or who get into somebody else's bed could have this complaint. The toilet is invariably approached from the wrong direction and the bed on the wrong side on return. A simple solution is to transfer beds to the most convenient side.

A drawing of a clock face, or the assembly of one of the educational variety will easily demonstrate the problem, as will the drawing of a house. (Fig. 5.3).

Other tests for body agnosia are to ask the person to point to various parts of his body and to use the Finger Agnosia tests. After a demonstration of the task the patient is asked to close his eyes, or is blindfolded. The examiner presses one of his fingers and requests the person to 'show' that finger on the other hand. There

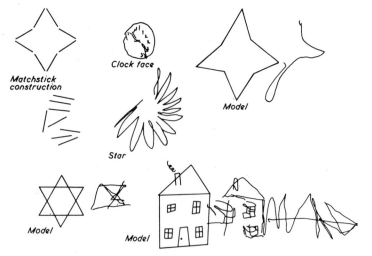

Fig. 5.3 Reproduction of actual drawings by a 70 year old lady with anosognosia — a left-sided neglect.

is a further test to see if the person can say 'how many fingers are there between that one and that one'. The examiner will press gently on, for instance, the forefinger and the little finger of a hand, and expect to receive the answer 'Two fingers' and so on.

As has been stated, unilateral spatial agnosia is almost exclusively related to the left half of space. Obvious exceptions would be people with right hemisphere dominance – usually left-handers. Other forms of agnosia include:

Tactile, or astereognosia, which is discerned by requesting identification of objects, particularly coins, by the sense of touch alone.

Prosopagnosia, failure to recognise faces. This was defined by Bodamer in 1947. Testing for this problem is through the use of photographs of familiar and unfamiliar faces. Occasionally, the person cannot even recognise self-reflection in a mirror.

Simultanagnosia, is an inability to perceive a whole while being able to interpret the parts. If a picture of, for instance, a floral festival is presented and the person asked to supply a suitable name for the picture, the task will prove impossible. Each single flower will be pointed out, even each blade of grass, but the scene will be too difficult to grasp. There appears to be some association with reading problems, for although a sentence can be written correctly it can only be read back letter by letter.

Awareness of agnostic factors has very practical implications. To use 'left' and 'right' as meaningful concepts for someone with spatial problems is obviously inappropriate. Words either written or spoken – depending on the impairment – are more valuable to those with such difficulties. A picture above a bed, a name in large print and verbal directions using colour or some meaningful symbol are more useful in retraining than spatial directions.

Acquired knowledge

There are other factors which should be checked in any neuropsychological investigation. Impairment of acquired knowledge may have more implications than that of global deterioration.

Agraphia – an inability to write properly. This includes spelling, letter construction and word organisation and is related to aphasia and tempero-parietal problems.

Acalculia – or difficulty with numbers, can also be related to parietal lesions, reading difficulties (alexia) and spatial disorders.

Alexia or dyslexia – is a disturbance in the relationship between visual and language functions, and can occur in association with a number of other conditions. From the management viewpoint, if someone cannot read it is hopeless to expect him or her to cope in situations where such ability is vital. Directions on medicine bottles, street or directional signs will prove meaningless.

Fig. 5.4 The Magazine Method. Using pages from a journal with clear, distinct pictures, words of varying size, columns, and colour in order to apply simple investigations of ability.

The magazine method of testing (Fig. 5.4)

A useful and unthreatening method of investigation is to use an ordinary, colourful magazine which can provide a wealth of information without stress. Using a suitable selection of advertisements from the two open pages of a magazine it is possible to test:

Reading – Can the person read, can only large letters be meaningful, can smaller ones be read or is reading impossible?

Comprehension – Can the implications and meaning of pictures be understood, as well as words? Are comments and memories produced, with encouragement, from the content?

Aphasia – Can the person use the right words and name the objects on the page with ease?

Agnosia – Has the person any difficulty in seeing the pictures, appreciating what they are? Is colour meaningful, can faces be noted, or parts of the body? Can the whole of a picture convey meaning, or are only parts of the picture seen?

Anosognosia – By watching the person's way of reading, and the initial direction of gaze it is possible to tell if there is one-sided neglect. If the farthest column on the right hand page is the first to be noticed there is a possibility of anosognosia. Check to see if there is difficulty in recognizing the existence of a left hand page and a column on the farthest left of that page.

Apraxia – Can be suggested by difficulties in turning pages and in pointing.

The 'magazine method' is by no means conclusive, but it is certainly very helpful and completely painless. It provides staff with information, useful interaction and the patient with some stimulation. This is, in fact, putting RO to use in an assessment situation. It is not vital to have strict assessment procedures with sick elderly people, what is important is to find out as gently as possible if there are impairments in certain functions. Using material from the natural surroundings provides a comfortable, unthreatening and easy way to screen for any possible difficulties which can be looked at in more detail, if necessary, later.

Frontal involvement

Though there are symptoms and signs associated with many locations in the brain, and much to suggest that localisation is not complete, discussion of these aspects is not appropriate here. However, some of the personality changes and function impairments associated with frontal lobe damage are of importance in understanding some of the behaviour frequently observed, and also helpful to the design of suitable therapeutic intervention.

Emotional lability can be very upsetting to relatives and staff. It is often the result of a stroke or other neurological trauma. Euphoria, inappropriate laughing and/or crying, the use of undesirable language, sexual exhibitionism and erotic behaviour are disturbing and they are usually out of character. The mechanisms of control have been lost and emotions can run riot. If the involuntary nature of this emotion is understood it is easier to use distraction than inappropriate sympathy which aggravates the situation. Lack of initiative is another common feature. This is not caused by paralysis, apraxia or confusion but an inability to voluntarily and spontaneously initiate a desired or automatic motor task. Recently it has been found that thought processes can also suffer from this inertia. Quite simply the victim cannot get going. There is a disorder of attention. Questions must be repeated over and over in order to elicit a response. This is linked to initiation difficulties. Similarly the patient forgets to remember. The information has not been forgotten, but the ability to start the necessary 'wheels' turning to make the memory process work is impaired.

Perseveration is common. On long-stay wards patients can be heard repeating the same phrase all day, or seen performing the same action again and again.

Writing and drawing show repetitions for instance:

The girl has a nice hat – can be reproduced as – The girl has has a has or when asked to copy MNMNMNMN – MNNNNNNNN is produced.

This form of perseveration has a bearing on the difficulty in changing set, or in progressing from one idea to another. When asked to complete a series of sequential tasks errors occur – such as the pattern in Fig. 5.5.

△△+○△△+ *please continue across the page becomes:-*

Fig. 5.5 Sequential Pattern Completion. One of the tests to help in assessing frontal lobe, or operational thought, impairment.

Similarly a set of wooden or plastic shapes which are also in sets of different colours can only be sorted into either colour, or shape groups; the alternative group cannot be found.

Luria (1963) has many suggestions for aiding rehabilitation programmes that are in difficulty because of this perseverative process. Though time-consuming they are effective. Distraction at the right moment is the key. The second an error in movement is commenced the action can be interrupted and distraction introduced. A comment on the weather on flowers or some nearby incident would be suitable. To ensure that the next movement in the task is correct physical guidance is used. To make a stitch with a needle, for instance, a hand guiding a hand can ensure the correct path and so help to stop perseveration of an incorrect action. Phraseology can be interrupted in a similar manner and reinforcement, usually praise and attention, can be given to non-repetitive talk. However, long-standing perseverations are very difficult to eradicate and early intervention is more successful.

Final comments

Understanding of some of the behaviour resulting from actual damage can improve the aims of programmes and rehabilitation. Relatives need to understand some of the changes that they see and cooperation from them can be increased. Examinations need not be threatening or stressful and the 24 hour RO approach can be used in aiding assessments. If the person's problems are related to damage, more appropriate measures of retraining can be used in conjunction with RO and with the reinforcement of behaviour modification methods. Goals can be set at a suitable level, the right kind of attention and encouragement can be discussed and

Table 5.1

Neuropsychological deficits		Simple tests
Language problems		
Expressive dysphasia	Difficulty in conversation	Listen. Word finding, odd words and sentences, little speech, or complete rubbish
Receptive dysphasia	Comprehension difficulty	Lack of appropriate response to questions
Agraphia	Writing difficulty	Write a simple sentence
Acalculia	Difficulty with numbers	Write numbers, add, subtract, multiply and divide simple sums
Alexia	Reading difficulty	Read notice on ward, on TV or from a magazine
Apraxia		
Constructional	Difficulty in putting things together to make a whole	Use matchsticks to make a star. Draw a star or a cube. Also use model for copying
Ideomotor	Difficulty in making a single gesture	Ask to be shown hair brushing, waving, clenching teeth etc.

Table 5.1 (contd.)

Neuropsychological deficits		Simple tests
Ideational	Difficulty in making complex gesture	Pretend to get out a cigarette, light it and start smoking
Dressing	Difficulty in dressing	Put on a coat, button it and take it off again
Agnosias		
Visual	Difficulty in appreciating meaning of objects	Use a letter or a number made up of other letters or numbers, e.g. a large 2 made of tiny 4s and see if both are recognised
Colour	Difficulty in appreciating colour	Naming, matching and association
Spatial	Difficulty in finding the way Unable to understand maps	Draw a plan of home
Autotopagnosia	Difficulty in recognising parts of own body, or another's	Point to parts of own body, and that of examiners
Anosognosia	Neglect of one side body	Watch dinner plate Draw clock-face or house
Astereognosis	Difficulty in recognising objects by touch	Name a selection of coins by touch alone
Prosopagnosia	Difficulty in recognising faces	Naming familiar and unfamiliar faces from photographs
Simultanagnosia	Difficulty in perceiving a whole	Name a picture with something suitable to describe its content
Frontal involvement	Personality change Euphoria or apathy Disinhibition Lack of initiative Perseveration Inability to plan	Watch Ask relatives about previous personality Use sequence of shapes or figures. Watch how games such as cards are played

applied, and simple management measures introduced. Furthermore such understanding will assist in better appreciation of such behaviour patterns that have been incorrectly attributed to dementia (Table 5.1).

ASSESSMENT OF GENERAL FUNCTIONING AND BEHAVIOUR

Three main approaches have been used with the elderly:

1. Rating Scales, where staff who know the person well assess the person's functioning from their general unsystematic observations of them in their own environment.

2. Direct observation in a structured situation, where the person is requested to carry out particular tasks, and then assessed on his or her performance.

3. Direct observation in natural settings, where a large number of systematic observations of the patient in his natural environment are made.

Rating scales

These have been the most frequently used forms of assessment in studies of RO, partly perhaps as they are less time-consuming than the other approaches. Typically ward staff are given a printed sheet for each patient, with areas such as toiletting, feeding, social interaction, etc., being rated on a five point scale according to the person's observed performance over the previous fortnight.

A number of different rating scales have been used with the elderly. They differ in areas rated, number of items, number of rating points, time period over which observations are made and so on. At least 10 different scales have been used in RO studies, and there are many more in existence. Lawton & Brody (1969) were impelled to say: 'The present state of the trade seems to be one in which each investigator or practitioner feels an inner compulsion to make his own scale and to cry that other existent scales cannot possibly fit his own setting.'

This tendency does make the literature rather complex, and hinders easy comparison of studies. However it is extremely difficult to find a rating scale that is useful for all purposes, and in fact the authors have had to devise their own for particular purposes! Only a selection of rating scales can be reviewed here;

others are reviewed by Salzman et al (1972), Goga & Hambacher (1977) and Hall (1980), who also provides a useful discussion and recommendations for devising scales. The major differences between scales are in which areas are covered and in how much depth each area is assessed. Some scales like the PAMIE (Gurel et

Table 5.2 Six behaviour rating scales used with the elderly

---

i. PAMIE, a 77-item scale producing scores on 10 factors:

1. Self-care dependent	6. Behaviourally deteriorated
2. Belligerent/ irritable	7. Paranoid/suspicious
3. Mentally disorganised/confused	8. Sensori-motor impaired
4. Anxious/depressed	9. Withdrawn/apathetic
5. Bedfast/moribund	10. Ambulatory

(Gurel et al 1972 Physical and mental impairment of function evaluation.)

ii. Physical Self Maintenance Scale (PSMS) – 6 five-point scales:

1. Toilet	4. Grooming
2. Feeding	5. Physical Ambulation
3. Dressing	6. Bathing

Instrumental Activities of Daily Living (IADL) – 3, 4 or 5 points per scale. Each scale applies to female subjects, but only scales 1, 2, 6, 7 and 8 apply to males.

1. Telephone	5. Laundry
2. Shopping	6. Transport use
3. Food preparation	7. Responsibility for medication
4. Housekeeping	8. Financial responsibility

(Lawton & Brody 1969)

iii. Geriatric Rating Scale (GRS) – 31 items, each with 3 points. Originally a total score only was utilized, but now can be split into 3 factors:
1. Withdrawal/apathy
2. Antisocial disruptive behaviour
3. Deficits in activities of daily living
(Plutchik et al 1970, Smith et al 1977)

iv. Shortened Stockton Geriatric Rating Scale – 18 three-point items gives a total score and 4 factor scores:

1. Physical disability	3. Communication difficulties
2. Apathy	4. Social disturbance

[Pattie & Gilleard 1979, Gilleard & Pattie 1977, now Behaviour Rating Scale (BRS) of CAPE]

v. Modified Crichton Geriatric Rating Scale – 13 five-point scales. The original CGRS did not include scales 6, 7, 8 or 13 but included ratings of the patient's subjective and objective mood.

1. Orientation	8. Social behaviour
2. Mobility	9. Restlessness
3. Feeding	10. Co-operation
4. Dressing	11. Sleep
5. Continence	12. Communication
6. Interest in environment	13. Complaints
7. Interest in others	

(Robinson 1977, Woods 1979)

vi. Holden Communication scale for the elderly – 12 five-point scales in 3 areas:

Conversation	Awareness & knowledge
1. Response	5. Names
2. Interest in past events	6. General orientation
3. Pleasure	7. General knowledge
4. Humour	8. Ability to join in games etc.

Communication
 9. Speech
10. Attempts at communication
11. Interest and response to objects
12. Success in communication
See Appendix 3

---

al 1972) cover many areas, including problem behaviours, in great depth. Others like the PSMS (Lawton & Brody 1969) cover fewer areas in much more detail; Table 5.2 lists six rating scales and the areas concerned. To emphasise the differences between scales, note that the Shortened Stockton Geriatric Rating Scale (now the Behaviour Rating Scale of the CAPE) has one item which covers *both* bathing and dressing, whereas the PSMS has five points each on these two areas. There are differences also in the way in which scores are derived. The PAMIE, GRS and SSGRS have a total score and sub-scores based on factor analysis of elderly people's performance on the scale; the others have a total score together with a profile of scores on the areas of functioning rated. Thus the former statistically groups items into factorial areas of functioning, whilst the latter has the structure imposed on it by the scale design.

The usefulness of these scales for the different aims of assessment is dependent on these differences. For selection purposes, and for eliciting factors relevant to progress in RO, a short general scale – like the SSGRS or the GRS – may be useful. Using the Holden Communication Scale in a geriatric population, scores above 25 usually mean the person is better placed in a Basic group, between 15–25 membership of the Standard group is indicated and obviously scores less than 15 imply suitability for an Advanced group.

For monitoring progress the GRS has been the most popular scale so far. It has reasonable inter-rater reliability. Plutchick et al report a correlation of 0.87 between ratings of 86 elderly patients made by two judges. The use of factor scores, developed by Smith et al (1977), is an improvement on one total score, but inspection of the scale suggests change would have to be considerable. This is largely due to each item being rated on a three point scale. To take an extreme example the item on incontinence has three points:

0 – never incontinent
1 – sometimes (once or twice per week)
2 – often (three times per week or more).

Thus if a patient who wets six times a day makes a dramatic improvement to wet only once every other day, the score would remain as 2, even though a clinically important improvement had been made. Where a patient has been withdrawn and apathetic for years and becomes more aware and sociable through RO the changes might be sufficient to be detected. Where changes are likely to be limited the GRS may prove insensitive.

For this aim then one of the 'profile' scales may be more useful, allowing more sensitive rating of each area. The PSMS and IADL are useful as far as they go, but lack any coverage of socialisation or communication. The Modified Crichton is wider ranging. Woods (1979) obtained an inter-rater reliability of 0.79 on a sample of 25 residents. No consistent improvements were found using a total score or scores for each area, and a lack of sensitivity on the part of the scale was suggested as one possibility for the discrepant results in cognitive and behavioural spheres. Holden & Sinebruchow (1979), using the same scale, did find a sensitivity to change however. A crucial difference between the studies is that Holden & Sinebruchow's geriatric sample was nearly twice as impaired behaviourally as Woods' Old People's Home residents. The possibility of differential sensitivity at different ranges of scores must be considered. In Holden & Sinebruchow's study the Holden Communication Scale was used for the first time. The scale is included in Appendix 3. As can be seen its coverage of behaviour is quite different from any other scale, having no items on self-care or mobility, but focussing on aspects of communication. It is of interest then that results on this scale paralleled those on the Modified Crichton. Correlations between the Holden and the Crichton were 0.78 (Leeds) and 0.85 (Merchant & Saxby 1981). From the latter study correlations were also made between the Holden and CAPE (cognitive) which were found to be 0.75 and 0.78 with the CAPE (behavioural).

Of all the rating scales available its content is certainly the most directly relevant to RO and it seems likely to be the most useful of these scales for this reason. Obviously if a self-care re-training programme was being evaluated rather than a socially oriented treatment, then other scales would be needed.

For identifying specific targets for treatment, particularly as outlined in Chapter 10, wide-ranging, detailed scales are needed. Some useful information can be obtained from the above scales, but generally scales are needed that emphasise the person's positive behaviour, those things the person actually does do, rather than the frequent emphasis on deficits and disabilities. An attempt at this is Cornbleth's (1978) Geriatric Resident Goals Scale. It consists of 85 behavioural 'goals' such as 'Washes own face', which are simply ticked 'Yes' or 'No'. The goals were established by asking staff what desired behaviour of the patients would be. Evidence of high inter-rater and re-test reliability (0.95) is presented, and of validity in that it is strongly related to independently made ratings of the patient's degree of independence and to cognitive functioning. Cornbleth suggests that the GRGS is a general procedure which can be adapted for any old age setting, with items being deleted or added according to the desired outcome of that setting. The goals set are observable, measurable, unambiguous and avoid vague terminology and interpretation by the rater. The setting of treatment goals for an individual from such a scale is very easy indeed. Different areas of function are to some extent broken down into small steps; this could be developed further depending on the impairment of the patients involved. Also the total score on such a scale could be used to monitor overall progress.

A further attempt at a rating of a person's positive behaviour draws its inspiration from the Adaptive Behaviour (AB) scales used in mental handicap facilities for several years (Nihira et al 1974). The Brighton Clinic Adaptive Behaviour scale (BCAB) is extremely long and detailed, and is only recommended for use where individual plans for patients are being developed. In such a situation, with a rater who has observed the patient closely, it can provide a great deal of information about the person's actual behaviour and areas where improvement might be possible (it is available from R. Woods). Again, as well as concentrating on positive aspects of the person's functioning, items are as specific as possible, with each area broken down into fairly small parts.

A welcome recent development in this area of assessment is the exploration of a more rational basis for the rating scales used. Most have been constructed by a process of trial and error. Recently techniques of Guttman scaling have been applied to these scales (e.g. Volans 1979, personal communication, Lyle 1980, Gilleard & Pattie 1980). The system used in a Guttman Scale is based on the principle that if the person can perform an item he will be able to perform all the lower items on that scale. Where the same skill is used in different areas of functioning, these scales allow some integration on a rational basis and also indicate possible patterns of deterioration.

Assessment using these types of scales is much more economical; if properly constructed, valid assumptions can be made about unobserved behaviour from observation of performance on key items. However, a great deal of work needs to be carried out to develop these scales, which are still at a preliminary stage.

More practically, how does one go about selecting and using a rating scale? The first and most important consideration is to select a scale that is acceptable in the particular situation. It needs to be short enough so that time is available for it to be completed – rather than it being left half-finished. It needs to be easy to use and understand, without difficult terminology. Scoring and interpretation should be simple also. It needs to be relevant to the situation; e.g. the GRS has an item on 'regular work assignments' that would be irrelevant in many situations. Item definitions must be clear and precise (Hall 1980). There must be no ambiguity or misunderstanding about the meaning of an item. Interpretation of behaviour reduces reliability e.g. the Crichton has an item on 'restlessness'; different staff have different criteria for such a term unless it is defined more specifically. Items should have single definitions; items like 'misidentifies persons and surroundings but can find way about' cause problems for the person who cannot find his way about, identifies people, but not his surroundings! Where items are ordered the sequence needs to be carefully examined, so there are no anomalies. Again on the Crichton a person who walks independently with a stick could receive a score of 2 or 4 on mobility depending on the staff member's interpretation of the item. Few scales have none of these faults; they are exceptionally difficult to avoid, particularly if a fresh scale is devised.

In using the scale, consideration needs to be given to who will make the ratings. The person who has most contact with the patient is the ideal choice; often trained staff members have less patient contact, so they may not be in the best position to carry out ratings. Training in the use of the rating scale should always be given. Making independent ratings of the same patients and then discussing reasons for any discrepancies is a useful exercise. The rating procedure needs to be clear; is the person rated as they are today, over the past week, month? Can the rater only use his own observations, or can he make use of what others have observed? What is the procedure for commenting on aspects of behaviour not covered by the scale?

It can be seen that there are many problems inherent in reducing the whole range of behaviour of the elderly person into a brief rating. Added to these are the difficulties brought about by fluctuations in the person's behaviour – sometimes related to different staff. None of the scales available is perfect, but used with common sense and again in conjunction with other available information they can play a useful part in assessment.

Direct observation – structured setting

This is a well-established assessment method, where the person is asked to perform certain tasks in the presence of the assessor, who then rates their competence in this structured setting. The best example of this approach is the Performance Test of Activities of Daily Living (PADL), described by Kuriansky & Gurland (1976) and used extensively in studies of psychogeriatric patients in New York and London. This consists of 16 tasks, all easily demonstrated in an interview situation. These include drinking from a cup, combing hair, eating, making a 'phone call and so on. Most need 'props' e.g. a cup, comb, spoon with sweet, 'phone etc., and it is recommended that these be collected into a portable kit. Performance on each task is broken down into component parts and whether or not the person carries out each part is recorded. Simple tasks are given initially to reduce anxiety, and the whole test takes around 20 minutes to administer.

Independent ratings of patients' performance by the interviewer and an observer showed high inter-rater reliability (0.90). Evidence of validity – in its relation to physical health, mental state and prognosis – is presented by Kuriansky et al (1976). The test is reported to be generally acceptable to patients.

There are advantages to this approach, particularly in as far as the person's capabilities are revealed, whereas in the ward setting opportunities for some skills might not be available or necessary. For the purpose of assessing RO this test might be useful if it revealed more ability than shown on the ward, providing potential areas to encourage and work on. However, this possible discrepancy between ward and test situation makes it less useful for monitoring RO, where changes in ward behaviour are desired. When specific programmes aim at particular targets included in the PADL, the sub-division of each task may be helpful in planning treatment and assessment of change. Unfortunately, the restricted range of items detracts from this application. There is no assessment of communication or socialisation.

Discrepancy between ward and test performance is also possible where the structured situation fails to elicit the person's best performance, which may occur more easily in some cases in a natural setting. Comprehension difficulties could lead to this, as could anxiety and insufficient motivation. Once more, reasons for failure need to be explored carefully; the person may not have grasped what he is intended to do or may be too anxious or apathetic to carry out the task correctly.

The test may be useful for selection of patients, establishing a dependency level, and for monitoring of some programmes focussing on specific aspects of the person's functioning. It could be utilized alongside ratings of the person's functioning on the same tasks in the ward setting.

Direct observation – natural setting

This is where the patient's actual behaviour on the ward, old people's home or day centre is observed and recorded. On the face of it if the aim is to change the person's performance within this setting, this should be the assessment method. It has been used extensively with children and the mentally handicapped, and to some extent in behavioural studies with the elderly; it has rarely been used to evaluate RO. Johnson (1979) planned to use direct observation, but found no effects paralleling the cognitive changes recorded and abandoned it because it was so time-consuming.

Two initial issues concerning direct observation both relate to producing manageable data from a potentially massive amount of observation. Firstly some method of sampling the person's behaviour must be chosen. By time sampling, a snap-shot picture of the person's behaviour over a longer time period is obtained. Thus observations might be made of the person every three minutes or every 10 minutes or every 30 minutes and so on, depending on the frequency of the behaviours being observed. A further decision must be taken as to whether to record over a short period (10–30 seconds, say) all the behaviours the person exhibits. If a very frequent discrete behaviour (smoking and shouting can be examples of this) is being observed then all the occurrences in a certain time period (say 15 or 30 minutes) might be counted at different times of the day. The second issue is to decide on what areas of functioning to observe, and at what level of precision. Often social behaviours or other readily accessible areas are chosen. The range of precision extends from the relatively crude categorisation of a person's behaviour as 'engaged' or 'disengaged' to the level of fine analysis of behaviour – for example, recording the person's direction and duration of gaze.

Some complex problems can arise. Readers are referred to Hutt & Hutt (1970) for a full exposition of direct observation. If it is desired to monitor a range of behaviours, the problem of the observer having to use too long and detailed an observation schedule will have to be faced. If behaviours occur infrequently, say once or twice a day, then they may be missed entirely by most time-sampling methods; direct frequency counts are preferable here. The observer needs to fit unobtrusively into the surroundings, so that his influence on the patients' behaviour is minimized. An adaptation period is needed for staff as well as patients. Staff may either keep well clear or arrange special events, which bias the picture obtained. Behaviours to be observed need to be defined carefully, without ambiguity, and a second observer making observations simultaneously but independently is helpful in ensuring this has been achieved. Time sampling is easiest when all patients are together in one place and very difficult if they are scattered throughout a number of rooms.

The simpler the observation method used the more reliable results will be. Jenkins et al (1977) used the concept of 'engagement' in their study of activity in old people's homes. Residents are said to be engaged if they are interacting with people or materials; non-engaged if they are doing nothing; a detailed manual is available with full definitions. The method is to enter the room where patients are being observed, count the number of people who are engaged and then count the total number of people present. A percentage is then calculated of the proportion of those present who are engaged. This is then a group method, which may be useful where changes throughout the home or ward are being monitored. McFadyen et al (1980) have extended the method by recording engagement for individuals, and by breaking the types of engagement and non-engagement down slightly. The definitions of Jenkins et al are given in such a way as to make this analysis quite straightforward. McFadyen et al made observations on each patient every half-hour over a 2½ day period. They found greater than 90 per cent inter-rater agreement on simultaneous observations of 20 patients. Their results showed a non-significant relationship of engagement with memory and information test performance, although ratings of self-care impairment did correlate significantly with active engagement in both a psychogeriatric ward and an old people's home.

This type of assessment, which because of its restricted range is reasonably manageable, would be useful in monitoring treatment programmes. It also makes possible the monitoring of staff-patient interactions, which are the basic therapeutic method in 24 hour RO. The necessity for ensuring changes do occur at this level has already been emphasised. This method would enable patients to be identified who have low levels of engagement or social activity; the reason for this could then be explored. It has been suggested that engagement is an indication of the 'quality of life' in an institution; if this is so then this method could help to identify the need for environmental changes of every kind in institutions for the elderly and help to monitor them.

ASSESSMENT OF THE PERSON'S AFFECTIVE STATE

So often it seems that the last people to be asked about the effects of treatment programmes are the elderly people themselves. Only one study of RO has included a measure of the effects of treatment on the person's feelings; MacDonald & Settin (1978) used a Life Satisfaction Index. The difficulty with this and other similar measures is that they are questionnaires that the patients fill in themselves. Their validity is doubtful in more severely demented patients, who may not be able to comprehend the self-report format.

For patients who are less deteriorated and can complete a brief questionnaire a number of mood, morale and life-satisfaction scales are available. Lawton (1971) reviews many of these.

An alternative strategy is for an observer to rate the person's apparent mood or level of depression. Kochansky (1979) describes several such scales. However, little attention has been given to the assessment of mood in demented patients. Generally the emphasis has been on differentiating solely depressed from solely demented people, with overlap being ignored. For the present it seems that there is very little available to enable mood to be evaluated satisfactorily in demented patients. Assessments of an informal nature, based on close knowledge of the elderly person and efforts to form a relationship with them, may be the most practical approach available.

STAFF ATTITUDES AND ASSESSMENT OF THE INSTITUTION

This is another extremely important – but underdeveloped – area. Change in staff attitudes was assessed by Smith & Barker (1972) following an RO Training Programme. They used the Oberleder Attitude Scale (Oberleder 1962) which originally was intended for assessment of elderly people's attitudes rather than care-staff's, and would need some adaption for that purpose. Other studies of staff attitudes (e.g. Melia 1979) have used structured interviews to elicit staff aims, expectations, aspirations etc. A standard scale, contrasting negative and positive attitudes to working with the elderly, would be extremely useful. The possibility of staff giving the 'right' answers, the expected positive attitudes, is a problem with any such scale, of course. Indirect measures, such as amount of staff-sickness or staff turnover may well reflect staff morale on a particular ward.

However, broad measures of institutional variables – including staff attitudes – have been developed. Lawton (1970) describes some of these measures, and makes a number of suggestions as to how institutional care may be assessed. More recently Moos & Lemke (1980) and Lemke & Moos (1980) have described aspects of the Multiphasic Environmental Assessment Procedure (MEAP). This consists of a number of scales which measure physical and architectural resources; policy and programme resources; resident and staff resources; and social-environmental resources in residential settings for the elderly. Some of these scales could have great value in identifying targets for institutional and attitudinal change, and in monitoring progress as efforts are made to modify the environment. Another important application would be in defining the type of institution in reports of more specific programmes; this sort of assessment could clarify some of the conflicting results obtained which may relate to differences in institutional structure and attitudes.

CONCLUSION

A good deal of work is needed if assessment related to RO is to progress beyond the current memory and information test and/or behaviour rating scale used in virtually every study to date. While these are useful, they have their limitations and it is to be hoped that in future it will be possible to more satisfactorily assess other aspects of cognitive functioning, the elderly person's adjustment and institutional and attitudinal variables, which would greatly enhance our knowledge of RO and other programmes, their effectiveness and their mode of operation.

Finally, although there is a study at Leeds (Holden) attempting to develop procedures to investigate the area, there is an urgent need to find methods of assessing relative's attitudes, their sense of strain and the extent to which they can use RO. The dearth of such measures could well hold back the evaluation of using RO with relatives in order to maintain elderly confused people in the community.

1(a)

1(b)

Plate 1 Good interaction using (a) flower and (b) different types of material.

Plate 2 Atmosphere in a pub situation.

Plate 3 Using a weatherboard.

Plate 4 Living again despite speech problems.

5(a)

GRESHAM HOUSE WARD ONE
BETHLEM ROYAL HOSPITAL
BECKENHAM
KENT.

THE NEXT MEAL IS SUPPER
TODAY IS FRIDAY
THE DATE IS 26th
THE MONTH IS JUNE
THE YEAR IS 1981

5(b)

5(c)

Plate 5 Signs and information boards can be extremely valuable in supplementing 24 hour RO. The dining room sign is the product of an RO session on food!

PART **TWO**

Reality orientation in practice

'How I long for a little ordinary enthusiasm. Just enthusiasm – that's all'. *John Osborn*

'There is great beauty in old trees
Old streets and ruins old.
Why should not I as well as these
Grow lovely growing old.'
(Seen in old churchyard in Cornwall)

6

The basic approach –
RO in everyday use

INFORMAL OR 24 HOUR RO

Reality Orientation in its broadest sense is a basic informal communication approach which is used by many staff unknowingly. In principle it could be used by all those in contact with the confused elderly. In essence the method is simple, obvious and practised automatically by many caring people. In this chapter will be discussed – in practical terms – how communication, even with elderly patients with dementia, can be facilitated using 24 hour RO. As the name implies, this is an approach to be used throughout the person's waking hours; in fact, every interaction is an opportunity for RO. In addition the approach demands certain environmental changes that will be described in this chapter also.

It is likely that difficulty in communicating with elderly patients is one factor in the frequent reactions of distaste, repugnance and rejection that occur in younger people faced with working with them. The barriers to easy communication may be many; some, at least, are potentially soluble. If they can be overcome then care-staff will find their work more satisfying and enjoyable, and patients will feel less rejected, frustrated and distressed.

Sensory deficits

The normal process of loss of acuity provides difficulties for both staff, relatives and friends as well as those involved in the actual loss. Eyesight is not as keen, nor often is hearing. The skin is less elastic so gesture is limited. Ageing bones, joints and muscles cause a decrease in mobility so fluency of action and movement change. As a result social contact and communication change (Bromley 1978). Because they do not hear, see or move as easily as in earlier years the elderly are often less aware of events occuring around them. A nurse can appear on the ward before breakfast and her general, cheerful 'Good morning' will elicit no response. Quite naturally she may feel upset and rejected. The patients may wonder why she becomes less friendly and helpful. A serious misunderstanding has occurred! The nurse was too far away, too impersonal, and spoke too quickly and too low. Even if standing fairly close to an individual a greeting or question may not be observed. If relatives mistake this lack of response for mental deterioration they begin to talk to each other as though their ageing parent was not present. The reaction of many patients in such a situation is withdrawal. Another misunderstanding!

Severe sensory loss is easier for staff and relatives to accept and understand; efforts are always made to help the very deaf and blind. The normal loss of sensory acuity, coupled particularly with any form of infirmity, is often overlooked. The attitudes of others caused by unawareness of the situation can lead to withdrawal which together with sensory loss has serious psychological implications.

In Chapter 2, the possible role of sensory deprivation in increasing the degree of confusion in elderly people was discussed. Sensory deprivation is the loss of sensory input for any reason; loss of sensory acuity and withdrawal are two ways by which a person's sensory stimulation may be reduced.

Two other processes by which withdrawal may be related to loss of acuity are probably common. Firstly, some patients may feel embarrassed about their failing senses, and suffer loss of self-esteem. A reaction to this may be to cut off from potentially embarrassing social situations. Secondly, some environments for elderly people may lack interest for particular patients; if they have a loss of sensory acuity 'shutting off' the unpleasant, boring situation is easy. In each case further sensory deprivation, and probably increased confusion, will result.

To combat these problems the barriers to communication should be attacked. Eyesight and hearing should be tested. When aids are required they should be used and checked regularly. Dentures should fit well, be comfortable and in their owner's mouth not in a glass or box! Thus the person's sensory and speech functions are aided as far as possible. Environmental help is also needed – lighting should be bright (but not glaring), extraneous noises damped down to a minimum. Staff need to remember that conversation should be at close range. It is better to be beneath the older person than to speak looking down at her. Slow, clearly enunciated speech is more appropriate than most quick-fire remarks. Shouting is usually unnecessary; clarity is more important.

To avoid sensory deprivation, as many of the senses as possible should be stimulated in conversation; the person is encouraged to feel objects, smell them, and taste them where appropriate. Particularly where one of the senses is impaired this sensory enrichment of the more intact senses is crucial in helping the person keep in touch with his surroundings.

Non-verbal communication

Non-verbal communication, or 'body language', is important in facilitating interaction. To join in a conversation people will move forward, or move away if they wish to escape. Gestures are vital in some cultures and have their place in every language. Not only limbs, but eyes, eyebrows, lips and the head can be used to express emotions, reactions and other messages. Close relationships have their own private system which is completely meaningless to outsiders. The movement of an eyebrow can mean anything from 'That's good' to 'Let's go' or, 'What a funny man'. Eye contact can be used to encourage the shy, to embarrass someone or to console her. It can imply concentration or interest and many other factors depending on individual ability and expressiveness.

Elderly people with sensory loss will be less sensitive to non-verbal communication; in normal conversation many of the signals given are subtle, and easily missed if eyesight or hearing is impaired. Staff need then to make their non-verbal messages slightly more clear-cut than usual. Thus a slow approach from in front of the patient is less likely to be misinterpreted as aggressive than suddenly appearing at the patient's side from behind. In face-to-face contact a warm smile expresses friendliness; eye-contact expresses the staff member's desire to interact and is useful in gaining and maintaining attention. The use of gentle touch should be encouraged – a hand over the other's hand, a soft stroking of a cheek with the back of the hand. These and other gestures are warm, reassuring and imply concern and friendship; touch is also helpful in attracting and keeping the person's interest and concentration. If the nurse, by these means, appears to the patient as calm, warm and friendly then the patient is more likely to respond and be relaxed and reassured. The nurse's aim is not to put on an act, but rather to express clearly, minimising the danger of misunderstanding, whatever she is trying to communicate.

In listening to elderly people, attention must be given to the messages they give non-verbally, as well as to what they say. Here it must be remembered that the ability of elderly people to give out messages may be impaired as well as their capacity to receive them. This is due to the decrease in mobility and dexterity mentioned above. However, as will be discussed later, the signals that are given can be important in making some sense of what the person says.

Personal distance

The distance between people effects interaction to some extent. This varies from culture to culture, from situation to situation and from person to person. Generally, total attention is required at a distance of about 18 inches; at four feet some communication is

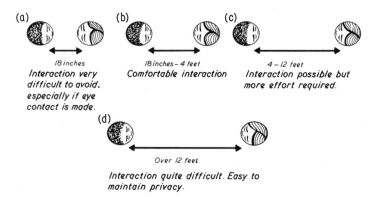

(a) *18 inches*
Interaction very difficult to avoid, especially if eye contact is made.

(b) *18 inches – 4 feet*
Comfortable interaction

(c) *4 – 12 feet*
Interaction possible but more effort required.

(d) *Over 12 feet*
Interaction quite difficult. Easy to maintain privacy.

Fig. 6.1 Effects on interaction of inter-personal distance.

indicated and a distance of up to twelve feet still provides the possibilities of social interaction. Over twelve feet allows for public space so it is possible to sit in a park, or on the beach or in a waiting room and maintain privacy even in a crowd (see Fig. 6.1). Sometimes, however, distance cannot be controlled and difficulties arise.

Difficulties caused by the need to manipulate distance occur frequently. For instance, the train is late, the station is very cold; to the relief of the passenger there is a fire in the waiting room. Before rushing to the only available seat the passenger notices that it is adjacent to one occupied by an undesirable, objectionable being. The need for warmth is greater than scruples, but precautions are essential. Non-verbal communication provides the answer. A newspaper is raised, a shoulder is turned to cut off direct view and any form of self-sufficiency is employed to illustrate the wish to preserve anonymity. How different the situation would be if both persons were attractive!

Elderly people can be lonely even in a residential home; the lounge can be like a waiting room, with little interaction occurring, and residents remaining strangers to each other. Staff need to bear in mind that some chair arrangements help, and others hinder, social interaction (see Chapter 2). It is difficult to converse side-by-side, it is much more comfortable to be facing the person

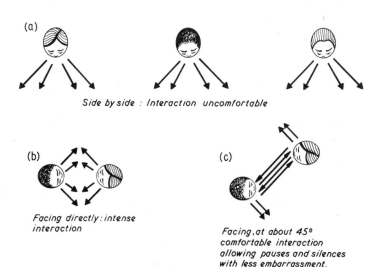

(a)

Side by side : Interaction uncomfortable

(b)

Facing directly : intense
interaction

(c)

Facing, at about 45°
comfortable interaction
allowing pauses and silences
with less embarrassment.

Fig. 6.2 Effects on interaction of inter-personal angular orientation.

(see Fig. 6.2). A lounge with many people in it will inhibit interaction; it is difficult enough for younger people to get to know 25 or more people at once; the problem is immense for the confused person whose awareness and recognition of others grows very slowly indeed. A smaller group, particularly if there are common interests and a shared task or activity, will greatly facilitate development of relationships and interaction. In this situation staff-resident interactions are made easier and more natural than when residents are dependent on staff for most opportunities for conversation; staff do not have to search for topics of conversation, as they are provided for them by what is happening in the group. This does not imply that all homes with large lounges have to be rebuilt; it is possible with room-dividers, partitions and careful furniture arrangement to achieve a great deal in encouraging the development of small groups (see Chapter 2 for references on and more details of the 'group living' concept). Table 6.1 gives a summary of the practical steps recommended so far to aid communication.

Table 6.1 Overcoming barriers to communication

1. Correct sensory deficits
2. Speak clearly
3. Use all the senses
4. Use eye contact and touch to maintain attention
5. Arrange environment to facilitate interaction

The whole person – basic attitudes

Far too often the need to treat the Whole Person is forgotten. Treatment programmes, either at home or in care, provide for the physical needs but ignore psychological and emotional needs. On hospital wards individuals can become medical diagnoses and the physical cure pursued vigorously. It is as if the identity of the person is forgotten. The patient in Bed 4 becomes a broken femur, the occupant of Bed 10 a heart condition instead of Mrs Anne Brown or Mr Peter White with their personal concerns relating to their rent, their possessions or their own individual personalities. The use of the Nursing Process can help to ensure that patients are persons in their own right. If the staff and friends know how to communicate they will know more about the whole person and be able to meet his or her individual need.

Elderly people have had longer to develop, and perhaps are more different from each other than younger people. Their psychological needs can only be heeded if they are seen and treated as individuals. They have had adult status for 50 or 60 years or more; to be then treated as a child will be potentially deeply upsetting. Even elderly people who are extremely confused may have an awareness at some level beyond that which they are capable of expressing. Interaction should then be attempted at an adult-adult level, however child-like the response may seem. Where it is obtainable, information about the person's background can illuminate present functioning and even help to make more sense of apparently random behaviour. Attempting to write a brief biography of the person can be a useful aid here.

Preservation of dignity and respect play a major role in assisting the elderly to cope with their problems. To lose independence suddenly due to hospitalisation, or by being placed in a home is disturbing in itself. When dignity is further upset by total strangers presuming (for instance) to use familiar Christian names, status is lost and self-esteem jeopardised. Some people do prefer to be addressed by their Christian names but some do not. For example a retired surgeon was taken ill and admitted to hospital where he became confused and difficult overnight. It was noticed that the staff were addressing him as 'Joey'; he was completely bewildered by a situation of unprecedented equality, as surgeons of the 'Old School' were notorious for their concern for personal dignity and aloofness. Once the staff began to call him 'Sir' he promptly regained his composure: within a few days he began to order everyone about in his customary manner and was quickly discharged!

Similarly a lady in her 80s was called 'Lavinia' by the staff. The younger nurses arranged her hair in pigtails and tied it up in pink ribbons. Until shortly before her illness she had been a very independent, arrogant spinster and a much feared and respected Justice of the Peace. In hospital she began by preserving her authoritarian demeanour but slowly lost her ability to dominate the scene. She stopped thinking for herself, lost independence, deteriorated into a confused institutionalised, childlike waif and simply faded away.

There are innumerable situations in which dignity and self-respect can be stripped from a person – often by lack of thought. Examples are: talking about a person in their presence, as if they were not there ('she doesn't understand'); leaving toilet doors open while occupied; doing something to a person (combing their hair, lifting them and so on) without first explaining to the person what is about to happen. The reader will be able to add many more instances; in short, any situations where the person is to some extent made to feel small, worthless or is humiliated are to be avoided.

Dignity and respect *can* be maintained. The individual's experience, standing in the community, achievements, and knowledge of the past are all aspects that can be used to retain his or her self-esteem. Explanations of what is happening, or will happen, are necessary. Day-to-day events, from the immediate environment or from national and international news, should be discussed. A concern for privacy, personal likes and dislikes shows courtesy which is appreciated by all age groups and preserves self-respect. Politeness is noted and invariably merits a response, particularly from people who grew up in a culture which valued good manners.

The attitude involved here might at first glance be characterised as behaving as if the person were not demented at all, as if the memory and behaviour problems did not exist. In fact, the approach is firstly, to treat the demented person as a *person*, and to recognise that because of this, dignity, respect, individuality and so on remain important. Secondly, however, the person must be accepted as she is now. This involves recognition of current limitations – but to see these as a starting point, as being possibly modifiable and not necessarily fixed. By doing this expectations and demands can be sensitively set at a level which does not place the person in a position of failure, whilst at the same time they are gradually increased as and when the person's functioning improves. Failure is avoided, as it leads to loss of self-respect, particularly when the tasks involved are still perceived as extremely simple. The avoidance of failure is not to be the passive 'if I don't do anything at all I can't possibly fail' variety. It is instead an active avoidance where those areas that the person can succeed in are emphasised. Too often the presence of dementia is unnecessarily demonstrated and made obvious by the use of direct questioning of memory, rather than allowing the patient to succeed by the skilful use of cues and prompts.

In summary, allowing dignity and self-respect is not achieved by pretending that any dementia is absent when it clearly is not; it is achieved by removing the focus from the disability onto preserved areas of functioning. This is of course exactly what happens with physical disabilities, and the same should apply to mental disabilities also.

Two further related aspects of the *whole person* need to be discussed, particularly in relation to the elderly person in institutional care. The first is choice; it is only too easy to remove choice and to place elderly people in a situation where they have little control over even the small – but none the less significant – features of daily living. For example, a cup of tea may be provided at breakfast time, when the patient had always been accustomed to coffee; or clothes may be laid out for the patient without any consultation about the selection. Complete freedom of choice is of course available to hardly anyone. In a communal setting inevitably there are restrictions; the approach here is to discover what choices can be made available and to present these to elderly patients. Encouragement may be needed to help them make their own choices, especially when they have become apathetic and accustomed to the staff deciding. This is an important part of being an adult, dignified, self-respecting individual.

The final aspect to be encouraged and developed is independence. Again, no-one is ever truly independent; we are all interdependent to a greater or lesser degree, and inevitably in communal settings particularly it is more difficult to be less dependent on other people. Once more though, many instances occur of patients being more dependent on staff than is necessary; thus patients are sometimes completely dressed by staff for the sake of speed when the patient can manage slowly with much less help; or sugar is put in the patients' tea when they are capable of adding it themselves. Self-help is important to a patient's self-esteem; the success of doing something for oneself, albeit slowly, can be rewarding. Interdependence was mentioned above; a neglected aspect of the whole person is often the extent to which they can do things for other people, the extent to which other people can be dependent on the patient. By helping the patient have a meaningful role, be it clearing the table, sweeping up, telling a story about the past, singing a song or whatever is appropriate and possible, again the patient's self-esteem is built up. The option of having privacy must be provided also. Hospitals and homes need to allow some space for privacy, plus the necessary arrangements to ensure it. Screens or curtains, the ability to display some personal items, personalisation of clothing, storage, thinking and entertaining space are vital to the quality of life.

Those aspects of the whole person that staff attitudes need to develop are listed in Table 6.2. These attitudes underly the whole RO approach. Without them any approach will fail at a human and emotional level.

Table 6.2 Basic attitudes

Staff attitudes must allow the elderly person:
1. Individuality as an adult
2. Dignity
3. Self-respect
4. Choice
5. Independence

24 HOUR RO – METHODS

Having covered barriers to communication, non-verbal communication and the attitudes underlying communication, the next section considers much more the content and form of communication with the elderly patient; in effect then what the staff member says is under consideration here. The guidelines are summarised in Table 6.3.

Table 6.3 Guidelines for 24-hour RO

Remind the person:	Useful tips:
A. Who he or she is	1. Use short simple sentences
B. Where he or she is	2. Encourage response and repetitions
C. What time of day it is	3. Use past experiences as a bridge to the present
D. What is happening in the person's surroundings	4. Keep conversation specific
	5. Encourage humour
	6. Provide a commentary on events

The aim is for each interaction that the elderly person has to be used for 24 hour RO. There are numerous opportunities during the day when even a short contact between the young and the old can be used to advantage. Waking people up, helping them to the toilet, serving meals are all natural situations for conversation.

The elderly person can be motivated into awareness of himself and his environment by simple methods of disguised repetition, and by attention to everyday, simple matters such as the weather, the day and the month, and the time. This can be done by drawing attention to what is happening indoors and outside the window; all the senses can be involved, as for instance by remarking on the lovely smell of breakfast or the feel of cold hands just come in from the snow.

Some examples of simple interactions are as follows:

'Hello, Mrs Smith; this place is called —— Hospital; yes, that's right, —— Hospital.'

'Mr Green, it's 12 o'clock now; time for lunch; that's right, the dining room is through that door there.'

'Your bath is ready for you, Mr Brown. Take off your jacket, then your shirt..; when you've finished undressing there's a nice hot bath for you.'

'My name is Jean; yes, Jean. I'm a new nurse here at —— Hospital. What's your name? I'm pleased to meet you, Mr White. Have you seen what an awful day it is today? Come and look out the window. Yes, it's pouring with rain; I suppose we can't expect good weather in November. It's good to be indoors today. At least —— Hospital is warm and dry, isn't it?' Note the frequent use of names (patients and staff) and the relatively short, simple statements and questions, which are intended to encourage a response and repetition, wherever possible, and *not* to make the person fail. The more opportunities for repetition that can be made the more likely is the learning process to be reawakened. Disguised repetition is necessary as elderly people are not children and naturally resent being patronised or treated as though they are inferior in any way.

There is a need to be aware of a short attention span or wavering concentration. In order to hold attention a number of related, sensorially stimulating items are useful. For example, when waking Mr Smith in the morning one may say 'Good morning Mr Smith; it's eight o'clock, time to be getting up for breakfast'. After a short time a further comment on the time can be followed by 'Have you looked out the window yet? It is really spring-like today, the sun is out and it's quite warm for March'.

At breakfast this can be repeated, 'Look, we've daffodils on the table. It's almost spring, don't they smell nice?'. Later in the day a calendar can be produced, the day and the month indicated and further reference to spring can be made. Repeated presentation of information may sound like a broken record to staff, but to the confused patient it may be only vaguely familiar!

The use of past experiences in comparison with the happenings of today allows reminiscence to play a vital role in a conversation.

The elderly know more about the past than their children or care staff. To capitalise on their experience helps to provide an opening to talk about the present. The old folk are aware of their superior knowledge and do not feel threatened by a possible exposure of inadequacies. Past experiences are used to help the person become more aware of the present – contrasts and similarities can be emphasised. When talking about past events it should be made clear to the elderly person by the use of past tenses of verbs, and so on, that current reality is not being discussed. For example: 'You used to work in a coal mine didn't you Mr Green?' or 'Before you came into hospital, you had lived in South Avenue for 30 years, hadn't you, Mr Brown?'. Note the attempt to provide a temporal context here.

One difficulty of communication with a confused elderly person is the frequency of 'crossed wires' in a conversation. The staff member is continuing on one subject, the patient drifts on to another, perhaps related topic, until the two diverge completely. The problem of many conversations is that they rely on memory of the words that have just been spoken a few sentences ago – this is very difficult for most patients with dementia. A way around this is to have a focus for the conversation. Words are spoken and then have gone, but if both the participants in the conversation have their attention on something specific – a picture, an object, an odour, a view from the window etc., – then it is more likely that the patient will remain on the same topic as the staff member. Although inevitably there will be some repetition at least both parties will be talking about the same thing! Avoidance of vagueness by the staff will also aid communication. In everyday contacts it will be of value if they are kept specific and concrete.

If a discussion of current events arose and one aspect, for example the Prime Minister, was chosen for discussion, rather than simply using words relevant items could be employed as a focus. A picture, television programme or a book about him or her would help. If the time of day is the subject a clock or a watch could be used. Conversations about relatives can be facilitated by the use of photographs from the past and present. Without such references the person could be talking about her daughter aged three, but the staff could be discussing the 50 year old lady whom they meet regularly!

Humour is to be encouraged. Laughing *with* the elderly person, never permitting the person to feel that he is being laughed *at*, are vital aspects. Humour breaks the ice, helps the patient to relax, and perhaps, makes it easier to cope with the reality of disability and impairment. No examples can be given, as what is funny depends on the situation, the people concerned and the timing. Its occurrence is a positive sign, especially when patients begin to initiate the humour and make gentle fun of the staff!

Conversation does not have to concentrate on major events; a straightforward comment on the day's happenings, however mundane they may seem, is important for the person who is having difficulty keeping in touch with reality. Physical care need never be given silently. Even if the patient is withdrawn and unresponsive the nurse can still talk about what is happening. It is not a rare occurrence to see two people attending an old person and talking to each other as though there was no third party present. 'I was at a party the other night. The band was great'. The friend will ask 'Was it punk rock?'. The discussion will continue as a duet. The older member of the trio could be included quite simply by enquiring 'What kinds of music do you enjoy?', or whatever may be appropriate to extend the conversation. Normal conversation is not impossible!

In hospitals or residential homes all staff and visitors can be encouraged to use 24 hour RO. The ladies who bring the flowers to the wards could make sure that the residents see the arrangements and touch and smell them instead of simply placing them on a window-sill or an out-of-the-way table. Flowers are beautiful, colourful, seasonal and smell delightfully. These qualities should be remarked upon and appreciated. Senior staff should watch the attitudes of regularly visiting services, as for example barbers, hairdressers and others, to ensure that dignity, choice and independence are preserved. No man should be shaved without being first consulted, and if he is being shaved should be treated like any other customer and not as an object. Similarly relatives and junior staff need to be encouraged to include the elderly in their conversations.

Finally, helping the person succeed is a major aim. In normal conversation questions are often asked to draw a person into talking and to elicit a response. With a confused person if a question is asked that the person cannot answer the disability will be exposed. Prompts should be given so that the patient is able to respond and join in the conversation. The amount of prompting and clues needed depends on the person; just sufficient to produce the response should be given. Answers can often be given in the original question e.g. instead of asking 'What's the weather like today?', the staff member might say 'What a lot of wet, showery days we're having'. In other situations it is appropriate to give the first few letters of the answer. For example, if conversing about a record the younger person might ask 'Who's that singing? Isn't that Bing something – I think it begins with C...Yes, of course, Bing Crosby. What was that famous song of his, remind me, wasn't it White something or other...?'

In this way memories may be reawakened, the older person being unable to recall them freely without this help from the younger one. Often information is remembered by the elderly to some extent, but they are unable to recall it fully, or the memory is slightly vague. Thus many elderly patients are, for example, unable to name the current Prime Minister, but some recall the name, if a special clue is given, 'it's a woman' or by using letters from the name, perhaps even by giving the first name. By using clues and prompts sensitively the elderly patient's limited memory can be used to the fullest extent.

Night-time confusion is well known. A calm response full of simple, reassuring information is helpful. A statement such as 'Mr Jones, it's three in the morning. Look it's dark, everyone is asleep. What's wrong, couldn't you see the clock?', will help him to reorganize his thoughts without exposing his genuine confusion. Restoration of the missing information will assist his self-confidence and calm him. The effect of waking up in the dark on a confused elderly person may be compared to regaining consciousness after an anaesthetic when even personal identity is lost and short-lived total disorientation occurs. By providing a confused old person with information, without questions which might expose his or her difficulties and thus cause him to lose face, confidence in the self and in the other person is restored.

Handling rambling talk

Confused people often produce rambling, confabulatory talk. A person may chatter away talking apparent nonsense about where she is and what she is doing, or may seem to live in the past. 'Oh, I just baked a lovely tea for this picnic. We're in the park I used to play in as a child. That's my sister over there eating chicken.' This kind of statement is commonly heard in the midst of a ward and possibly in the midst of winter. The only thing in keeping with reality may be the fact that it is mealtime. Rambling talk like this shows that the person is mixing past events, experiences and present events indiscriminately. Reactions can include impatience or sharp correction, acceptance of the remark as indicative of a dementing mind, or agreements with the incorrect statement to 'humour' the elderly person.

It is sometimes thought RO always involves 'putting the person right'. As Table 6.4 makes clear the important principle is to never agree with rambling talk; after this there is a choice of strategies depending on the person and the situation.

Table 6.4 Rambling and confused talk

Do not agree
1. Tactfully disagree (on less sensitive topics)
   or
2. Change the subject – discuss something concrete
   or
3. Acknowledge the feelings expressed – ignore the content

Gentle correction is possible, particularly in situations where sensitive topics are not involved. These corrections should be tactful, so that they can be accepted without loss of dignity. For example:

'Actually it's Tuesday today – but one day does seem much like another here.'

'This is a hospital in fact, but we like to think that it is as good as any hotel.'

'That's Jim Smith, one of the other nurses, perhaps he looks like your son Bill.'

Such statements could be possible corrections for confusions of day, place and person. Where more sensitive areas, such as a bereavement, are concerned it is wise to first ascertain the type of response which occurs after correction to errors on a more general plane. If these responses are usually reasonable then it would be feasible to attempt open discussion about the more emotionally loaded situations. The important point is to choose appropriate occasions for correction – when the person is calm and there is time available. If a bereavement is to be discussed, it may appear fresh to an old person, almost as if it was new information. Therefore the same procedure should be followed as when it is necessary to break bad news to someone. Time, also, should be allowed for this and for sitting with the person as he or she grieves. It is not such a terrible thing if the person cries – indeed it may be more abnormal not to cry in the circumstances.

On many occasions – where time is limited or there is already some agitation or confusion and talk is vague and incoherent – it is better not to correct confabulatory statements. Instead of emphatically denying that such a thing is possible it is better to ignore the content of the rambling talk and use distraction. A gentle touch on the arm, eye contact and an attempt to attract attention by speaking in a firm, clear voice should be followed by a distracting statement. The use of an interesting item such as a flower accompanied by a suitable comment 'Ellen, Ellen, what do you think of this?', will usually suffice to promote a definite response. If proper direction of attention is enforced rambling will stop. Moving the person's focus of attention onto something in the surroundings is important in any attempt to change the subject of the conversation – everyday objects and pictures can be used to achieve this.

The final possibility for responding to confused talk is relevant when it seems that a statement or remark is an attempt to express a feeling. This feeling is hidden, perhaps because the appropriate words are not available. Possibly non-verbal methods are used to convey the message e.g. 'I'm sorry, I must go home now and get my Dad's tea.' The lady is 84 years old, had been hospitalised for three years and her Dad died 20 years ago. Pointing out these facts to her would be inappropriate in many situations. The 'hidden' meaning may well be the simple one that she is expressing boredom or a feeling of insecurity for the moment and wishes to escape. The response is to acknowledge the feeling – but not the actual words. Here it might be 'We've done enough for today haven't we, let's get a cup of tea on the ward', which allows the person to retire with dignity.

A further example would be 'My mother is coming soon' – when the patient's mother had died several years previously. The response to this might be 'It must have been a good time of life when you were with your parents, and they were there to look after you.' The feeling communicated was again one of insecurity – a need to recall that time of life when the patient was very dependent, but had her mother there to provide security for her.

Here background knowledge of the patient is important as there are homes where both mother and daughter are residents!

An interesting case of the 'hidden message' was an elderly lady who talked to her 'sister' in a mirror. She knew it was a mirror but had constructed a fantasy world where she was able to pass the time of day with her own reflection. Again responses like 'It's great to feel you have relatives near by', seemed more appropriate than outright correction, which the patient resisted. The point may be reached where one can say 'You know it is a mirror and I know it's a mirror but if you want to say you're talking to your sister, that's fine.' However, in situations like this the possiblity of involving the person in activities and interests that were previously enjoyed should be seriously considered.

A refusal to cooperate often indicates a reaction to stress and an avoidance of a situation which might be threatening to self-esteem. Sudden deafness is an example of this! By smiling broadly and remaining silent, by being inattentive or by confabulating, anxiety is avoided. 'I don't want to answer any more questions', is an attempt to control a situation; once this is achieved cooperation usually follows. Old people may buy time in order to think, to control and to make sure that they understand the implications of a situation. 'Oh, I've forgotten my glasses' or 'I must go to the toilet' can be useful excuses to allow a delay. The importance of helping the person succeed, by not making demands or asking questions that will lead to failure, is clear. Helping the person to feel reassured, relaxed, and self-confident can thus reduce the amount of rambling talk.

Environmental aids

If a normal person is finding his way around an unfamiliar place he will use signs to guide him. When we want to know the time we consult a watch or clock; for the date we look at a diary, calendar or newspaper. If normal people sometimes need memory aids, how much greater is the confused person's need!

Table 6.5 Environmental aids: use orienting cues in the person's environment

Clocks		
Calendars		Large
Signs	*Ensure that they are*	Clear
Pictures		Accurate

Table 6.5 indicates the type of aids that are required to reinforce the information given to patients by staff members. The aids must be large and clear enough for the elderly person to see; above all they must be accurate – or confusion will be increased! Getting these details right is an important – and inexpensive – part of RO.

Patients may need to be taught where the signs and aids are, and encouraged to make use of them. This initial effort is well worthwhile in view of the time saved later.

Colour plays a large role in creating an atmosphere. Bright covers on beds assist identification as well as looking pretty, toilet doors are easier to find if they are painted a special colour as well as bearing a printed notice. Attractive curtains, cheerful walls, interesting pictures, gaily patterned tablecloths and colourful crockery provide a varied environment with plenty of landmarks to aid orientation. The staff are helped by the memory aids too! They act as a reminder to use 24 hour RO in every interaction. Here as well as clocks and calendars, boards with clearly written information about the Day, Month and Weather, colourful pictures or collages of food, national leaders, places, children, seasons, occupations, maps etc. should also be on view. A daily newspaper and journals of particular interest should be easily available. There is always time in the day for comments on these, and they are valuable aids to communication, providing a visual reminder to the patient of the topic.

Consideration should be given as to whether there are any environmental features which used routinely may cause acute distress and hasten the process of withdrawal. The use of cot sides is still, unfortunately, a common example of this. Restless patients, elderly stroke cases and others could wake up to a world cut off by bars. This must confirm feelings of rejection. If he wishes to use the toilet and no one is around he either attempts to climb over the bars – and has the accident the bars were meant to prevent – or is incontinent. Dignity and independence are lost – perhaps permanently. Similar problems are caused by the *routine* use of geriatric chairs, or even beds that are too high from the ground, floors that easily become slippery or even just look very shiny, and large open spaces.

COMMUNICATING WITH DYSPHASIC PATIENTS OR THOSE WITH SPEECH PROBLEMS

People who have had a stroke, head injury or some neurological disorder resulting in damage to the parts of the brain responsible for speech will suffer from some form of speech disorder. This is a complex field; fuller definitions are given in Chapter 5; here three major types of speech problems will be indicated.

1. Dysarthria

Here it is the actual production of speech that is affected; words and sentence construction may be correct, but the articulation is poor. The listener finds the speech indistinct and difficult to understand. Temporary dysarthria is familiar after a substantial consumption of alcohol!

2. Expressive dysphasia

This takes various forms; essentially the person is impaired in his ability to express himself and the words and sentences do not come out correctly. There may be difficulties in finding the right word leading to a high frequency of 'thingumajigs', 'whatsits' etc. or to long-winded or circumlocutory speech when e.g. the person says 'a small piece for fastening articles that people wear' instead of 'button'. Words may be invented, reversed or omitted. There may be difficulty in reading, writing and calculation. Automatic speech such as 'Monday, Tuesday, Wednesday . . . . .' or 'one, two, three . . . . .' may be possible, as may be singing; these do not represent the overall level of functioning as they are so well-known to the person. The person may well feel frustrated at his inability to make others understand, which he is able to perceive.

3. Receptive dysphasia

Here the patient has difficulty in appreciating what is being said. There is incomplete or even no understanding of conversation, directions or questions, which leads to a considerable degree of isolation. Some associated problems include reading, writing, calculation and spelling. The person is placed in a world of which he is unable to make sense; he is likely to be bewildered, perplexed and frightened. The nature of the difficulties of comprehension is such that the person is also often unable to express himself clearly; a person's own speech is continually monitored by the receptive system, so expression is also likely to be affected by receptive difficulties.

Communication

Wherever possible a speech therapist should be consulted to guide, advise and treat. However there is a great deal that can be done by care staff – as the success of 'stroke clubs' and volunteer speech after stroke schemes has demonstrated.

The first step with these – and other – impairments is to recognise and accept that they are not within the person's control, that the impairment arises however hard the person tries to overcome it. Secondly, speech impairments may make people appear more deteriorated and confused than in fact they are. Here the basic RO approach of not writing anybody off, but continuing to treat them as a person, is of great value. Thirdly, particularly where a stroke has led to the impairment, improvement may well be possible. Where the speech problem is a feature of a dementing illness, more restricted aims will be appropriate.

More specifically the problem of communicating with the receptive dysphasic is the most challenging of all. They should not be included in group settings and communication should be on a one-to-one basis. The group situation aggravates their sense of worthlessness and frustration. Others appear to be enjoying themselves, but they do not understand what is so pleasing to the others in the group.

On a one-to-one basis communication must be simplified as much as possible. Non-verbal signals are very important; sudden movements, or an approach from behind may be misinterpreted as threatening and lead to aggressive lashing out. Gentle touch, an open and warm approach and voice tone should be employed to encourage a feeling of security and acceptance. Verbal messages must be simplified, avoiding complex concepts; sentences must be short and involve one idea at a time only. Words should be backed up with demonstrations, gestures, pictures etc. Every possible effort to understand the person's attempts at communication must be made; again non-verbal signals and gestures are important in making sense of what the person says. Any communication abilities the person does retain should be capitalised on, whether it be reading, writing, mime etc. With interaction being so difficult there is a tendency to avoid such patients; if only some feeling of warmth and acceptance is conveyed then something will have been achieved.

Patients with expressive dysphasia or dysarthria do well with RO both in groups or in informal interaction.

Mr D, a 79 year old who had a right-sided hemiplegia and severe expressive dysphasia resulting from a stroke, could say an occasional word, but more frequently said 'Five, five, five,' or 'Go to Hell!'. He was incontinent, negativistic, a little aggressive and cut himself off by burying his head in his arms. Though included in an RO group, he remained isolated for two weeks. Suddenly he began to write with his left hand and made several meaningful and distinct drawings. Gestures, eye-contact and interest in the materials used in the session began to increase. As his gestures and the therapist's understanding of them improved his needs could be interpreted. He showed his delight by increasing his efforts and warmth of response. His drawings became so meaningful that it was possible for him to give an account of himself and his past life. His intelligence was put to use in finding ways to tell his new friends about his experiences. His improvement was dramatic and his family were pleased for him to be discharged home.

Mrs V had a severe form of receptive dysphasia as a result of a stroke. She was extremely depressed and weepy, but there was little that could be done to communicate with her. Initially, before the problem was clear, she was included in a group. It soon became apparent that there were many problems and the situation was becoming intolerable for her. Individual therapy was instigated. Using warmth, information from her past, much respect and by introducing items that she recognised, it was possible to build up a happy relationship between her and the staff. Simple things, as for example bringing her a posy of the flowers with a similar name to herself, pictures of places she had visited and the use of gentle touch, all aided in at least improving her life on the ward. It also encouraged her to attempt to express herself non-verbally, so that the staff were able to learn more about the things which pleased or interested her.

Mrs F had a mild stroke one evening and in the morning was unable to speak properly. She was frightened and disturbed and the staff anxious. By using sentences which required the minimum of response – initially 'yes' and 'no' – it was possible to calm her and to gradually increase the span of response. For example 'Would you like some tea?', would become 'Would you like some tea or coffee?' Later, perhaps in a day or two, as she improved, a calm voice would enquire 'Would you like to get dressed this morning? What would you like to wear?' This permitted the use of 'yes' and 'no', but also allowed longer responses. These were aided by 'What about this?' or 'Do you like the pink jumper?' In an atmosphere of calm and of minimal demand on speech confidence can return and normal processes of recovery can be aided, with the minimum of stress.

These are some of many examples of how RO can be used to help those with speech problems. Special allowances must be made for them. Patience is vital and the patient should be given time and encouragement in order to appreciate that others are willing to help. The atmosphere should be one in which the patient does not feel that heavy demands are being made for him to express himself, whilst being friendly and inclusive. As in other aspects of RO the person's disability is not to be exposed and demonstrated once more, but again help is given for the person to find success. He or she should be greeted, materials used by others should be shown, brought near or left in reach. Reactions such as eye contact or gestures should be noted and a response made to them. Again non-verbal responses are useful – touch, warmth, gesture and so on, but here there is more scope for verbal responses and reassurance. A reaction should not be forced, but any effort, however small, should be greeted with interest and attention. Too fulsome a response could be inappropriate, but warmth and moderated praise are indicated. 'What do you think of that, it's nice isn't it?' or 'You can do a lot with that left hand can't you? I like your drawing.' Lack of speech does not mean lack of intellectual ability, but it does mean that everyone has to try harder to understand and be understood.

Where some speech is retained but there is perhaps a word-finding difficulty then the patient may be able to indicate a choice from several alternatives; he may not be able to name something, but may be able to match it with an identical object. Any communicative ability at all should be capitalized on, and the speech therapist may indicate certain aspects that are less impaired. The dysarthric patient may need to be taught to talk more slowly and precisely, and to use non-verbal means to provide a context for what is said. Words are easier to understand if the listener knows roughly what is likely to be said. In all cases isolation and withdrawal are possible consequences of the speech impairment; the work of 24 hour RO is to ensure this does not happen, by helping the person feel accepted, and to some extent understood and – importantly – unpressured.

CONCLUSION

Reality Orientation used as an informal or 24 hour approach should be used consciously by those in contact with elderly people. There is a need to be aware of dangers; sensory deprivation, neglect of the whole person, poor environment, poor communication and lack of understanding of individual problems are the main concerns. Awareness of these leads to better planning, more stimulation and increase in quality of life. It is vital to preserve dignity, self-esteem and an interest in life. Volunteers, friends, relatives and caring staff should use every opportunity to reassure and encourage the elderly by drawing their attention to everyday events. The use of simple forms of sensory stimulation – such as flowers, pictures, seasonal items – can be employed even by grandchildren. The past, old experiences and knowledge with comparisons from the present are valuable aids to conversation and the reawakening of interest in the self and the environment. Social contact is equally important.

Efforts to understand the person's words and actions should be made; do they suggest anxiety or insecurity? Do they make sense in view of their previous personality, interests, occupations etc? Is the person wandering along the corridor opening each door in turn really behaving aimlessly; perhaps he is looking for something that seems familiar (as many people do when lost); with a severe memory deficit everything looks new and fresh, nothing is familiar, unless known to the person before the memory problems began. Alternatively the person may be searching for the toilet!

Encourage and praise all the person's efforts at reality orientated behaviour; all their successes and achievements; their appropriate conversations. Praise and staff attention are powerful motivators where staff develop warm relationships with the elderly patients;

they can help define that appropriate non-confused functioning is the aim for the ward or Home by reversing the common trend for most attention to be given to confused behaviour.

Above all never write off the elderly person as a *person*: by getting to know and understand older people and all that has brought them to where they are now, communication, on a person-to-person level, becomes possible.

'If you really want to hear about it, the first thing you will probably want to know is where I was born, and what my lousy childhood was like, and how my parents were occupied and all before they had me, and all that David Copperfield kind of crap, but I don't feel like going into it'. *J D Salinger*

7

RO structured sessions

RO structured sessions consist of regular meetings of a small group of elderly people, when RO is carried out intensively for from 30 minutes to an hour. They are variously described as RO sessions, RO groups, RO classes or formal RO. Group leaders may include care-staff, nurses, OTs, speech therapists, psychologists, volunteers and so on; no formal qualifications are implied by the use of the term 'therapist' for these group leaders.

In many ways formal RO is the more immediately obvious and perhaps more dramatic aspect of RO. It usually seems to attract more attention than the more mundane hour-by-hour 24 hour RO described in the previous chapter. This is unfortunate as the RO session is intended to supplement 24 hour RO and not to replace it.

While informal RO assists in developing helpful attitudes and responses towards the elderly in any day-to-day situation, a formal session run by therapists provides an opportunity for intensive stimulation, guidance, and retraining. During the session it is possible to learn more about participants, to obtain an insight into their history, personality, individual characteristics, experience, likes and dislikes. Such information reinforces those working with the elderly and helps them relate with greater ease during the day.

As group member and therapist learn more about each other mutual understanding grows and becomes generalised into all contacts. Even difficult patients can become easier to handle because of this increasing awareness and greater insight which has developed between all parties.

Therapists become aware of the patients' capabilities and the elderly people feel more secure and closer to those who care for them. A bond is developed which can greatly aid rehabilitation.

This chapter will describe how to lead an RO session. Before RO sessions can be organised there are issues of staff-training and support, patient selection, programme co-ordination and feedback to be considered. These are covered in Chapter 9. In Chapter 5 assessment is discussed, and Chapter 8 includes many examples of possible equipment and aids to be used. However before describing actual sessions the overall atmosphere to be aimed at will be outlined.

SOCIAL ATMOSPHERE

As with 24 hour RO a basic aim is to help the elderly person succeed. For this to happen he needs to feel relaxed and unpressured. Many programmes in the USA use a classroom setting, with the nurse acting as a teacher, and possibly having gradua- tion' ceremonies when progress is made to a higher level of class- es. Many elderly people in the UK in our experience find the classroom an anxiety-provoking setting, and they do not function at their best there. The classroom setting seems to emphasise the child-like level of knowledge and skills of the elderly person. Whilst recognising the good results often obtained with the RO classroom our preference is to emphasise the social aspects of the session. Clearly much depends on the cultural background of the elderly people involved; if adult education becomes more widespread the classroom may become more attractive!

Where should the session take place? Ideally a special room should be used. The atmosphere should be colourful, warm, sunny and relaxed and be designed to stimulate interest and response. Large external windows are an asset. The ward atmosphere is not conducive to concentration or relaxation. It is associated with ideas of Hospital, authority, routine and medical treatment. Even in community Homes the idea of a club or social activity room implies a change from routine and the possibility of being amused and diverted.

In the room a social atmosphere can be created with comfortable chairs, interesting and bright pictures and posters, small tables, flowers and plants, colourful curtains and so on. More elaborate settings can be devised. In Leeds RO rooms have been established with a 'pub' atmosphere. In Great Britain one of the most popular meeting places is the Pub. In this situation people relax, amuse each other and talk freely. There are inevitably those who take the drinking aspect too seriously, but the vast majority go for the company and some may only sip at an alcoholic drink or simply stick to fruit juice. In former years, when current elderly patients were in their youth, most pubs tended to be male preserves. However when female patients were asked if they would prefer a tea-room they unanimously chose the pub — perhaps feeling slightly wicked in so doing!

To produce a simulated pub at low cost is comparatively easy. It is often possible to find old cupboards with the correct elbow height. Beer advertisements are on posters, ashtrays and labels. Help may be obtained from a kind local brewery. The hospital furniture store may have an old barrel and cash register. In everyone's home rests an object or two which would prove invaluable to such a setting. Enthusiasm and imagination on the part of the staff can work wonders! As most hospitals and residential homes have a little-used supply of beer, sherry and fruit juice for their elderly, there is generally no problem in finding the stock for the bar. It is more appropriate to have a drink in the right surroundings than by a bedside or simply at a meal table. Certainly it is more stimulating.

There are, of course, other kinds of suitable surroundings. One group in London is fortunate enough to have access to a swimming pool for their hemiplegic patients. They have instigated an RO type situation beside the pool where they can sit, relax and talk while not actually taking part in the water therapy.

Another ideal situation is an old-fashioned living room. The comfortable armchairs, old sideboard, table and dining chairs together with a real or simulated focal point fireplace provide a useful scene to stimulate social response. A family sitting room demanded social response to visitors, required politeness and involvement in conversation and the playing of 'host and hostess'. It necessitated the need to entertain and produce tea and some form of refreshment. Old well-learned reactions are allies to RO therapy and in a living room such learned social behaviours are much more likely. A small female unit in Leeds used such a room imaginatively. Apart from employing it for formal sessions each patient had the opportunity of occupying it at least once a week. This resulted in a greater awareness of the day of the week as each lady awaited her turn with eagerness. Once in occupation – usually in threes – each patient took over her chair produced her crockery and utensils and adapted the room to suit her purpose and needs. Independence interest and interpersonal relationships developed.

All is not lost, however, if a special room simply is not available. RO sessions can be carried out in a quiet corner of the day-room or in the dining room; the use of screens can partially remove any excessive distractions. If a special room is used the distance from the ward day-room is important as a great deal of time and effort can be expended simply getting the patient to the room if the distance is too great.

A further aid to a social atmosphere that should be considered is the avoidance of staff wearing uniforms in RO sessions. Uniforms, so often a sign of authority, can be changed or disguised suitably before a session. However, more deteriorated patients may find uniforms useful aids initially to the identity of staff-members; any change into everyday clothes should not change the staff member's appearance so much that she cannot be recognised as the same person by the patients! Also removal of uniform does not necessarily remove authoritarian attitudes; attitudes for RO sessions are identical with those for 24 hour RO (Table 6.2).

LEVELS OF RO SESSIONS

RO sessions are flexible and should always be geared to the needs of the group members, rather than adhering strictly to a rigid formula. It is useful if patients in groups are at a roughly similar level of functioning with one another so that some do not feel left behind, and others do not become bored. Three levels of groups may usefully be identified, with different emphases and slightly different methods but identical principles. There is always an overlap between them which allows flexibility in finding the right approach for individual needs.

The Basic Group consists of those whose confusional or deteriorated intellectual state is severe. They are those who take hardly any interest in events, in their surroundings or in themselves. They are severely disoriented and unresponsive; attention and concentration are very limited.

The Standard Group consists of those who are more responsive and who can take a little interest in people and things. They are not as disoriented and confused.

The Advanced Group consists of those who are much more alert. This is a maintenance level for those who need to be kept stimulated, independent and involved. This group is for short-stay hospital patients, those about to be discharged, and for those who simply need a boost to encourage them to keep their interests and independence. It may be appropriate for elderly physically handicapped people, for many elderly chronic psychiatric patients, in clubs for stroke victims, and can be employed for some residents in old people's homes and attenders at clubs and at day-centres.

Helping the elderly person achieve success – and thereby greater self-esteem and confidence – is the aim of the social atmosphere and of the methods used at all three levels. RO also brings the person into contact with reality, by helping him be aware of what is happening around him, and by re-awakening interest and involvement in the environment. The groups differ in the scope of awareness that is covered but all attempt to do this; all recognise that current reality makes sense only in relation to the past, so all use the person's store of past memories to some degree. Finally each level combats withdrawal – a process by which dementing elderly persons may appear much more impaired than in fact they are. At each level communication is encouraged, with the leaders and with other group members. Conditions are created where this can take place. These aims are summarised in Table 7.1.

Table 7.1

All three levels aim to help the elderly person to:

1. Succeed
2. Know what is happening
3. Communicate

Basic group

This group should meet daily, for half an hour. In view of the severity of the problems there should be a maximum of two or three patients per therapist, so all can be kept occupied and their attention retained. During the first few days the therapist must break through resistance and withdrawal with gentleness and courtesy, whilst encouraging trust and response. A situation in which failure might occur must be avoided carefully, so the aims are simple. A routine is established during which basic information such as names, days, months and the weather are discussed. At this stage repetition is an essential aid to the relearning process. Repetition is more useful and interesting if a variety of methods are used. The session is commenced by a handshake and a personal greeting. 'Hello, my name is . . . .'. After the initial introductions it is appropriate to return to each individual with a further extended comment on names.

'Have I written your name properly? How would you like to be addressed – Mrs Jones, or would you prefer Mary?' 'Can you say my name?' If the therapist's name has been forgotten write it down and ask for it to be read. Simply writing the name, showing it and saying 'Look, this is how you spell my name' usually suffices. Large clear name badges can be useful in a small group, so that there is a visual reminder of group-members' names. If errors in reading occur further repetition is required. Names can be useful means of reaching out to the group. Discussing other people with similar names reinforces the learning process and provides added interest.

The therapists in groups at this Basic level are extremely active in presenting information, directing the subject matter of the group and in sustaining the patients' attention. A board of some description is essential for the visual presentation of information. This can be fixed or portable, depending on the setting. If it is fixed it should be clearly in the view of group members; writing on it should be large enough to be seen by all. Boards are available with magnetic letters, or words on cards that slide into slots on the board or may be a simple blackboard, with information written up in chalk. One commercially available board is a 'Weather Board', which is approximately three feet by eighteen inches, and has information regarding day, date, month, year and weather on cards that are slotted in appropriately.

As part of the routine this board can be completed during the session. The participants are asked what day it is, usually individually. If the response is wrong the reply should be sufficiently gentle so there is no loss of face. 'Well, it is almost the weekend. It is Friday today', or 'Yesterday was Tuesday, so today it is Wednesday'. If the answer is correct praise is given. Reading the correct day from the board reinforces this process. Prompts and cues are useful here; if a blackboard is available the day can be written letter by letter until someone guesses the answer. If no one guesses the group can read the complete name, so whatever happens the correct response will be achieved. The clue of the first few letters could be given verbally of course. If the board is completed before the session then members can be encouraged to take their cue directly from the board, and so again be spared the risk of a wrong answer. A similar pattern is followed for the remaining information – month, year date, whereabouts of the hospital or old peoples' home and weather are the basics. In considering the month, help can be obtained from the view through the window. The introduction of seasonal flowers and fruit or calendar-like pictures can also be of assistance. The members are encouraged to look outside, to notice the sky and the state of growth of trees and plants. The look and smell of a spring or summer bouquet of flowers or a collection of fallen autumn leaves emphasises the season.

If answers to questions are vague, slow, unforthcoming or consistently incorrect the right answer is supplied gently and conversationally. Direct criticism or contradiction should be avoided as confidence could be destroyed. 'I just told you that or 'No, that's wrong' are destructive remarks.

Once these areas of information have been covered the whole board is re-read by group members, with the therapist prompting those with reading or speech problems. Diaries are commonly used in RO for those without reading or writing difficulties. Some people enjoy keeping a diary and complete it in detail; generally only simple routine facts are recorded. This adds variety to the repetition, and members can read out their diary entries to the others. Large letter-cards can be used by patients who have lost the fine motor control required for writing; they can be given the letters needed to spell their name or a short word and asked to put them in the right order.

A further aspect of information to be given is time. Initially this may be in terms of morning, afternoon and evening, but where appropriate a large clock with adjustable hands can be used to show current time, time of meals and so on.

This level of group is quite demanding on the therapists, as they have to maintain the group members' attention throughout, because their concentration span is usually exceedingly short. Preferably there should be two therapists to support each other.

The group is made up of adults not children. To patronise, or talk down to the elderly is to guarantee that they will remain withdrawn or become agitated or resentful. Friendliness and courtesy create the right atmosphere for response. The session should always start and end with handshakes, hellos and farewells. Interruptions and 'observers' who do not participate are not helpful. In order to establish rapport with this level of group the subject matter may seem childish. As long as the therapist is gentle and unthreatening this initial period is necessary in order to establish a relationship of trust and expectation. Once the confusion begins to lift it is imperative that the simple aim be changed and the group member moved on to the next stage. Table 7.2 summarises the features of this level.

Table 7.2 *Features of the Basic group* (for most severely disorientated and withdrawn patients)

2–3 patients per therapist. Daily. 30 minutes. Social setting.

Emphasis on basic information – presented and repeated. Repetition varied – reading from board, writing in diary etc. Many clues provided to guarantee successful response. Use of RO, or Weather Board. Also calendar, large letter cards (for those unable to write) and a teaching clock etc., also useful. Therapists extremely active in sustaining attention, directing group, presenting information. Patients moved into Standard group as soon as possible.

Standard group

This is the most flexible level of RO, and according to group members' needs can resemble the Basic group at one extreme or the Advanced group at the other. Rigidity in the programme will be demonstrated by complaints from individuals about being treated as though they were in school, or a refusal to attend because of boredom. It is better, though not always possible, to avoid such a situation by being prepared for improvement. The therapy must be adapted to the group not vice versa. As soon as there is some evidence of improved response – by assessment, observation or even as a result of some signs of restlessness — the aim, scope and methods are broadened.

Introductions, names and warm greetings remain the natural starting point for the session. Again the RO Board is used to present basic information, but this is achieved more quickly in this group. The information too may be in more depth and detail. Diaries are likely to be particularly useful here.

Following the basic information part of the session, a wide variety of activities is possible. They aim to make a contribution to one or more of the following:

The fostering of interpersonal relationships, social awareness and interest

The connection and comparison of past and present, capitalising on the person's previous experiences to build up interest in the environment

The stimulation of one or more of the person's senses. The type of activities and equipment needed are described in Chapter 8.

Sessions are slightly less directed, and therapists will use the responses of group-members to develop a theme or to change tack entirely! Thus pictures of food may have been intended to start a discussion on shopping, prices etc., but may elicit more response on cooking and favourite foods. There is scope here to pursue topics flexibly, as long as the discussion remains reality oriented, with past and present being distinguished, as well as fact from fantasy!

It is important to have knowledge of individual histories, experiences and interests. More personal orientation is encouraged at this level. Age, date of birth, names and whereabouts of family members, previous occupations and interests, places where the person has lived are among the items that might be covered over a number of sessions. Staff need to know this information themselves so they can reinforce the person appropriately. A separate index card with these details on it for each group member is of great value for this purpose.

Although the therapists are slightly less directive, their role is still demanding. Before sessions they need to plan topics and collect relevant materials. They need to guide discussion, encourage social interaction, gently praise appropriate responses, watch for patients who are bored through the level being either too basic or too advanced, and modify the methods used accordingly. Group sessions can last for up to an hour, where staff time permits.

In encouraging social relationships, common backgrounds, occupations, interests and experiences are important. Topics that are likely to establish such links include old and new pictures and maps of the area where patients used to live, common occupations and industries of the area; everyday items from the past.

For each topic a tangible focus is essential; a picture, an object, a newspaper, slides, a short film, materials, and even a collection of smells. Everyday objects such as fruit or even a cup and saucer, can lead to consideration of colour, shape, taste, smell, texture, preferences (in the case of fruit) or material (bone china or plastic!), design, texture, function, and memories of tea parties (in the case of a cup and saucer). The latter discussion would end of course with a cup of tea for the group!

The group does not have to be static in the RO room. If mobility and weather permits, why not make a collection of autumn leaves. If the topic is the hospital or home why not have a tour, with members pointing out 'landmarks' – the lounge, dining room, their own sleeping area etc.

At this level, as at the others, where gaps occur in members' memories cues and prompts are given, so that the person does not fail. Rambling talk is dealt with as in 24 hour RO.

Humour is important; a group where laughter is frequent is likely to be much more useful and effective than an over-serious group. For example, one 93 year old man caused a stir by describing how he had made his wife *walk* several hundred miles to meet his family. Female group members castigated him for his irresponsible behaviour, and he with a broad grin responded by adding more outrageous detail, to the delight of all concerned.

In another group a series of everyday objects was being named; one was a woollen tea-pot cover which one group-member then put on as a hat and proceeded to dance a jig around the room, whilst everyone collapsed with laughter.

Reality is not of course constant happiness; the whole range of emotions may arise in the group. Topics should not be banned in order to 'protect' the elderly people. A moving group session was stimulated by a poppy, reminding participants of the 1914–1918 war and the awful loss of young men there.

Rather than banning religion and politics the topics can be usefully employed to arouse active response and healthy emotion.

Sex, love and marriage should not be taboo either. Relationships between the sexes can do a great deal to combat withdrawal, and the group should be mixed for this reason. Their attitude towards sex is often humourous and teasing and they can turn the tables to tease the therapist when so inclined. Some useful and most amusing sessions can develop as a result of open discussion on their attitudes to sex and members of the opposite sex.

Death too is something that is too frequently a taboo subject. If one of the group should fall sick, or there should be a death on the ward or in the Home there is no reason to fear open discussion. Those in contact with the elderly often underestimate their ability to cope with natural emotion and can become overprotective.

Table 7.3 lists the main features of this group and Chapter 8 should be referred to for detailed ideas for sessions.

Table 7.3 *Features of the Standard group* (for majority of moderately disorientated patients)

2–3 patients per therapist. Daily 30–60 minutes. Social setting.

Begin with basic information. Follow with wide variety of activities, topics for discussion etc. Stimulate all senses. Encourage social awareness and interest. Past is bridge to present. Prompts, clues used as necessary. Weather Board used initially. Then a variety of sensorial aids. Reminders of the past. Money, pictures, everyday objects, food, newspapers, fresh fruit etc. Therapist needs to plan, collect relevant materials, watch for boredom, guide discussion. Patients move on to Advanced level if possible, but may remain in the group for some time.

Advanced group

If an elderly person – or a whole group – makes a great deal of progress with the Standard RO group, then he/she can be moved on to this third and final level. Realistically, this 'graduation' will not occur for most patients, in view of the progressive nature of their disorders, but some patients are able to advance in this way.

The Advanced group is usually a maintenance level used for less deteriorated short-stay patients, people who have recovered from an illness and need stimulation in order to be sufficiently motivated to return home, and those who have physical problems that make total independence impossible. Those in the community who are beginning to show signs of impairment or confusion will also benefit. 'Stroke' clubs and day-centres may find these methods relevant for some of their members. The aims at this level are those of independence and self-determination. The number of participants can be increased up to 10. The therapist acts as an adviser and guide, encouraging activities and achievements and monitoring progress. A watch is kept for signs of regression or deterioration so that early preventive steps can be taken. Self-help and self-care are included in the aims. Leadership can be from the members themselves. They decide what activities are needed, and direct the sessions themselves. Relatives and friends should be included where appropriate, to help them use this approach at home.

Meetings can be less frequent – perhaps once, twice or three times a week depending on practicability. Basic information is still mentioned and an information board is present, but the scope is directed towards awareness of the wider world. Introductions, names, social relationships, past and present comparisons and sensory stimulation continue to be emphasised.

Outings and visits start during the Standard group but should be extended and become more ambitious. The therapist can make suggestions and advise, but final decisions come from the group. General needs are the responsibility of the therapist, who also watches for the more submissive and retiring people so that their needs are not overlooked. Responsibilities can be shared. Group living plans could be introduced where appropriate in residential settings. Active participation in hobbies and pastimes including gardening, painting, handicrafts etc. are to be encouraged. Places of interest can be visited, parties, picnics and competitions organised. Events for sessions require planning: a committee of the elderly themselves would be ideal. Film shows and the use of audio-visual equipment have a place here. Extensive use of reminiscences about the past and comparisons with the present would also be appropriate.

Major features of the Advanced group are summarised briefly in Table 7.4.

Table 7.4 *Features of the Advanced group* (for mildly disorientated people – useful in community settings)

Larger groups feasible
Less frequent
Social setting

Group self-determination of activities where possible. Mention of basic information but extended towards awareness of the world and community. RO Board present. Other material dependent on group needs and choice. Cooking, shopping outings, music, active involvement. Therapist acts as guide, encourages, assists and advises. Patients in group for some time. Maintenance procedure.

FINAL POINTS

The atmosphere for RO sessions must be relaxed and non-threatening. Therapists must approach the situation with an awareness of the individual and of the dangers of rigidity. Withdrawal can result from boredom, too fast a pace, or by setting aims too high; these factors are under the influence of the therapists. Too many questions can prove very threatening and unnatural in a social situation. Conversations are not one-sided or composed of questions and answers. Retraining needs to be subtle and hidden in conversation. An interrogation where questions are asked as quickly as the patient fails to answer them is not RO! Failure must be avoided as it could prove disastrous to the patient's progress.

If the aims are low initially success becomes more probable. As each step forward is achieved praise is given and another simple aim set. Praise can be freely given even for minor successes. Many elderly people with dementia have received very little praise, because of their difficult behaviour. Aggressive, domineering people need to be encouraged to help the less forceful so that they do not receive more than their fair share of attention. Praise can prove too fulsome for the more independent and may sound patronising. In this situation reinforcement can be satisfactorily achieved by a gentle, matter-of-fact comment of approval. Generally the enjoyment of social interactions and achievement is reinforcing in itself.

Therapists need feedback as well as patients. The coordinator can ensure that results and progress are made available to the staff. The expectations of staff must be realistic. Changes may be very slow or only minimal in certain cases. RO is hard work and demanding. Initially the elderly patient may be too confused or unable to respond without considerable effort on the part of the therapist. It requires good planning, realistic aims, energy and imagination to obtain worthwhile reactions and progress.

SUMMARY

1. Create atmosphere. A special room modified for use as a pub, living room or clubhouse is ideal. A social setting helps remotivation and resocialisation.

2. Routine consists of the basic information concerning day, month, year, place and weather in Basic and Standard groups. Different ways of repeating them need planning.

3. Confused elderly people have a short attention and memory span. Constant stimulation is required to maintain interest and cooperation.

4. Constant repetition is necessary; this must be varied.

5. Praise and approval can reinforce re-learning

6. Informal RO is necessary to reinforce the achievements of the structured session.

7. The patient may be confused and withdrawn, but he is not a child. His knowledge and experience are buried and need restoring.

8. Friendliness, courtesy and knowledge about the individual are vital aids in re-establishing confidence.

9. Therapists and clients should know and use each other's names — the formal title or the intimate first-name basis must be decided among them.

10. Signs of authority do not help relationships. Uniforms can be changed or disguised.

11. Rigidity is retarding. A relearning programme once assimilated indicates the need to progress.

12. As soon as possible, individuals should be involved in group activities as social interaction is important to rehabilitation processes. Interpersonal relationships can be encouraged even in the early stages of therapy.

13. Sensorial stimulation should be used — interesting smells tastes and the feel of things are as valuable as visual material.

14. Clients must be placed in appropriate groups so that suitable levels can be provided and realistic aims set.

15. The therapist needs to be friendly involved and capable of using imagination and initiative.

16. Relatives can be included but need guidance and monitoring as family attitudes can cause reversal.

17. Basic to the therapy is the capitalisation on the client's long-term memory stores. Their prime of life — roughly 1920–50 — is the period they remember the best. They are secure in discussing this era. This makes it possible to direct their attention to the present and bring them up to date by comparisons between then and now.

18. Patients can be helped to succeed by the use of clues and prompts, and by avoidance of exposure of disabilities.

8

101 ideas for formal RO sessions

Frequently it becomes difficult to think of a topic or to plan a day-to-day programme for RO sessions. As a result the session deteriorates into a time when the staff and patients/residents just sit about and talk vaguely and without purpose. This can also arise when the therapists are tired or have been too busy to have time to prepare topics. The following suggestions are intended to help in such situations. They are not exhaustive, but illustrate the range of possibilities. Leaders should select and adapt topics and ideas carefully to be appropriate for the abilities and interests of the par- ticular group. From the ideas here, and others that can be added, a set of 20 or 30 different programmes for RO sessions, suitable for a particular setting, clientele and group level, can be constructed. A card is then chosen at random and can be used to give structure for the session; also any equipment needed can be assembled just prior to the session. Example cards are shown in Table 8.1; these were used with a Standard group in an old people's home with residents having senile dementia. Use of such a system ensures variety in the sessions and helps when therapist's creativity runs dry. They should be quickly ignored when a group leader has a new or better idea or if something emerges from the group. They are to fall back on rather than to be used rigidly.

A cupboard for accumulated items of interest is essential, pref- erably in the RO room. An alternative approach to planning a

Table 8.1 *Examples of possible Programme cards*

A	B
1. Introductions – greet each other by name.	1. Introductions – greet each other by name.
2. Enter day, date, name of home on RO board; change calendar; copy into personal diaries.	2. Enter day, date, name of home on RO board; change calendar; copy into personal diaries.
3. Use spelling boards to rearrange mixed-up words. Start with shorter words and use longer words only when residents gain confidence.	3. Enter age and date of birth and place of birth in diary. Discuss who is oldest, youngest etc.
4. Bring in common objects: cup, saucer, plate, spoon, comb, hat, pencil, key, umbrella etc. Name the object and its colour; what shape is it? What does it feel like? Cold, warm, rough, smooth, hard, soft? Draw round the object.	4. Discuss weather using weather board. It is as expected for time of year? Is it changeable? What weather is forecast? What clothes would be needed outside today? Find appropriate weather picture.
5. Prepare a menu of residents' favourite foods. Compare with actual menu!	5. Play picture dominoes; small prize for winner.
Equipment: Diaries Spelling boards and letters Common objects Pencils and paper	Equipment: Diaries and pens Weatherboard and pictures Picture dominoes Small prize

topic is to start with a piece of equipment. A small box of cards in two sizes can be used as an index. Each piece of available equipment can be given a separate large card, e.g. MAPS, HERBS AND SPICES, CLOTH, etc. Under each of these headings an appropriate letter or letters will indicate which of the smaller cards to consult. Placed in alphabetical order the small cards supply suggested topics that may be relevant to the use of the equipment. For instance under T suggestions for topics could include Travel, Taste, Touch, Transport, Tailoring etc. So in order to find suggestions for the use of a bag of cloth the therapist would look up the card headed CLOTH and find, for instance, the letters TCOH. On consulting the smaller card 'C' appropriate topics would be Clothing, Cost, Colour; under T, Tailoring, Touch; under O, Occupations; and under H, Household jobs, Homecrafts, and so forth. Each provides a useful starting point for discussion and stimulation. The topics included depend entirely on the experience and imagination of the therapist which can by this means be used collectively. Cues are needed by staff as well as by the group members!

Ideas for sessions are best described by breaking them up into those suitable for each group level. The following ideas are not intended to inspire rigidity, they are simply suggestions. A group may have interests which require other avenues not included. There are differences in every group, and in people from every area and cultural background. After only a few meetings these differences are noticeable and should be recognised.

BASIC GROUP

1. Introductions – always a good (and necessary) starting point. Shake hands – use large name labels.

2. Large Weather Board, comprising main board and a collection of smaller slot-in pieces on which are written the Days, Months, comments and pictures about the Weather. Can be made or obtained from Educational Equipment suppliers. Used to present relevant information and stimulate some discussion.

3. Personal diaries – those who retain writing skills can copy basic information into their diaries, providing further repetition. Also scope for personal entries about past, current and future events. Gives person ongoing record to refer to.

4. Large letters: on wooden squares, or on cards (as in 'Lexicon'), or plastic letters with magnets attached for use with metal spelling boards. All can be used to spell out simple items of basic information, particularly where group members have difficulty writing. For instance, they could be used to spell out the day of the week, letter by letter, until someone guesses the correct answer.

5. Flowers – fresh and seasonal, to emphasise the time of year and stimulate sight, touch and smell. Also fallen leaves in autumn.

6. Fruit – again fresh to emphasise seasons and stimulate senses – including taste!

7. Food – other items of food can be brought in where appropriate – cakes, sweets. Raw ingredients – flour, salt, raisins etc., vegetables, sandwiches etc., to stimulate senses and discussion, once they have been identified.

8. Drink – provide various beverages – tea, coffee, fruit drinks, sherry, wine, beer etc. for taste, identification, smell and enjoyment!

9. Maps – plastic or wood shapes of Great Britain, America, Australia and Europe etc. Large, clear map of local city or town.

Maps help in orientation, discussion of 'where we are' and 'where we come from'. Several members may be from the same area, so the maps help to identify possible neighbours or common knowledge. In later stages, 'where we have been' is another topic arising from maps.

10. Large Clock Face with movable hands (as realistic as possible). The clock can be used to indicate present time, breakfast, dinner, and bed time.

11. Chalkboard and chalk – has many uses in repeating and reinforcing whatever is discussed. More able patients should be encouraged to write on the board for others.

12. Collages – these can be made in the group; members search through magazines looking for pictures that illustrate the particular theme, cut these out and stick them on a large piece of paper.

13. Collages of seasons – to aid discussion of time of year.

14. Collages of food – can emphasise time, by depicting different meals for different times of day. Also discussion about preferences, ingredients, prices etc.

15. Collages of children – to emphasise sense of life-span, memories of their own childhood and their own children, grandchildren etc.

16. Collages of places – local pictures or further afield, can be used in conjunction with maps. Reminders of the group's previous 'haunts' – the main street, shops, local landmarks and so on – assist in recreating a temporarily forgotten daily existence.

17. Picture cards illustrating occupations e.g. – postman, window cleaner, miner etc. Occupation cards can be useful in reminding people about everyday jobs which provide day-to-day contact in the environment. The postman, the butcher and the bus conductor are part of everyday reality.

STANDARD GROUP

By using visual and other stimulation and by encouraging reminiscences through related materials elderly people can be persuaded to respond well. Learning more about them as individuals with specific interests can assist in the search for suitable equipment and relevant approaches, all of which can be exploited in building up good relationships.

18. 'Then' and 'Now': Most towns have produced a book full of photographs of places and familiar landmarks of Then and Now. These are invaluable for discussion, showing how the town has changed since group members were children. If such a book is not available then libraries etc. often have collections of old photographs, copies or slides of which could be obtained, together with up to date comparisons. If there is an area where most of the group live, it is possible that they also had schools in common. They have memories of the buildings, streets and activities of the district, and may well have mutual friends and acquaintances. They may have shopped in the same shopping centre, been married in the same church etc. Finding such things in common can greatly help a group interact.

19. Old newspapers, national and local, again provide a stimulus to reminiscence that can aid grasp of current reality as it is brought up-to-date into the present. Libraries often have collections of old newspapers.

20. Gardening – pictures and books may elicit memories and knowledge of plants, flowers, vegetable etc. Advanced groups could try indoor gardening – bulbs, plants, cress and so on – as a continuing activity.

21. Cookery – pictures and recipe books are useful (as well as real food). Discuss favourite recipes, particularly for traditional foods. More advanced groups could carry out simple cookery – all can help mix ingredients for cakes and sweets as a group exercise, and enjoy the smell of cooking, as well as sampling the finished product!

22. Clothes – books and pictures of fashions over the years, may prompt fascinating reminiscences; current fashions always produce interesting comments! If costumes from the patient's young days can be obtained these can be 'modelled'.

23. Occupations – in any given region or area there are many employed in particular local industries or occupations and knowledge of these is a valuable too. Any relevant material from such industries inspires discussion and reminiscences. It also provides therapists with opportunities to introduce present-day comparisons. Pictures of coalmines and miners in the 1920s and 1930s can bind a group together, in a mining area, for instance. Many members of groups may have spent some time in domestic service. Local or national firms may prove helpful. Films can be hired, there may be a library or museum on the subject, and most homes

have objects or materials which would prove invaluable — old typewriters, miner's lamps, models of ships, old tools, looms etc. Things lying around the home for years unnoticed suddenly assume importance as they could provoke memories and experiences. It is equally important to have a supply of modern material to show how things have changed.

24. Royalty – in the UK books and pictures of the Royal Family past and present often stimulate interest; tracing the Royal family tree through the use of pictures gives the elderly person a sense of their own ageing and development.

25. Cars – group members will have lived through massive changes in the motor car (and other forms of transportation). Old and new pictures and models are useful here. Members may recall their first car, or their first journey.

26. Homecrafts – members may have had previously interests in sewing, embroidery, knitting, crochet and so on. Discussion of these crafts, together with finished articles and pictures, may produce a number of memories, and may encourage members to attempt some tasks themselves.

27. Travel – a number of topics arise from this theme; members can describe their furthest travels, the method of travel, speed of journeys and so on. Pictures of places near and far will aid such a discussion.

28. Animals – pictures would be the stimulus here; have you ever seen a lion? ever ridden a horse? milked a cow? The questions draw on well-learned knowledge, and may evoke memories e.g. one old seaman vividly described his experiences with whales.

29. Pets – the real thing can be provided here, as well as pictures. It can start a discussion of pets people have had and the sometimes harsh reality of not having them in the Hospital or Home. Different breeds of dogs and cats may also be a discussion topic, using relevant photographs.

30. Birds – this topic could be developed as above, with pet birds and wild birds being observed 'live' or in photographs. A bird table just outside the ward or home would facilitate this, and provide a daily routine of feeding the birds.

31. Art – interest in paintings, drawings and sculpture could be explored with the help of large colourful reproductions. Some popular paintings will be identified; others can be appreciated or

in some cases can be the cause of group bewilderment! According to ability, a group art session of painting, drawing, modelling in clay, simple printing, sticking on of coloured shapes or whatever can be a good activity.

32. Stamps – even if members have not been avid collectors, interest can be aroused by colourful stamps from around the world (use with a map) or using a range of stamps from the person's life-time, the historical changes (and changes in price of sending a letter) can be a cause for comment.

33. Coins – different value coins (and notes) can be identified, and used to carry out simple arithmetic. The dates and heads on the coins are also worthy of discussion. Coins and notes from around the world could also be used; in the UK pre-decimal coins could evoke memories and comparisons.

34. Holidays – a rich source of discussion – prompted by picture postcards, brochures etc. What sort of holiday – seaside, country; hotel, camping, boarding house; home or abroad. Where did members go on holiday? What did they do whilst on holiday? Where would they like to have gone?

35. Famous houses, castles, palaces and so on – particularly if local. Pictures will help recall visits to such places.

36. Countryside – pictures of local country areas may remind members of country walks, the rural life, the country year and so on.

37. Mountains – pictures of grand mountain scenery provide another topic, with mountain sports and dangers being possibilities for discussion.

38. Racing – pictures of famous horses and jockeys of the past, together with comparisons with the present scene will interest former racing followers.

39. Small antiques – pieces of furniture or bric-a-brac brought into the group can promote discussion of the purpose of the items and whether group members had anything similar; what would be used now?

40. Old toys – again a comparison can be made e.g. between lead and plastic soldiers, clockwork and electric trains, china dolls and dolls whose hair grow! Computer games defy comparison!

41. Traditional cards – greetings cards and postcards were collected by many families, and make a fascinating contrast in materials and design with their modern counterparts.

42. Souvenirs – the small ornaments people brought back from holiday – often china miniatures – will again evoke memories of the time and places.

43. Jewelry – compare old and new pieces; many group members will have some jewelry – a ring or brooch; does it have special significance. Naming precious stones, trying on necklaces, bracelets and so on.

44. Old kitchen equipment – bring in the oldest kitchen utensils that can be found or borrowed – discuss all the gadgets and labour-saving devices of today – compare pictures of automatic washing machines with the 'dolly-tub' and so on.

45. War memories – pictures of life during the world wars; memories of air raids, women at work, fire-watching, friends who were lost in action, and so on. The Flanders poppy is an evocative visual aid around Remembrance Day.

46. Medals – what were they awarded for? Action in World War 1, and in the Second World War; where were they stationed? What did they do? What was it really like? Some will have pictures of themselves in uniform to show the group.

47. Ration books – and other reminders of the effects of war on life at home; how did members stretch the rations allowed – special recipes or menus? Comparison with present-day standards of food and clothing.

48. Mementoes of war-time leaders – pictures, other mementoes of Churchill; the 'V' sign; a brief tape of his voice.

49. The depression – pictures of life in the 1930s; mass unemployment, huge marches and so on; how were group members affected? Comparison with present-day levels of poverty and state benefits.

50. Emigration – did members consider emigrating, or have they actually emigrated? Any family abroad? Pictures and maps are useful here.

51. Prices – pictures of food and other items; discuss current prices, prices in previous years; also rise in wages. Make up a typical shopping basket for £1, £5 then and now.

52. Religion – what beliefs do members have? Did they go to church because they had to or because they wanted to? Do they attend church now? What other beliefs are there?

53. Marriage – were they (or are they) married? Where did they get married? What sort of wedding? (photograph albums here are a great help). What do they think of marriage now? What do they

think of people living together – without being married? . . . .

54. Education – where did they go to school? What age were they when they left? What was it like? What did they learn? Were there opportunities for further education? Were they trained for a particular job as an apprenticeship etc? Did they go to college? Would they have liked to?

55. Local festivities – many towns have long-established traditions of annual fairs, festivals and celebrations. Pictorial comparisons of past and present will jog memories in the group about them.

56. Families – using family photograph albums, each group member's family history can be pieced together pictorially: pictures of the person when young can be compared with ones taken as they are now; the development of their own children into adults and (possibly elderly people themselves) can be seen.

57. The role of women – a brief illustrated article on 'women's lib' can stimulate a useful discussion about changing roles – particularly in a mixed group.

58. Sports – old newspapers, magazines and illustrated books provide the material for a discussion of sporting interests; sporting heroes of the past – and what has become of them; teams supported by group members, changes in sports clothing, athletic ability, styles of play.

59. Local public transport – use old pictures of trams, horse and motor drawn, trolley-buses, early buses and charabancs, together with modern counterparts. Fare prices might also be discussed.

60. Film-stars, singers and other celebrities – a scrap-book might be made of favourites from the group members' younger days, with pictures showing the stars in their prime, and also as they aged. Reminders of particular films, songs and catch-phrases would be relevant here.

61. Old-fashioned shop goods – old tin boxes (which preceded packets) might be unearthed; old adverts from newspapers and magazines; 'then' and 'now' comparison.

62. Special events on TV – it is not always necessary to oversee viewing particularly when the observers are deeply involved, but frequently the proceedings are meaningless to confused elderly unless someone directs their attention to certain aspects of the proceedings. If a video machine is available, this could be used to repeat such events.

63. Music – unlike other sounds used in isolation, music is

extremely useful in RO. Music for enjoyment's sake is more part of 24 hour RO, where it should be remembered that tastes differ widely. One use of music in RO sessions is to play a tape made up of brief extracts of singers well known in the group members' younger days; these can be combined with pictures of the singers as in 60 above.

64. Music to reinforce RO – a second use is in aiding the repetition of basic information; appropriate songs and rhymes are sung to back up the current information; e.g. 'April Showers', 'White Christmas', 'Easter Bonnet', 'Here we go gathering nuts in May' etc.

65. Music-making – a third use is as a coordinated group activity; simple rhythm instruments can be made in the group – shakers, blocks of wood to hit together, kazoos and so on.

66. Movement to music – simple, gentle group physical exercises are carried out to music; this can be done with group members seated.

67. Touch – Hot and Cold. The weather or the temperature can be stressed by a pair of cold hands just in from the snow or frost. The temperature of the room can be shown by the warm hands of the residents. Use a thermometer to show the temperature. Food and drink is hot or cold; bring in some ice! Parts of the world have different temperatures (use maps and pictures).

68. Touch – Soft and Hard, Rough and Smooth. Many things can be used to discuss these concepts. Skin, fabrics, animal fur, surfaces, pumice stone, rock collections, scouring pads and powders, wallpapers, clothing, sand and tissue paper. Fruit – apples, bananas, oranges etc. Food can be examined to tell, by feel, if it is fresh, ripe or rotten.

69. Touch – Dry and Wet. Spills of liquid can be used. Travel cloths, sponges, mop heads, towels, washing.

70. Cloth – provide a bag of pieces of material for the group to feel; they will reminisce about old fabrics such as chenille, flannel, tulle and cretonne. They will dismiss a piece of denim as something which is too 'rough' and be surprised by the cost of trousers made from it! Drip-dry fabrics will produce stories of difficult ironing problems. What would different types of material be used for? What colours and patterns go together?

71. Heating – old and new – pictures of old-fashioned stoves and fires; discussion of work they involved; pictures of modern heating systems – advantages and disadvantages.

72. Smell – some elderly people, particularly men, appear to

have lost their sense of smell, but generally this is a very rewarding sense to use as a tool for RO. A box of smells made up with the help of a kindly pharmacist is needed. Little bottles containing for example: attar of roses, lemon, peppermint, almonds, cinnamon, cloves, lavender, orange, menthol, cherries, Sloan's liniment. The bottled smells can be used as in a game, with clues and quick identification so as not to lose interest. The purpose is to arouse memories and excite discussion of use. For example the smell of almond essence provokes thoughts of Easter and Simnel cake, Christmas and Christmas cake.

73. Smell – herbs and spices. Discuss the smells and uses of collections of herbs and spices from the kitchen shelf, potpourri and collections of fresh herbs from the garden: Thyme, Sage, Rosemary, Mint, Lavender, Chives, Marjoram. Uses in cooking, as air-fresheners and for keeping clothes fresh.

74. Smell – fruit and flowers: Fresh Flowers: Roses, Carnations, Sweet peas, Lilac, Daffodils as available. Fresh Fruit: Tangerines, Oranges, Lemons, Apples, Bananas, Strawberries etc. Also discuss colours, likes, dislikes, of flowers and fruit.

75. Smells in the kitchen – kitchen smells, coffee, soaps, moth balls, ammonia, cooking, polishes etc. Compare carbolic and per-fumed soap. Cooking smells can be introduced in an actual ses-sion by providing half-cooked bread from the supermarket. Old herbal remedies and medicines provoke memories that are often amusing and provide easy comparisons with today.

76. Smells – perfume; compare various perfumes, lavender water, eau de cologne etc. Current toiletries – deodorants, after-shave, talc etc.

77. Taste – this is closely associated with sense of smell. A game can be made of identifying foods and drinks from their taste, with eyes closed. Tea, coffee, beer, fruit, bread, cake etc. can be used in this way.

78. Taste – sweet and sour; contrast sweet and sour food, lead-ing onto discussion of preferences etc. Lemon juice, vinegar, unsweetened cooking apples, rhubarb etc. compared with sugar, jam, syrup, treacle, sweets, cakes and so on.

79. Tastes – unpleasant and disputed; medicines, cod liver oil, taste of cigarettes, cold tea, stale food, disliked food, bitter aloes, alcohol, real v. instant coffee, tea bags v. tea leaves; all to stimu-late discussion and response on food memories, preferences, cur-rent opportunities.

80. Tastes – hot; peppers, spices, curry powder, radishes, raw onion, salad dressing, sauces, chillies and so on.

81. Menus – popular and unpopular food. Modern tastes. Wartime food – dehydrated eggs, milk etc. Potatoes for flour in cakes. Funny recipes for icing sugar and almond paste. Wartime recipe books. Foods and tastes once enjoyed, now unobtainable. Food from other countries. Prepare typical menus from different times of members' lives, including the present. Discuss choices available – or lack of them.

82. Newspapers and journals on the tables provide day-to-day current information that can be incorporated into discussions about current events. The TV pages stimulate discussions about favourite programmes and personalities; the horoscope encourages members to recall their birth-date; some groups have been seen to attempt a simple crossword.

83. Magazines – are similarly a potentially rich source of discussion starters; a short paragraph from an article or a letter can be read out (perhaps from the problem page!); pictures accompanying articles and advertisements can also be used in this way – in addition to their use in collages mentioned above.

84. Current events – local, national and world events can provide a continuing topic. An election for example could be the subject of a large poster with names and pictures of those involved, and the polling date clearly indicated. Reminiscences about previous elections, political argument and interest in the outcome could be stimulated. Posters of other continuing news stories could be made – e.g. royal tours, strikes, wars etc.

85. Current events – politicians; pictures of current leaders could be mounted on a poster or in a scrap book with their names, parties and office. A montage of former Prime Ministers or Presidents going back to the early years of this century, will allow comparisons and a historical perspective.

86. Current events – sports; major sporting events, Olympic Games, Soccer's World Cup or FA Cup Final, Cricket Test Matches, Tennis Championships and so on can be discussed in advance, the outcome predicted and watched. Major horse races could form the basis for a sweepstake, depending on the interests of the group.

87. Everyday objects – any common articles can be brought into the group, identified, and their use demonstrated; discussions of shape, colour and so on can be stimulated. Cups and saucers,

knife, fork and spoon, shoes, hat, ball, light-bulb, umbrella, sauce-
pan, key and padlock, purse and radio are among the sort of
objects that could be used in this way.

88. Anagrams – large letter cards or blocks can be used; a word
is given in mixed-up order for the group member to rearrange into
the correct order. The difficulty can be adjusted according to ability from two letters upward!

89. Word games can be played with letter cards – turning up
say the letter E and then naming a word beginning with E. If the
next card is T, thinking what word could be made from ET....

90. Number games – use a simple version of Bingo, with only
the numbers 1–20 to bring the game within the confused person's
memory span. Each person would have four numbers on a card to
cover when they are called out; dominoes can also be used – with
different colour spots for each number and large size dominoes.
Small prizes for winners are essential.

91. Picture Games – the picture equivalent of the above. In picture Bingo each person has a card with four or five easily identifi-
able pictures on it; there could be 20 or so pictures altogether,
taken one at a time from a bag – the winner being the first to
match all his pictures. Picture dominoes is another possibility,
with pictures of common objects replacing the usual numbers.
Again prizes should be given.

92. Shape puzzles – these are games where a number of plastic
or wooden shapes are fitted into corresponding holes in a board.
These can spark off discussion on shapes – squares, triangles, cir-
cles etc. – what else is a triangle? point to the two squares and so
on; and also colours, if the pieces have different colours; find
another the same colour as this; what else is green? Has anyone
any clothes the same colour as this? Use matching where naming
is difficult for group members.

93. Jig-saw puzzles – these can be a useful activity if the
number of pieces is small, the size of the pieces is large, and the
finished picture is not childish. The completed picture can then be
a topic for discussion.

94. Outings – these assist memory, remotivation and resocialisation. Relevant visits can be made to the home area, shopping
area, churches where people were married; parks; picnic and
beauty spots well remembered. Where physically possible visits to
shops and new supermarkets and shopping precincts are valuable.
Local pub outings are always welcome.

ADVANCED GROUP

Much of the material and techniques used for Standard groups would be relevant. The aims for this group are Independence, Self-esteem and Self-help. The group should be encouraged to initiate their own programmes and make their own decisions as far as possible.

95. Events – a number of special events can be arranged; a fashion show, a brief film show, a school band or choir and so on can arouse interest.

96. Demonstration – by gardeners, beauticians, cookery experts, artists, local theatre, dance groups, handicraft experts and so on may be within the attention span of this group.

97. Cooking – a complete group meal could be possible, with stronger members of the group helping and encouraging the more infirm.

98. Games – more complex card games and so on will be feasible; perhaps competitions can be organized.

99. Parties – with a special or relevant theme; Halloween, Christmas, Easter bonnet competitions etc. The right food, the right decor, suitable entertainments can all be organised between the therapist and the group.

100. Making decorations – for parties at Christmas and for members' birthdays.

101. Reminiscence Theatre – a local group putting on a show with music hall items and memories of life in previous years could be appreciated by this group.

Each group can indicate where their interests and abilities lie, and with suitable support and imagination on the part of the therapist can succeed in their aims and so increase their own self-esteem.

RECORD-KEEPING

Each day immediately at the end of the session a written record should be made of the group. A large book can be used with a page for each day.

Record: Group members present
             Group leaders and other staff present.
             Times group began and ended

Topics discussed, equipment used
A brief note about each group member's reaction
Anything discovered in the group about likes, dislikes, interests, abilities – things that should be developed, things that should be avoided!
General appraisal of the session.

See Appendix 4 for a possible programme over two months at the Standard group level.

9

Practical issues

In this chapter are discussed some of the key practical points that may arise when care staff seek to introduce RO into their work with elderly people.

Intensity

How often must RO be 'done' to be useful? Is a weekend break harmful? Can it be omitted when there is a staff shortage? Would sessions twice a day be more beneficial than sessions once a day?

At first sight it seems that these are important questions in the operation of RO which have implications for the amount of staff involvement required. In fact they reflect a total misconception of the basic principles by assuming that RO is like a pill to be taken so many times a day after meals! They ignore the importance of the basic approach, of the use of every interaction between staff member and elderly person to increase awareness and orientation. RO is in fact a continuous process for the person in a hospital ward or old people's home (the situation of community residents will be discussed later). In some settings staff-resident interactions are few and far between. Sometimes RO sessions are perceived as an alternative to a satisfactory level of interaction throughout the day. There is no substitute, however, for such consistent support. Sessions supplement 24 hour RO, and help staff and residents to get to know each other better, in a friendly, relaxed atmosphere; this then facilitates the continuous daily contact.

The following points can be made regarding intensity:

1. The amount of staff-resident contact needs to be increased as far as is possible, and encouragement given to use RO in each of these contacts. In some settings talking with the residents is seen as avoiding real work; though in many senses, if it is done properly it is perhaps more demanding than other more physical forms of work. Many of the routine physical tasks of the Home or ward can be carried out whilst talking with a resident quite easily.

2. Generally speaking the more intensive RO can be, the more the resident will benefit from it. However, the elderly person must be allowed to respond to information supplied so that it can be absorbed gradually.

3. The more confused and disorientated a person is the more intensive the RO needs to be in order to stimulate learning. This may be reflected in the slower pace of learning and the much lower level of information required. Two and a half hours a week is hardly adequate to promote change. Even in a group it is vital to provide individual attention, but the social atmosphere always proves a valuable aid. Very disturbed and restless deteriorated patients may particularly benefit from individual contacts, if their concentration is too limited for a group session.

4. There is relatively little benefit in having more than one RO group session per day, and the additional time could be utilized with briefer individual sessions. There are suggestions that not having group sessions at weekends may tend to detract from some of the gains previously made, and if at all feasible group sessions should be seven days a week rather than five.

Consistency

It is important that all staff work closely together to increase a patient's level of awareness. It is possible for inconsistencies to occur as the staff are made up of individuals. Each of them can perceive ward or home policies, and the way to implement those policies, in their own way. Furthermore if team spirit is weak, understanding of such policies is limited. For example, in a situation where most staff members are employing RO principles with a particular patient their efforts to help her to realise where she is could be destroyed by the faulty approach of a single staff member. Without appreciating the consequences this nurse could seek to reassure the patient by telling her she is in a hotel at the coast! The effects of RO would be weakened if messages received by patients were inconsistent. In effect they would reinforce confusion.

When team feeling exists and is encouraged such problems will be minimised. This relates particularly to how an RO programme is implemented (see below). The necessity for staff to feel involved in the programme must be emphasised – rather than it being presented as another chore. Other staff who might not normally be included in a staff training programme e.g. cleaners, domestics, orderlies, porters etc., have in fact often a great deal of contact and interaction with patients. It may well be important, if a consistent approach is to be maintained, that they are at least informed of what is happening and the rationale behind it. Similarly visitors to the ward, volunteers and most importantly relatives need guidance on how best to communicate with patients on the ward. A brief printed sheet may be helpful, giving details of the approach, but perhaps the best way of getting the approach across is by the care-staff being seen to put it into practice at all times themselves. In many ways RO could be a uniting force among staff, helping all to feel there is something useful that they can do, that they are important and valuable members of the care-team, whether or not they have degrees, qualifications or certificates. If these feelings, can be nurtured – and they stand in marked contrast to the feelings of helplessness and uselessness so often experienced by staff working with the confused elderly – then the all-important consistency of approach is more likely to be achieved. It should be borne in mind of course that it is consistency of approach that is needed, and not necessarily consistency of method. Thus in RO to help sessions be more enjoyable for all concerned variety is important. There is here a great deal of scope for individual personalities, flair and imagination.

Limited goals

However encouraging the results of studies of RO might be, we have attempted to emphasise that the gains have often been quite small, and often not as clear in the person's general functioning as in their mental state. RO is not a cure for dementia; severely demented people will almost certainly not be discharged in their hundreds from long-stay hospitals if RO is introduced!

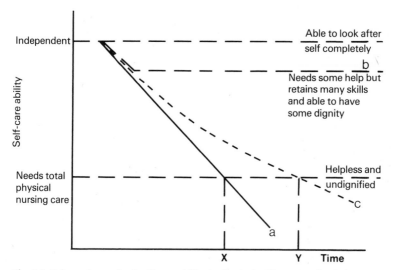

Fig. 9.1 Schematic graph of self-care ability in dementia, illustrating that halting or even slowing down deterioration can be useful aims.

   a represents 'usual' deterioration in dementia

   b represents stabilisation of self-care ability at an intermediate level

   c represents a slowing down of deterioration resulting in a higher quality of life for (c) as compared with (a) for the period of time X–Y.

    The potential of RO and other similar approaches lies in the nature of dementia. Figure 9.1 is a notional graph of self-care ability in dementia. Line (a) illustrates what generally seems to happen in dementia. Initially the person is independent but gradually needs more and more assistance as skills decline, until there is a need for almost total physical nursing care. At this point, when the person is virtually being dressed, toiletted and washed etc., it is difficult to see how any semblance of dignity can be retained, however caring and sympathetic the care-staff may be. Line (b) represents a stabilisation of self-care ability at a level where there is considerable independence; if a therapeutic approach could achieve this, then clearly this would be an acceptable aim as the stage of total nursing care is not reached. Line (c) represents a slowing down of the deterioration, with the person taking somewhat longer to reach the area of greatest indignity. Thus by comparison with line (a) we could say this person has overall a better quality of life as more skill has been retained and there has been more independence. Slowing down of deterioration can then also be an acceptable goal. In addition, total physical nursing care is costly in time and in the extra stress and burden for staff. However there is a problem here; if slowing down deterioration is the aim then the care-staff will continue to see their patients deteriorate despite their best endeavours to carry out RO, and cannot know for certain that they are achieving anything. Untreated comparison groups are probably the best way to ascertain possible changes as a result of intervention. It is not always possible to use these so it is often difficult to show that deterioration is being slowed down. Those using RO need to be aware of the variability of deterioration in individuals and of the importance of close communication with patients in order to note even the smallest of changes in their behaviour, or in our interaction with them.

Aspiration levels should not be set so high that only dramatic changes are expected. Such expectations are courting disappointment and will lead to lack of confidence in the approach. While some patients can show impressive changes the improvements of those with degenerative disorders may only be minimal. To miss small changes could prove disastrous to the programme as there would be no appreciation that a step forward had been achieved. A number of little steps can combine into a substantial one. Realistic attitudes can help to analyse the progress and so permit staff to set or reset appropriate goals by lowering or raising them as is necessary.

RO is not a therapy in the sense that it can be applied for a few months and then withdrawn with improvements being then maintained. At the present time it does seem that if RO is withdrawn the effects are likely to wear off fairly quickly. RO is perhaps better viewed as a continuing part of the person's environment. Hopefully the person will be able to progress to higher levels of RO but it is unlikely that they will cease to need support completely.

In summary then, RO needs to be a continuing process: improvement may be limited but the possibility of small changes should not be overlooked. Although more impressive changes can occur, a slowing down or stabilisation of deterioration may well be an acceptable aim for degenerative processes.

Staff attitudes

Attitudes underly and colour so much of what we do or say, so no apology will be made for dealing with this topic at greater length, in this and succeeding sections, in view of its importance in pro-

grammes like RO (see Woods & Britton 1977). If we have a negative approach to a task we will probably do it badly; if we have a
negative attitude to a person then we may say pleasant polite
words to them, but our real attitude will probably be communicated in the way they are said. Conversely positive attitudes are
more likely to lead to enthusiasm and to convey warmth.

What are our attitudes, firstly to elderly people in general, and
secondly to those with memory difficulties who are the focus of
this book? If this question were asked of the general population a
wide variety of replies would be received. These could range from
those who believe in advocating euthanasia for all elderly people
to those who would find it difficult to see elderly people as a group
and would talk about attitudes to individuals who happen, by
conventional arbitrary criteria, to be labelled 'elderly'. How do our
attitudes to elderly people develop? One powerful learning experience may have been the way in which elderly people in our own
family were treated when we were young. Were they revered and
respected, or were they despised? Were they frail – or were they
strong and powerful? These types of considerations may lead to
our first ideas about elderly people. The attitude of society itself is
another strong influence, as are the attitudes of those sub-groups of
society to which we belong. Society often seems to emphasise
youthful qualities like speed and productivity, and to devalue the
mature contributions of experience, perspective and emotional
stability. A third major influence may well be our fantasies of what
being elderly would be like, our projection of our own old age,
which must have associated with it some of our feelings about
death and dying. Given the various influences and learning
experiences that each of us have undergone it is hardly surprising
that in any group of care-staff there will be a multiplicity of
attitudes. There are even a number of different reasons for being
involved in work with the elderly at all, from genuine interest to
purely economic ones.

It is important for all staff members to think about their own
attitudes and to consider what experiences have led them to their
current position; it is useful for staff to discuss their attitudes
together, noting both agreements and differences. Attitudes cannot
be changed overnight; what is necessary is a willingness to try
alternative strategies of working with elderly people, and not to
reject them out of hand. When elderly people previously considered to be confused and totally dependent actually respond in an

RO session, then attitudes begin to be modified. When the face of the elderly lady – who had previously seemed rather ugly and unapproachable – lights up as an item from the past acts as an entry into communication with her and as we begin to see the person behind the 'geriatric patient' stereotype, once again we begin to change our ideas.

Not all staff are so willing to try new ideas, of course, and it is important that change proceeds at a rate that does not leave some staff feeling railroaded and coerced by others. It is important that staff at all levels really do communicate with each other, about their aims in their work and what they see as the means of achieving them. This may happen informally but is perhaps more likely to occur if there are regular, frequent meetings of the staff-group.

Again the importance of all staff being involved must be emphasised. This is not only for reasons of consistency, but also because if a small group of staff is chosen to lead RO sessions tensions may result. The staff omitted may see RO as a higher level activity than the general chores and feel resentful. At the other extreme RO may be seen as an officially recognised way of avoiding the 'real' (physical) work that needs to be done, so those leading the sessions will be regarded as idle when they laugh and chat with the elderly people! To allocate the work of therapist to certain staff members may seem satisfactory in delegation of responsibility, but in practice it is not to be recommended. The result can isolate the staff, be the cause of jealousy and feelings of strain, and furthermore will make consistency of approach from all staff impossible to obtain. The programme would be jeopardised by sick and holiday leave, not to mention staff changes. In 1980 at Leeds seven people representing different disciplines acted as therapists in a two month study. Video tapes of the sessions suggested that it was not necessary to involve the same staff. The group related well to all the therapists and it is in our view the consistency of approach that is important.

The basic approach to RO involves an awareness of the elderly person's psychological, as well as physical needs. Attitudes need to allow the elderly person individuality, dignity, self-respect and choice. There is a need to avoid the sort of caring that stifles the person's attempts at independence: 'Let me help you with that, it takes you such a long time on your own'; that treats the person as a child rather than as the adult they have been for 50-odd years: 'What you want is . . . .' or 'Come along now, eat it up'; that treats the person as an object: staff member to visitor in front of resident, 'Now this man here is very confused and incontinent'; that misunderstands positive approaches: 'Why interfere, leave them alone, it is our turn to do things for them'. The person needs to be nurtured; allowing as much independence of us as possible. As with the parent-teenager relationship this can be a painful process. We must hold back, suppressing the desire to take over and dress the person who is having difficulties, because we know she will manage eventually on her own. It means sometimes taking risks because to be wrapped up in cotton wool is to be deprived of freedom.

Finally, we need to be positive; if we are not our negative feelings will show and may simply add to the helplessness of the situation. A realistic optimism and expectation that some change is possible may help to increase elderly persons' self-confidence, and so in fact make change more likely to actually occur.

Selection of patients

If RO is seen not simply as a daily 'therapy' group for a proportion of our patients or residents but as a 24 hour approach, as part of the elderly person's environment, then the issue of which patients are selected for the group is transformed into the question of which aspects of RO are best suited to different types of person. That it is suitable for a range of elderly people is seen in its successful application in psychiatric and geriatric hospitals, nursing and residential homes, day hospitals and day centres etc. The following principles may be useful:

a. Severely demented patients have been reported in some studies as receiving least benefit from RO sessions in isolation from the basic approach (while others have found them to respond as well as less demented patients). With this type of patient it is especially important to continue the re-orientation process throughout the day.

b. Moderately impaired patients benefit from both RO sessions and the basic approach. Particular care needs to be given to finding the appropriate level of activities so that they do not find the sessions boring or insulting to their intelligence.

c. The same consideration applies when non-demented patients receive RO. These may be patients who have had a stroke or in some instances patients who have been in a psychiatric hospital for a number of years. Where disorientation is not evident then the basic approach should aim to draw out from the patient what is happening in their surroundings – both in the immediate vicinity and more generally in the world. Consideration should be given to activity sessions at a higher level than conventional RO groups.

  d. Severely deaf patients, where the hearing loss cannot be corrected, often do not fit well in an RO group because of their hearing impairment and may require more individual orientation work.

  e. Patients with very poor eyesight may have difficulty with a number of the tasks often included in a RO session. Again individual work is indicated, or a group specifically aimed at utilizing the other senses.

  f. Patients who are extremely restless and cannot sit in a chair for a few minutes are not suited to a group approach in view of the disruption they cause. RO here may have to be done literally on the move – around the lounge, down the corridor...! If they can concentrate for a few minutes it is better to use those minutes intensively with that person, perhaps several times a day, aiming to gradually increase their span till they are settled enough to remain in a group session.

  g. Patients with speech problems need careful help. Those whose major difficulty is in expressing themselves may not find the group situation too stressful, whereas those who have particular difficulty in understanding the meaning of what is said may well find the group session a threatening experience; they are then best helped on an individual basis.

Group membership should not be constantly changing. If in the early stages a member appears to be unsuitable a closer investigation is advisable. Problems may concern behaviour or specific disability, but the person may just be slow to respond. If essential, exclusion should be made, but individual aid should be considered. Choice is to be respected. To force attendance at a session is unacceptable. However, a refusal must be realistically assessed. Staff will be able to judge the genuineness of the response according to previous experience, and often a little gentle persuasion can result in happy participation. Perhaps if the group was brought to the person concerned for one occasion attendance at another session would be encouraged.

In summary then, the basic RO approach is flexible enough for it to be used with a wide range of elderly patients. If only a proportion of patients can be accommodated in RO sessions a good rule of thumb is to work with the most restless and disturbed patients on an individual basis, to encourage the least impaired to initiate their own activities (providing materials and interest) and to work with the other patients in RO groups, i.e. those who are moderately severely impaired. Often these are a comparatively neglected group, needing less physical care than the severely disturbed group and being less able than the mildly impaired group to interact with the care-staff.

Application to community residents

Most of the aspects outlined so far – and indeed virtually all the research that has been carried out on RO – has been primarily concerned with patients in hospital or residents in old people's homes. Yet it has been established that for every elderly person who is institutionalised with dementia there are four more who live in the community, perhaps alone or perhaps with relatives (Kay et al 1964). The reasons for the primary development of RO within institutional settings are clear and include the greater impact of demented people grouped together in a ward or home as compared with those scattered in the community, the greater ease of carrying out and evaluating intensive treatment programmes consistently and the availability there of more experienced, less emotionally involved care-staff.

Current thinking, rightly in our view, stresses the importance of maintaining elderly persons in their own surroundings, if this is their wish, providing the necessary support, and, especially important, support and relief for those such as relatives involved in their care. What part has RO to play in this endeavour?

a. Work by Greene and his colleagues in Glasgow (Greene et al 1979) has shown that some impact can be made on the demented person's orientation and awareness by RO sessions three days a week in a psychogeriatric day unit. One of us (R. Woods) has established RO groups in a Newcastle psychogeriatric day hospital; patients here seldom attend more than twice a week and staff resources only allowed for one group session a day, but even so improvements in verbal orientation in the majority of patients participating were noted. With this low intensity level of RO clearly it is the mildly demented person with a fairly specific memory disorder who will gain most benefit. As well as day-hospitals a number of day centres and clubs which cater for some confused elderly people perhaps on a longer-term basis are now being established.

RO sessions could certainly be utilized here, and if attendances are more frequent then more impaired persons may benefit. Volunteer helpers might be able to lead sessions in this setting, with suitable training and support.

b. For the elderly person living alone there are major difficulties in carrying over work done at a day centre into the person's home. Obviously regular visitors to the person's home – home help, neighbours, meals on wheels attendant, volunteer visitor, etc., can be given some guidance as to the RO approach, but some memory aid is needed for the times when the person is alone. It may be that in the future microprocessor technology will allow the use of electronic memory aids in the person's home – giving reminders and acting as a source of current information (Jones & Adam 1979). For the present however, less sophisticated measures have to suffice. Many elderly people have a newspaper delivered regularly and keep the current one available as a reminder of the date, others leave notes in strategic places. Some have a large diary to refer to; in one case the home-help assisted in keeping this up-to-date and the elderly person learned to consult it, whenever something arose about which she was uncertain. A large electric clock, perhaps with an automatic calendar, might also prove useful. Basically of course these are memory aids that most people use at one time or another. The problem with the confused elderly is to teach them to make use of these aids, and it is here that much useful work can be done in the person's own home. They might for instance usefully make a list for shopping but need to learn where to keep it so it can be easily consulted in the shops. The person may well continually 'lose' a purse or handbag and needs to be taught to keep these sort of items in particular places. Thus an RO session can actually be carried out in the person's home, with the emphasis being on developing and using memory aids and reminders.

c. The situation of the elderly person living with relatives seems much more immediately amenable to an RO approach, with the relatives being given guidance about the techniques of RO. Indeed the RO Training Programme in Tuscaloosa has produced a brief leaflet for relatives with this purpose in mind, and others are available from the Scottish Health Education Council and Leeds. A note of caution must however be sounded. Living with a confused elderly person is often very difficult for a relative and in many cases, however caring the relative is, and however good the relationship has been, there may well be some tension, anger and resentment in the relationship. Occasionally, particularly when the relative receives no relief or support, rejection of the elderly person occurs. We would reiterate the importance of the basic attitudes on which RO is dependent: dignity, individuality, self-respect, choice, the person being treated as an adult. Where there are difficulties in the relationship between relatives and the elderly person some opportunity is necessary to allow the relative to air these negative feelings and the possible resultant guilt. It may then be possible for the relative – with continued support – to allow the elderly person dignity, adulthood etc., where previously the difficulties in the relationship precluded these attitudes. If it is not possible for this change to occur – perhaps the tensions and resentment and bitterness being too entrenched – then we would not recommend teaching the relative to use RO.

Be this as it may there is no doubt that any procedure of this kind is more difficult for a relative to carry out than for a nurse because of the long-standing emotional attachments and expectations that have built up over the years. However the relatives do have certain advantages in using RO. They are much more aware of the person's previous interests; they see the elderly person in familiar surroundings; there is ready access to family photographs, souvenirs etc. from the past right up to the present time; they can work with one individual only; and they can involve the elderly person in tasks around the home.

There has been little study of the use of RO by relatives. However it does seem likely that an effective way of working with relatives would be to set up relatives' groups, preferably made up of people living close by each other, and using these to train, guide and support the relatives. Relatives may well be able to help each other through such a group by sharing experiences, difficulties, problems and solutions, and might be able to help each other in practical ways e.g. providing relief for an afternoon or evening on a reciprocal basis.

There is no doubt that some relatives are actively seeking information as to how best communicate with the confused elderly person; at present they often feel helpless in the face of the seemingly inevitable deterioration. It may be that procedures like RO will help the relatives feel some purpose in their interaction with the elderly person and to draw from them their maximal level of functioning. One of us (U. Holden) is currently involved in a study where two groups of relatives are being taught to use RO. One group will have the support additionally of a relatives' group. Comparison will be made with a group receiving normal community services support. Volunteer visitors to conduct an RO session with the elderly person (much as has been done, in stimulating speech after stroke, by Eaton Griffith 1975) might also provide the relatives with a relief from the continual burden of care and RO!

Setting up and maintaining a programme

It would be misleading to suggest that setting up a programme like RO is easy in what remains essentially an institution – however homely and relaxed a ward or old people's home might be. This being the case it would be virtually dishonest even to imply that maintaining such a programme once it is commenced does not have its pitfalls!

All the evidence that has accumulated over the years in various fields – with the mentally handicapped, children, chronic psychiatric patients etc., indicates that it can be extremely difficult to establish any positive psychological programme in an institution and that once established these endeavours are liable to encounter difficulties of various kinds. Often such difficulties lead to the programme being discontinued or simply drifting into disuse. This process, it should be emphasised, may occur independently of the demonstrated effectiveness of the therapeutic intervention. It seems to be related to the well-documented difficulties in caring for people in institutions of any kind, where the needs of the institution are given greater importance than those of the patients they are intended to serve, and where change seems to be resisted and blocked.

As far as RO is concerned little has been written about these sort of difficulties, perhaps because workers in the field are reluctant to document what may be perceived as 'failures', but the experiences of Wallis & Cope (1978) are almost certainly not unique.

Briefly, they attempted to initiate RO on two psychogeriatric wards; a previous effort by medical staff to initiate RO had encountered resentment from the nursing staff who saw it 'as yet another imposition on nursing staff without any help from anyone else'. In this case however, some additional help was available in the short-term from Wallis & Cope's research team. The establishment of the programmes became at one point embroiled in an ongoing conflict in the institution (viz. who gets the patient up in the morning – day staff or night staff) and was supported with varying degrees of commitment by the nursing staff involved. The programmes on both wards were short-lived, apparently because it was felt patients became more agitated following RO sessions. It seems likely however that the lukewarm commitment and even antagonism of some staff towards the programme may also have been an important factor. Other factors were the frustration some staff felt with the institution's authorities who failed to supply commodes and some staff feeling threatened by the research team who were looking at the activity of staff and patients on the wards and feeding the results back to staff.

Every setting is different of course and it is impossible to lay down specific rules for overcoming these sort of difficulties. What we will attempt to do is describe some general issues that seem to be of some importance and which need to be borne in mind in work of this nature.

1. The initiative

The first question to be raised is where does the initiative and impetus for the establishment of RO come from? Does it emanate from an 'outsider' e.g. a psychologist wanting to set up RO in a residential home, or from someone in a position of authority in the hierarchy of the institution e.g. a senior nursing officer or a consultant, or from someone in a position of authority within the ward or residential home unit e.g. a sister on a ward or a superintendent of an old people's home, or from 'shop-floor' level e.g. a care attendant or ward nurse.

Clearly there may be different reactions to each of these initiators. The 'outsider' may find that staff feel threatened. The very suggestion of change in the pattern of care may be perceived as a criticism of current standards and procedures; there may be a mistrust of outsiders – 'they can never know our patients as well as we do, we know what is best for our patients' may be the staff response. The institutional authority figure may encounter resentment, that *more* work is being handed down for the already short-staffed and over-stretched ward staff to do. The programme may be begun grudgingly, but the chances are that before too long a reason for abandoning it will be found. The attempts of the sister or superintendent depend on their position in the Home or ward; if viewed as another of sister's strange ideas it will be abandoned immediately she is off duty; if as an unnecessary disruption to the smooth running of the ward it will soon be proved useless, potentially damaging and certainly impractical! The care-attendant or ward nurse may find that her efforts to start a programme are blocked perhaps from above – with the various other duties to be done on the ward clearly pointed out – or perhaps from her fellow care-workers or nursing assistants, who may see the time being spent talking to patients as avoiding real work.

This is clearly a particularly gloomy view of the implementation of a psychological programme, and we are not alleging that these attitudes are representative of the caring professions generally. However we have come across all the reactions described above at one time or another. What we do want to emphasise here is that if one person is taking the initiative their first task is to persuade staff at *every* level of the value of the proposal. This may involve much discussion and perhaps some demonstration of what is involved; perhaps a visit to another centre where RO is being carried out. It is extremely useful to identify within the ward or home the natural leaders among the staff group – these are often not those with designated authority, but are heard, respected and influential. If these people become enthusiastic about the programme then there is less chance of the staff being divided and antagonistic.

If despite all efforts staff remain uninterested in RO though criticism and pressure have been avoided, but there is still antagonism, then it is advisable not to attempt to push the issue. Instead ongoing discussion on the ward of our aims as a staff group, of our attitudes, of the patients' needs, of the difficulties and frustrations we face, of the pleasures we enjoy in our work should be attempted. This would examine and possibly, over a period of months, modify attitudes to the point where some demonstration RO sessions may be organised. On some wards where attitudes are more neutral a small pilot project may be all that is required to generate enthusiasm; on other wards the staff may, with one voice, declare that RO fills for them a long-felt need for some positive guidelines in their approach to the demented patient. Even here, though, it is important that the backing of staff further up the hierarchy of the institution is also forthcoming.

2. Training and support

Crucial to the success of a programme of this kind is adequate training, so that staff feel confident in what they are doing and so that their uncertainty is minimized. Training will be dealt with more fully below, but it is important to emphasise that it must be on-going, with new staff being involved when they begin on the ward. Staff need a great deal of support if the programme is to be maintained, especially in view of the limited goals mentioned above, which mean that rewards from the programme itself may be few. The repetitive nature of RO can result in staff finding it boring at times, especially if it is applied unimaginatively. Here support and encouragement from other staff can be a great help; if the sister or superintendent, doctor or senior nursing officer shows a real interest in what is happening care-staff may be better able to see the value of what they are doing. If communicating with patients or residents is generally valued in the institution then staff carrying out RO will see it as important; if having a spick and span ward is seen as more important by those in authority, their efforts will be devalued and the programme undermined.

Rewards and satisfactions experienced by the staff as well as patients are important for the success of RO. If the RO session is enjoyed because sufficient time is set aside for it to be relaxed and unhurried, because it is allowed to be a social occasion and because sufficient guidance is given for staff to feel comfortable in their leadership role then the quality of RO will be better. If the staff can learn to look for small changes then there is the satisfaction of seeing an elderly person responding. If the staff are praised for using RO on the ward and encouraged not to walk through the lounge in silence and not to speak solely to other staff whilst carrying out physical care on a patient again they will experience more satisfaction from the RO approach. This will then increase the possibility of it being successfully maintained.

3. Maintenance

If RO is to be continued once implemented, it needs to become part of the routine of the ward not an optional extra to be carried out when all other chores are completed. It may be necessary to establish a rota of staff to carry out RO sessions, to avoid every staff member leaving it to everyone else to lead a group on any particular day. This also ensures that as many staff as possible are involved in the RO sessions which help to give the staff intensive practice in the basic approach. Perhaps the testing time for a new RO programme is when the first staff shortage occurs – what priority will RO be awarded then? There will of course be times when it is extremely difficult to carry out RO sessions as such – an example of this is a Home where there was an outbreak of gastro-enteritis among residents and staff – and other situations which are difficult to legislate for! However it is important to plan what will happen during the more predictable staff shortage periods – at weekends, in winter when staff sickness reaches its peak, in summer when many staff will be enjoying a well-earned holiday, in March when perhaps many staff are on leave to complete their holiday entitlement for the year. If RO grinds to a halt at times like these then only a small portion of the year will remain when it will be fully operational.

What is needed is of course an emphasis on the basic approach which takes relatively little additional staff time together with a manageable number of patients involved in daily sessions. It is better to restrict sessions to a small number of patients rather than include a large number involving more staff resources than can always be available.

It may be tempting to include more patients by having a larger group in a session at any one time. Our view is that the group size should be no larger than the staff leading the group can keep fully occupied whilst maintaining attention. Depending on severity of deterioration this usually precludes a group size larger than 4–6. If it is desired to include eight patients it might be advantageous to split the time available between two groups of four rather than struggle to maintain the concentration of eight confused patients together.

Consideration should be given to the use of volunteers to help lead sessions, given suitable training and support of course. Having a structure like RO to work within can help a volunteer worker a great deal to contribute something useful to the care of the elderly person with dementia, and can help reduce the uncertainty and feelings of uselessness that lead to many a voluntary worker only coming to the ward or Home once or twice and not returning.

Other resources may also be explored, and it should be emphasised that the task of leading an RO session does not have to always

fall on the care-staff – occupational therapy staff, or speech therapists, psychologists etc. may also be willing to be involved in this
way. However when several groups of workers are involved
exactly how the duties are to be shared should be made explicit.

4. Aids to staff

Everything possible should be done to ease the staff's taxing task of
seeking to communicate with the confused elderly person. To help
the staff member who comes to the RO session having had a busy
morning with no time spare for planning an RO session a number
of cards should be made available each with a different suggested
programme for an RO session on it. Equipment should be readily
available for the appropriate activities; the physical setting should
be as attractive and comfortable as possible; cards giving details of
the elderly person's background – age, number and name of children, occupation, interests etc. – should be available so the staff
member can respond appropriately in conversation.

A written record should be kept of each session, listing all those
present, subjects discussed, how each elderly person responded,
any particular successes made, difficulties encountered. This is of
great use when different staff lead sessions each day, so they can
ensure variety and can build on previous successes and avoid
previously discovered pitfalls. Senior staff can also use the record
to monitor progress made by the elderly person in the sessions,
and to help staff over any difficult issues that arise. It can be seen
then that implementing and maintaining an RO programme
requires careful advanced planning and the involvement of staff at
every level. There are no guaranteed methods of carrying this out
that will work everywhere, but it will be clear that both
enthusiasm *and* persistence will be required!

Staff training

The need for adequate training has already been emphasised.
Without it staff may feel uncertain of themselves and what they are
meant to be doing or they may inadvertently misinterpret some of
the RO principles and techniques. Training must be ongoing to
keep up with the inevitable turnover in staff and to refresh those
who remain. Who is to lead the training? This implies imparting

knowledge and skills so the training should be led either by people who already have some knowledge or skills or by people who are prepared to do some background reading, some visiting of other centres etc. The work may fall on a few people with prior know-ledge or experience or on a larger group of staff prepared to learn together. If only a few staff are to lead the training obviously those with the ability to communicate – from whatever profession – will be most useful.

What form should the training take? This depends very much on the individual situation, but we have found the following compo-nents of training particularly valuable.

a. *Lectures*. These should be informal and provide plenty of opportunity for discussion throughout, thus helping the 'lecturer' to ensure real understanding. The subject matter should include:
The rationale underlying RO
The general principles of the basic 24 hour approach
Examples of the use of the 24 hour approach
Dealing with rambling and confused talk
General guidelines for RO sessions
Specific examples of methods for use in RO sessions
Goals and limitations of RO
How RO is to be applied in the particular setting.

b. *Audio-visual aids*. However interesting the lecture, there is no doubt that carefully chosen audio-visual aids are extremely use-ful in bringing the subject matter to life – particularly when the subject matter is as practical as is RO.

Slides are particularly useful in illustrating what happens in an RO session or in setting the scene for 24 hour RO. They can be used in conjunction with snippets of audio-tape recorded in RO sessions to show what staff can do to draw the patients out and how they can respond appropriately.

In fact a tape-slide programme providing a recorded talk on RO illustrated by a set of slides can be extremely useful. It enables the same talk to be repeated on several occasions – which is helpful in view of shift work. When new staff join the ward they can work through the tape-slide programme and so receive some training without another course needing to be established. Staff can work through the programme at their own pace. A set of questions to accompany the tape-slide programme is useful to direct the staff-member's attention to the key points.

Another useful form of audio-visual aid is a video tape, showing parts of RO sessions and illustrating the communication that the leader attempts to establish. Careful editing is needed to ensure that salient points are made – it can be difficult to watch a video tape of a whole RO session as the pace is somewhat slower than TV programmes to which staff are accustomed! A commentary directing attention to particular principles and methods is also advisable.

c. *Hand-outs* – for staff to keep, peruse at their leisure and refer to when necessary are very important to reinforce the lectures and talks given. They should cover briefly the main points made in the lecture, giving examples as well as guidelines.

d. *Demonstration* – of the application of RO techniques again clarifies and helps to make tangible what is covered in any lectures given. This may be provided by a visit to a centre where RO is already taking place. A person with prior experience could lead a small group with other staff members observing, or someone could lead a session with some other staff role-playing the parts of the patients and others observing. It is in this demonstration that staff observe how the principles are actually put into practice, how the staff member can be encouraging rather than patronizing, how even the most deteriorated person can be helped to succeed rather than having their failure reinforced yet again. After each demonstration plenty of time should be allowed for comments and discussion of what took place. This should then be followed by:

e. *Role-play*. Here staff in training take the role of group leader whilst other staff play the confused elderly patients once more, and other staff observe. This is valuable not only in giving the leaders a gradual exposure to running an actual RO session, but also for those role-playing the part of a confused elderly person and seeing RO from the recipient's angle. The role-played group sessions should be interrupted frequently for observers to make suggestions to leaders or patients and for leaders to ask for help if uncertain how to respond to a patient or how to involve them in the group. This then leads on to:

f. *Feedback*. Where other staff (including those who played the patients) tell the group leaders in the role-play what they thought helpful about what they did and said and about their attitude that came across, and of course what seemed to be less helpful. Giving feedback is never easy, particularly if it is negative. It is important that these training sessions are relaxed and open and that it is remembered that RO involves certain skills which can only be learned properly if we are able to have our perfor- mance monitored – just as when we are, for example, learning to drive a car. If access to video tape equipment is available this provides a way in which the staff member can see his performance for himself and, in a sense, provide his own feedback in addition to that of others.

From feedback the training session may lead on to further demonstrations, more role-play and more feedback. For example in one training session, in a role-play one staff member tended to 'interrogate' the 'patients', pressurising them with questions they were unable to answer, leaving an uncomfortable pause in which the 'patient' seemed likely to become acutely aware of having failed. Feedback was given on this point and a further demonstra- tion showed how the same areas of information could be covered without making the 'patient' feel threatened. The staff member then repeated the role-play and was able to be much less inter- rogative, helping the 'patients' to find the answers for themselves. Feedback was then given by the other staff on how much better this second role-play now was and on the noticeable change there had been, and how the 'patients' responded much better to this more gentle approach.

Feedback should not be confined to training sessions, and it can be helpful in preventing staff from slipping into bad habits once they have been involved in RO for a while (again the analogy with driving a car applies!), and in encouraging them as they find innovative ways to deal with the variety of situations that arise in RO sessions and elsewhere. Feedback should be mutual, not just given by senior staff! What is needed is a continued willingness to learn and to improve the skills in RO, not to become over- confident and above all to continue to be sensitive to the elderly, their needs and what *they* can teach us.

Negative effects of RO

Can RO change patients for the worse and perhaps be harmful to them? Woods & Britton (1977) reviewed reports of negative trends occurring generally in psychological programmes with the elderly. They concluded that some reports (none involving RO, inciden- tally) indicated a change in the patient from being non- complaining, uncritical, and acquiescent to becoming more criti- cal, demanding and challenging due to improvement in general functioning and a better awareness of reality.

The change, perhaps, is from being an 'ideal' patient, presenting no nursing problems, to a person becoming aware of a reality which is often by any standards unsatisfactory, who seeks to bring about change by being more complaining and critical. This type of 'negative' change can be seen as in fact healthy and adaptive.

Possible harmful effects of RO incorrectly carried out will be considered in the next section. It must be emphasised here however that even if properly executed RO does not always make patients happy, because reality itself is never all roses. However tactfully we discuss the death – even some years ago – of a patient's spouse or discuss events during the World Wars these cannot be dismissed with a joke. Reality covers the whole range of emotions, however tempting it is to only look at one side of life. Respect for the patient's dignity may sometimes mean staff facing up to issues that they find painful to talk about also, and so would rather avoid. We do need to be aware of negative reactions, however, and instead of blaming RO for them, be prepared to work through them with the elderly person, providing warmth in our support of them as they come to terms with what is happening to them, helping them where possible to express their feelings – which their mental state may make it extremely difficult for them to do unaided.

A further word of warning when beginning work with a new patient; it is important to take note of their previous environment. If they have been sitting quietly, withdrawn and non-responsive on a psychogeriatric back-ward for some years it is not sensible to rush in and stimulate them too quickly, and a gradual approach is more likely to succeed. Change presents difficulties for most people, and in a ward generally gradual changes will be much less anxiety-provoking – for staff as well as patients!

Misuse of RO

We have become increasingly concerned that a 'little knowledge' of RO can lead to it being misapplied, often inadvertently through lack of adequate training or from misunderstanding of the complexities of RO which, on the surface, seems so simple.

An important article by Gubrium & Ksander (1975) is of particular relevance here. They observed RO in two nursing homes and came to question what they saw as the implicit assumptions of RO. One particular interchange they report is illustrative of the misapplication of RO they observed. The aide leading the group had indicated on the RO board that it was 'raining'. He asked the patient what the weather was, she looked outside, perceived that the sun was shining (the rain having abated), and said it was sunny. The aide disagreed with her until she read 'correctly' from the board that it was raining, whereupon she was praised warmly.

What is being described here is an inflexible, unthinking, mechanical approach to RO and we feel Gubrium & Ksander are right to ask what is the 'reality' of RO in these circumstances. The staff member has learned to go through the RO board, helping the patients to recite the information there. What he has not learned to do is to try to understand the elderly person's viewpoint, to look for what he is seeking to say, and go beyond the rigidly structured session to a situation where real communication can take place. This mechanical type of RO can occur when it is applied without warmth. We would emphasise the importance of staff approval in RO in rewarding appropriate behaviour but this means more than an automatic 'very good' or 'well done' if it is indeed to be rewarding.

The dangers of being too interrogative have already been mentioned in previous sections, but this does seem to be a common pitfall, often with the question being emphasised to the detriment of the answers which are glossed over as the next question is put to the beleaguered patient! An emphasis on putting the person right at all costs can lead to difficulties e.g. staff feeling they have to keep telling a patient his wife is dead when other strategies such as distraction might be usefully employed, especially as it is difficult to be continually tactful!

It is mistaken, in our view, to see RO as a replacement of other approaches to encouraging independence, and we would see it as part of a total programme, rather than standing in glorious isolation. Social, recreational and domestic activities are all necessary and the basic RO approach can be used in conjunction with them, rather than in place of them.

Finally the level of RO needs to be adjusted depending on the particular patient. The range of abilities in dementing patients is vast, and when RO is applied to elderly people with other difficulties the range becomes even larger. Some studies of RO (e.g. Voelkel 1978, MacDonald & Settin 1978) seem to have applied relatively low-level RO to patients with more ability, who have accordingly felt insulted by the topics covered. Similarly the converse would be unlikely to produce benefits to say a severely deteriorated, incoherent patient faced with a discussion of current political leaders. Again flexibility is the key-note, a readiness to adjust the activities to the particular group. For example, if a group is thought to be relatively undeteriorated, day and date could be covered by each person keeping a diary, beginning with the day and date entry, before moving on to higher-level topics, rather than feeling obliged to spend 10 minutes on repeating the day and date etc. simply because that is how the book says RO is to be done. A group of widely different levels can result in boredom and stress for patients and staff, as it makes this flexibility difficult to achieve.

To summarise the various misuses of RO perhaps it is fair to say that the application of the attitudes underlying RO is necessary rather than rigid adherence to the methods, and to examine our use of the methods in the light of these attitudes. It does not come amiss for any RO leader to ask 'Did I in that session allow Mrs X dignity and respect? Did I help her have self-respect; did I see her as an individual adult person rather than as just another old demented patient?'

By keeping these issues alive in our minds we then have more chance of avoiding some of the pitfalls described here.

10

Beyond RO

A MODEL FOR FURTHER DEVELOPMENT

Although it has been emphasised that RO is not a cure-all, it is equally true that surprisingly consistent changes have been noted when it is used with those suffering from dementia, and other disorders which lead to confusion. So much therapeutic pessimism prevails among those caring for these patients that RO becomes a particularly welcome development. The wide applicability of the basic approach is also very valuable as, used flexibly, the methods are appropriate, one way or another, with the majority of these elderly people.

It will be apparent that RO tends to have a specific focus on cognitive aspects of functioning i.e. current knowledge, concentration and so forth. This may be a factor in the often disappointing generalization of improvements to areas such as toiletting, dressing, and other self-care skills which appear far removed from the context of RO.

However, RO has shown that when learning is encouraged in the right conditions and the environment has been suitably modified the elderly dementing patient can learn. This implies that RO can be used as a model for intervention in other areas. If learning is required to improve basic self-care and social skills then the right atmosphere and specific schemes must be created in order to encourage the relearning.

Quite simply, we are advocating that RO can be seen as part of a broader relearning and rehabilitative programme incorporating other relevant approaches and using behavioural methods in order to maximise the opportunities for relearning. This broader programme could be as useful with these other areas of functioning as RO has proved to be with orientation.

The next sections will describe how the behavioural approach can be used more generally. It must be borne in mind that research in this field is at a very early stage in comparison to the successful applications of behaviour modification in other areas such as mental handicap. Inevitably this chapter remains speculative until large-scale studies can be completed. We have drawn on the findings of smaller investigations conducted by ourselves and others interested in the ageing process. Hopefully this will provide some practical guidance towards a means of developing and improving psychological intervention in treatment of the elderly.

The individual programme

If patients are to show changes in their actual functioning their problems, deficits, assets and needs have to be examined on an individual basis and plans made for each person.

The immediate problem is the issue of practicability. Staff-patient ratios can make it very difficult for patients to be seen as individuals. Inadequate staffing levels would cause this approach to fail. However, in many situations the more efficient use of staff would allow more time for contact with the patients. Obviously if patients can become more independent and efforts to achieve this are successful, then there will be a saving of staff time in the long run. How to obtain extra time is a problem that must be solved according to the demands of each particular situation.

Current literature indicates that hospital staff are examining closely the 'regimes' in use at present on wards. Reorganization of the day's activities is being achieved by reconsideration of priorities. This may imply less rigid enforcement of ward routine, making each nurse responsible for a small group of patients and the use of the nursing process, which all show an overall effort to make individualisation of care a reality. This individualisation we see as a basic right of the elderly person.

There are many advantages in certain staff members developing close contact with a designated group. Such contact provides the opportunity to really know and to build relationships with a more manageable number of elderly people. As there is less staff change, staff are recognised by patients more readily. Therapeutic optimism is increased when the patients stand out as individuals from the back-drop of deterioration. There are, of course, practical difficulties in allocating nurses to particular patients, but it is certainly worthy of consideration in any setting.

As it is impractical to provide immediate individual plans for the entire ward, a realistic strategy would be to start with new admissions. The first stage of setting up an individual programme or plan is the selection of targets or goals which must be attained to achieve the aims. The plan will then have to specify how these aims are to be realised. In many ways the stage of selecting the appropriate goals is the most important as the rest of the plan follows from them. The first goal of any plan is to correct or alleviate any medical conditions and sensory deficits wherever possible. The following sequence of questions should then be asked, explored, investigated (and even answered) by all the staff involved with the particular patient – nurses, doctors, OTs, social workers, psychologists etc. can (and should) be involved where resources allow.

1. What does the elderly person want?
2. What assets, abilities and interests does the person have?
3. What problems does the person have?
4. What inconsistencies are there in his behaviour?

1. What does the elderly person want?

What are his or her objectives? What are seen as problems? What does he or she want from us? It is hard to believe that the necessity of posing such questions can come as a surprise. Those 'in charge' sometimes take it for granted that they know best and so ignore the wishes and needs of the person whose life is being organised. Even if poor memory, poor decision-making capacity or other problems exist the right to be heard must be retained. Respect does not imply complete subservience to the needs and demands of the elderly. There are wishes which are totally unrealistic, practically impossible or even encroaching on the priorities of others. However, the views of the individual must be considered when any decision is being discussed. This question is placed first deliberately.

To make a decision about what an elderly person wants based on 'when I'm 85 I will want to...' is to impose our own, possibly faulty conceptions and fantasies on the individual. It is essential to discuss the situation with the individual concerned, and to take into account biography, abilities and personality in order to fully appreciate the situation. To accept at face value expressions of helplessness and weakness can lead to further misunderstanding about real needs and feelings. These can be signs of depression and withdrawal which can prove misleading and which may well recede as the person becomes more active and more in control of life once again.

2. What assets, abilities, and interests does the person have?

Detailed observations of behaviour are of importance. There are various methods available to assist in achieving this, for instance rating scales (see Chapter 5). These can provide information on a variety of functions. It is vital to ascertain what a person can still do, what skills are retained – self-care, social, other acquired skills, capacity to perform domestic tasks and so on. The emphasis is on assets not deficits. It may be that tasks are carried out slowly, or some prompting is needed; what is important is to recognize that the person does have some skills and abilities and the eventual plan will seek to capitalise on these.

It is equally important to know what the person's interests have been, what was enjoyed and some idea of background and life history. This provides valuable information in building up a picture of what the person would be like without the present disabilities, in individualising recreational and constructive activities, in providing guidance as to topics for conversation and in selecting suitable rewarding items and events.

The question of the very deteriorated patient is often raised. What skills, abilities, and interests can possibly be retained? Here a more basic level must be considered; perhaps the person cannot use utensils for eating, but succeeds well with fingers; perhaps verbal communication is poor, but a smile is offered in response; despite apparent total withdrawal a sudden noise elicits a turn of the head; music and rhythm lead perhaps to joining in a dance or a song. Under these conditions very careful observations are necessary. There is a need to stand back and allow the patient to attempt something for himself before automatically doing it for him. This permits the expression of whatever remaining skill there may be. Above all else a patient must be seen as a living being who must not be 'written off' no matter how deteriorated appearances suggest him to be.

3. What problems does the elderly person cause?

Again the placing of this question is deliberate. Too often it comes first – understandably enough — as it is the problem behaviours that make life difficult for those in the caring role. It is placed low down the list of questions to avoid the possibility of perceiving individuals only in terms of problems. Frequently patients are described as personifying particular behaviour. As a result they become known as 'the screamer', 'the wanderer', 'the hoarder' etc. In any plan the emphasis must be on the person's assets if the problem behaviours are to be improved at all. Negative aspects of behaviour cannot be seen in isolation from neutral or positive features. If the aim is to reduce the frequency of a problem behaviour e.g. wandering, the aim should be to increase the frequency of other – preferably incompatible – positive behaviours. In this example, the amount of sitting, reading a magazine, or joining in a group singing session could be usefully increased.

In specifying the possible problems of each patient several issues need to be examined:

a. the problem should be stated clearly

b. the frequency of its occurrence

c. the situation in which it occurs

d. any clues about events preceding its occurrence, or which could act as a catalyst

e. What follows as a result of the behaviour. In other words what are the reactions of staff and others in the situation, what benefit or gain does the person obtain and what are the losses?

It is necessary to say much more than 'Mr Jones is aggressive'. A more correct account might be 'Mr Jones hits other patients once a week. This occurs when someone sits in his chair in the living area. The staff try to restore peace by removing the other patients from the lounge so that Mr Jones can have his seat back'.

Specific descriptions of behaviour are required; this is essential for an individual plan to be developed. Abbreviated notes such as 'confused', 'attention seeking', 'demented', etc., are insufficient and may have quite different meanings for different staff members and disciplines. The word 'confused' can be used by one member of staff to describe continual wandering about the ward, whereas to another it would imply an inability to name the day and time of year. Particularly misleading is 'attention seeking' which can even be used as a derogatory term for unpopular patients. It rarely proves informative; after all, human beings are all seeking some form of attention! Problems can arise over the nature of the attention seeking and the amount demanded. Once again the nature of the problem in each case should be explicity specified.

Mrs R and Mrs S were both described as 'attention seeking'. Mrs R was an obese diabetic who found it impossible to stick to the prescribed diet and so had a constant thirst. She would call for water whenever a nurse passed within earshot – even though she might have a glass already in her hand. Her call was loud and insistent. Enumeration of this behaviour indicated that she shouted 'Nurse, nurse' approximately 30 times in an hour. The appearance of a nurse acted as a trigger. Reactions varied – she was ignored, told to be quiet, some attempted to calm her down and others provided her with more water. Reactions of other residents were consistently negative, urging her in the strongest terms to 'pipe down'.

Mrs S complained of nausea in order to 'seek attention'. She felt sick at the meal table and invariably had to leave halfway through. Her nausea was worse with difficult-to-digest foods. The other patients responded negatively and objected to being put off their own food, and although initially sympathetic the staff eventually became matter-of-fact in their approach. Medical investigations showed a partial oesophageal obstruction and so treatment plans were directed towards a special diet.

Two quite different situations and yet the same label – 'attention seeking' – illustrate the point that greater detail is necessary in order to avoid the consequences of what is undoubtedly pejorative terminology. Careful medical investigations are usually indicated when there are complaints of physical symptoms which may not appear to have a physical basis. Even when these are negative it should be borne in mind that some studies have shown that the elderly patient's self-evaluation can be a better predictor of survival even than that of the doctor's!

Finally, several studies have shown that there is very little staff-resident interaction in some long-term care environments. To those rebelling against routine and not being 'model' residents the label of 'attention seeking' can be attached and natural independence can be stifled. To be a 'model' resident too often it is desirable to accept without question and to ask for nothing. The behavioural approach must not be employed to achieve such an undersirable state of depersonalisation. Rather it should indicate a need to modify the environment as a whole providing the residents with more personal contact, more choice, more individuality and more scope to be individuals in their own right with reasonable control over their own lives.

4. What inconsistencies are there in the person's behaviour?

This question should provide further clues as to capacity for change. It highlights aspects of behaviour that vary from situation to situation, or behaviour that depends on the presence of a certain staff member, or is inconsistent within an area of function.

An example of a situational variation in behaviour would be the patient with senile dementia who sits alone and withdrawn in the lounge of an old people's home but in the pub becomes sociable and chatty (this precedes the ingestion of alcohol!), or the lady who is able to cook a meal at the day centre but never at home. These variations demonstrate the retained capacity but suggest that some situations lack sufficient stimulus.

Different reactions to different staff are commonly observed. One nurse will say Mrs Brown cannot dress herself, another will say she can. Such inconsistent observations are extremely valuable and should not be concealed; they provide clues as to the best ways to help the lady concerned. On this occasion perhaps one nurse may have stood back a little more, allowed Mrs Brown more time and managed to find the right way to help her. Other staff could then benefit from the discovery of the particular 'trick' in their own interactions with the lady.

It is in examining the inconsistencies of behaviour that 'excess disabilities' (see Chapter 2) may be identified. These are deficits that seem worse than the person's level of actual impairment would suggest. Here multi-disciplinary assessment is particularly valuable; some specific deficits e.g. in dressing, eating, language and so on may be related to damage to particular areas of the brain (see Chapter 5). Knowledge of these kinds of deficits will help staff understand the patient's difficulties, enable suitable aids and adaptations to be provided and realistic goals to be set. Excess disabilities are identified where staff have some evidence to suggest that given the right conditions the person could perform a task which currently he does not. An example of this would be a person whose language functions are clearly intact, but who never initiates a conversation; or someone who has been observed to use a knife and fork once or twice, but who usually uses fingers.

THE PLAN

When these four questions have been examined they should provide most of the information required to formulate a plan. This will consist of two parts – a set of goals or targets, and a set of procedures by which these can be achieved. The targets will be set according to what seem to be the most important deficits and excesses in the person's behaviour.

Any inconsistencies from situation to situation or with different members of staff should be borne in mind. 'Important' relates to the patient's and relative's wishes and not simply to the convenience of the staff. If particular problem behaviours have been identified then the targets will, where possible, include the encouragement of activities that are incompatible or which will reduce the frequency of the problem behaviour. Targets should be defined precisely so that the staff will be able to judge the level of achievement.

An indication of the actual frequency of the behaviour and the desired change may be useful, e.g. Improve Dressing would be an imprecise target, evaluation would be difficult. It might be better to use 'Improve frequency with which patient puts on shirt and trousers with only verbal assistance, from present level of only once a week'. Further examples of targets will be given below.

It is beyond the scope of this book to provide details of procedures for behavioural change – those interested in pursuing this are referred to one of the standard manuals (Kanfer & Goldstein 1975). It is relevant to outline some of the principles, as if appropriate goals are chosen then relatively simple and straightforward strategies will enable some limited change to occur.

Accurate recording of the patient's behaviour is very useful indeed; e.g. if the target is to increase the patient's rate of self-initiated visits to the toilet then each visit should be noted on a record sheet. Recording is invaluable in providing staff with both a reminder of the target and reinforcement for their efforts. It is necessary to obtain a pre-treatment level for comparison. This is done by daily recordings of the behaviour until the baseline measurements represent a reasonably consistent assessment of the patient's functioning. As different people tend to interpret observations in an individual manner it is advisable that staff should discuss any discrepant findings so that a high degree of consistency is obtained. The less confused patients might benefit from being given a graphic chart of their own progress.

Four basic methods of bringing about change will be considered:

1. Reward
2. Modelling
3. Shaping
4. Backward chaining.

Reward

The fundamental principle in encouraging change is the use of a reward for desirable behaviour, and no reward for inappropriate behaviour. A 'reward' consists of something enjoyed by the patient. As individual tastes and values vary enormously it is vital to know what the patient's likes or dislikes include. Undoubtedly, elderly people most appreciate staff approval and attention, so good interpersonal relationships have a strong motivational force. The word 'behavioural' is often mistakenly equated with 'mechanical', but warm and affectionate relationships are of prime importance and preclude the possibility of mechanical and automatic responses being the rule in relationships. Apart from approval other practical rewards might include a favourite drink or food, a special event or outing, even cigarettes, any of which could be used to encourage new behaviour initially. Some studies have used tokens as a reward. The token can later be exchanged for rewards of the patient's choice. Token giving structures staff approval. If it is difficult for the elderly person to remember or to perform the necessary actions to exchange the token it is probably only a useful reward system for them in as much as it reminds staff to give their attention appropriately.

The use and relevance of rewards should be considered. It is illogical to reward a full stomach with food; a cigarette for a patient with a packet in his pocket is like coals to Newcastle; if someone wants to sleep he is not impressed by extra attention.

To delay a reward is to lose an opportunity. A very confused person forgets quickly and might not connect the praise with her own response: it is also advisable to make clear what is so pleasing. In the initial stages the rewards should be given virtually every time the desired behaviour occurs. If the behaviour becomes well established they can be slowly decreased, though continued, if only infrequently.

If rewarding the behaviour of elderly patients appears difficult and artificial it should be borne in mind that people are rewarding and failing to reward each other all the time—often without being aware of it. We all smile at those we like, listen attentively to what they say, yet ignore those to whom we are indifferent; these are examples of reward and lack of reward in everyday life. What is being advocated here is the use of these everyday phenomena in a planned, structured way to bring about specific changes in a patient's behaviour. Praise and encouragement are part of all good training programmes, and where the elderly are concerned many of the skills were previously in their possession and only require relearning.

One problem in using a reward system is to ensure that the behaviour to be rewarded actually occurs in the first place. For instance if a patient never goes to the toilet without prompting how can he be taught to go on his own? There is nothing to reward. Clearly the behaviour must be elicited before it can be rewarded. Several strategies are possible. One method is to increase the probability of it occurring. The environment can be adapted so that the patient sits nearer to the facilities instead of a long way from them. He could be taken for a walk in the vicinity so that when he sees the toilet he might feel disposed to make use of it while close at hand. If social interaction is the target a patient could be invited to join a small group in order to play a game or have a drink in company. In such circumstances the desired behaviour becomes more probable, so then it can be immediately rewarded. Three other possible strategies are discussed in the succeeding sections.

Modelling

A second approach is to demonstrate, or model, the required behaviour. To increase recreational involvement an actual game can be shown; mime can be employed to show how to get dressed, how to wash, or how to eat correctly. A group already engaged in discussion can demonstrate to a withdrawn patient that by conversing they can obtain attention and praise from the staff.

Shaping

Here successively closer approximations to the target behaviour are rewarded, and as each stage is achieved the demands become a little stricter. If, for instance, the normal use of a fork and knife is the target the reward system could commence at a very low level:

Any sort of self-feeding, even with the fingers, then reward only for an attempt to use a utensil, then only when a fork is used. Finally, only when the correct use of utensils is observed.

Similarly if the target is to be self-initiated toiletting:

A visit to the toilet even when accompanied. Then managing with less and less help in getting up and walking there, then only response to verbal reminders is rewarded. Then these too could be faded into non-verbal cues – initially a mime, eventually perhaps a simple nod of the head. Finally the only reward to be given is for self-initiated toiletting.

The entire procedure would consist of initial response to guidance, response to a verbal reminder, then a non-verbal prompt and finally no reminder at all.

Consistent use by the staff of the minimum prompt needed to begin or continue the behaviour in question is very important. When dressing a patient, for example, if verbal prompting does not get a response the patient's arm might be placed gradually in the sleeve of his shirt with firm pressure until he begins to continue the movement himself, when the pressure is relaxed and the patient praised. As soon as the patient stops the required movement the guiding hand of the nurse becomes firmer until he takes over again and can be praised once more. Thus small amounts of dressing behaviour can be reinforced and become more likely to occur again in the future.

Shaping involves the setting of intermediate goals in order to achieve the main one. If aims are set realistically it will enable the patient to obtain encouragement along the way and so increase the likelihood of complete success. Breaking goals down into small attainable parts is necessary in order to progress. If goals seem a long way off they discourage both patient and staff.

Backward chaining

The final related technique to be mentioned is backward chaining. Many target behaviours in fact consist of a sequence of smaller behaviours, for example toiletting includes:

Get up from seat in lounge

Walk to toilet

Remove clothing as necessary

Urinate in appropriate receptacle

Adjust clothing.

As the term implies, backward chaining involves starting at the end of the sequence, establishing that behaviour, and then going on to work on the preceding link in the chain, establishing that before going on to the next part of the sequence.

Thus, in the case of toiletting, the person's dressing ability should be checked, perhaps arranging for any necessary adaptations to clothing, and practice in dressing skills should be provided so that these parts of the chain can be performed. Next there is a need to ascertain if the person connects urination with being at the toilet. If when on the toilet urine is not passed, then this part of the chain requires assistance until the person reliably uses the toilet area (experience with mentally handicapped adults suggests that increased fluids and very frequent supervised visits to the toilet are useful at this stage). Then comes the 'approach response' which is the actual decision to go to the toilet, finding the way to it, walking to it and so on. As with any skill, the component skills of toiletting or dressing etc. may be learned (or here relearned), by repeated practice with rewards of praise for success.

In the case of a person who has lost the skill to feed herself, backward chaining might involve initially praising the person for opening her mouth to allow the spoon in, then letting her help to carry the spoon the last inch or so into her mouth, then encouraging and praising her for gradually taking over more of the complete sequence of actions that constitute independent feeding. The importance of backward chaining is that the completion of the chain has in it the reward of fulfillment – in this case food. This acts best on those responses closest to it, until these are well-established and can then be extended to include appropriate preceding responses.

Maintenance

The previous sections have concentrated on procedures for bringing about behavioural change, building up new behaviours, and re-establishing old ones. What must be understood, however, is that for change to be lasting the person's environment must maintain the new or re-established behaviour. When targets are set, maintenance of the targets must be considered. For instance, if we teach Mrs Jones to make a cup of tea for herself, will she continue to do so when there are six cups of tea provided daily in the Home? If we help Mr Smith to use the toilet independently will he continue to do so if most of his fellow patients are incontinent and so receive extra staff attention? Will Mrs Brown continue to dress herself if being dressed had been one way of obtaining staff attention? Having taught Mrs White to cook her own meals at home will she continue to do so when her neighbour provides her with a meal on most days? Although the emphasis may have appeared to have been on changing the individual's behaviour, behaviour-environment interactions are always present. How the environment must be modified to maintain the changed behaviour is as important as the actual change.

Reactions to problem behaviours

Sometimes the behavioural approach is characterized as 'reward good behaviour and punish (or ignore) bad behaviour'. The saying 'ignore it and it will go away' is only true in so far as the behaviour can be completely and consistently ignored – if it is rewarded at all, even infrequently, it will persist for a long, long time. To ignore a problem behaviour is usually an extremely difficult task for residents, relatives and staff. We are advocating an approach where the focus is on building up incompatible behaviours to take the place of those that are inappropriate.

Punishment is used in one form or another in everyday life – and not just with children. Everyone does or says things other people will not like, to get revenge for some real or imagined wrong. Withdrawal and moodiness may be used as punishments.

However, on ethical grounds we would not wish to see the development of programmes for the elderly (or anyone else for that matter) based on punishment. Care staff have – whether they realise it or not – a great deal of power over those in their homes or wards. Power to use wisely but also power that can damage, hurt and even destroy. The great majority of care staff use this power sensitively, responsibly and constructively. Inevitably there are those who do not; in institutions under pressure of poor facilities and resources experience in other fields had shown that systems using punishment have lent themselves too readily to abuse. Too quickly the aims of treatment are forgotten and punishment has become a way of running a ward or home for the convenience of the hard-pressed staff.

How can problem behaviours be treated if they arise before alternative positive responses have been established? What reaction is appropriate if one patient literally throws another onto the floor because she has taken the chair she usually sits in? Obviously this would be difficult to ignore; clearly, if the offending patient reclaims 'her' chair she will have succeeded and may continue forcibly ejecting 'intruders'. One possibility would be to take the offender to one side (having ensured that help is being given to the patient on the floor) and reiterate in a firm, clear, calm voice, looking at her directly face to face, that violence to other patients is unacceptable. A good way of calming the situation might be to take her out of the lounge, or to her own room. However, the plan must not stop there. Positive preventive measures are required. In this instance a decision must be made on the contentious issue of ownership of chairs! If it is held that chairs are common property then patients should be encouraged to sit in chairs in different parts of the lounge; the pros and cons of each chair could be discussed – position, view and comfort for instance; a wider field of interpersonal relationships could be encouraged so that a number of chairs would be attractive alternatives. On the other hand if 'ownership' of chairs is accepted the 'owner's' name could be attached as an indication to others that this is 'reserved'. The patients could be encouraged to practise asking others, politely, to move and being allowed to call the staff for assistance if the chair was not vacated.

A second example could be the case of an elderly man who is incontinent of urine, but who is otherwise fairly good at self-care.

His wetness cannot be ignored – some reaction is inevitable whilst his clothing is being changed. In this situation it is easy to make a critical remark which will only add to the humiliation of the whole event for the patient. The situation should be dealt with calmly in a matter-of-fact manner – so the patient is not given a lot of positive attention which might reward his being wet. The patient is prompted to get changed – as far as possible independently – and to take responsibility for the event — perhaps rinsing through the underwear, taking his trousers to the laundry room, or mopping up the puddle – as far as he is able. This does not constitute a plan for controlling incontinence and it is still necessary to train the person to visit the toilet as has previously been described. The desirable behaviour has to be established so that the problem of incontinence will decrease; the person is less likely to be incontinent if the toilet is used correctly.

It must be ensured that inappropriate behaviour is not rewarded – however unwittingly. The example of the person obtaining attention for being wet is clear, but in some situations a more subtle reward system might operate. Aggressive acts may be greeted by severe and critical responses which may prove to be rewarding enough to encourage further aggression. Even removing the aggressors to their own rooms may be rewarding for some patients; the accompanied walk, the peace and quiet of the room, the change of scene may be perceived as pleasant consequences of the aggressive act.

This area is one of great complexity and illustrates why problem behaviours can prove resistant to change. Considering the consequences for the particular event only and ignoring the totality of individual functioning can lead to errors. For any problem behaviour it is necessary to bear in mind that reactions to it may be encouraging its recurrence; in each case a consistent, humane response which minimises this should be planned.

Review of progress

Having established a plan for the individual patient consisting of targets and procedures for achieving them the task is not complete. The plan cannot be an inflexible and unchanging statute for all time; it has to change to meet the changing events that occur once it is put into action. Responses may be unexpected or even undesirable; some targets may be quickly achieved, others may take longer or show no progress at all. The next stage is to review progress and to establish fresh targets where necessary. If previous targets have been realized then more difficult ones can be set; if progress is slight then the level of difficulty must be lowered– using, perhaps, intermediate goals. Limited goals are important in all work with elderly people. The ideal aim is complete independence, but to be realistic more independence of functioning in a particular area would be a desirable improvement. Limited goals are of tremendous value; they are frequently overlooked but their occurrence indicates a positive move forward. If encouraged, they can increase self-esteem, confidence and effort on the part of the patient and have a real effect on staff morale while also releasing more time for rehabilitative work.

EXAMPLES OF INDIVIDUAL PLANS

Obviously these examples are much abbreviated, but are presented to illustrate the points outlined above.

Mrs A

This 78 year old lady was a resident in an EMI Home, (a residential home for the elderly mentally infirm). Her diagnosis was senile dementia. She reported that she felt a bit of a failure as she could not remember things and often felt useless. She liked to be kept busy and to socialise with other residents. She had a family, and previously had been a fit, active person with a warm personality. As regards her abilities, her self-care was largely independent, her mobility and dexterity good. She socialised well, making relationships with particular residents, but had difficulty in learning their names, and in recognising relatives when they visited. She knew her way around the home, but tended to get lost outside. She only rarely took part in domestic activities such as preparing food etc.

Mrs A caused no specific problems in the home. Although her memory was poor and she tended to ramble on in conversation, her behaviour only fluctuated when she suddenly became unhappy and weepy.

A tentative plan would aim to help Mrs A feel better about herself by encouraging and praising her activity and by providing support for the memory difficulties.

Plan

General	Specific
Increase domestic activity	(These are *aims* not orders) To make her bed at least two days out of three To tidy and dust her own room at least one day in three To help with laying the table once a day To help drying up after meals once a day
Increase cooking activity	To make a pot of tea daily To make a snack (e.g. sandwiches) one day in three To cook a meal one day in seven
Increase social activity outside the home	To attend an Over-60s Club once a week
Improve and support memory	To participate in daily RO sessions Pictures of relatives to be obtained for use in RO sessions To use memory aids about the home To keep a diary as a memory prop Frequency of rambling talk to be reduced from initial level

Record-keeping would indicate the degree of success in reaching the targets and what level of prompting was required – with the aim of eventually reducing prompting. Rambling talk would be the most difficult to evaluate, and would require definition of what is meant by rambling talk and in what situations it would be monitored – one method could be to count the number of times she had to be brought back to the point in a half-hour RO session.

Mrs B

Mrs B was another resident in an EMI home with the diagnosis of dementia. It was difficult to obtain a clear picture from her of exactly what she wanted. It seemed that her major goal was to be with her daughter – she had previously lived with this daughter and had been very dependent on her for physical care. The daughter's marriage had been jeopardised so she was unable to continue to care for her mother at home. Previously Mrs B had been socially very active and very much involved as an organiser in various charitable bodies.

The care staff completed a detailed behaviour rating scale which showed that toiletting and eating were normal; that she communicated well and that orientation about the home was good. Poor mobility curtailed domestic activities. She lacked confidence in walking and would desperately hang on to people and things, sometimes so fiercely that people would fall over with her. She refused to dress herself and was resistant to looking after her personal cleanliness.

The major problems the staff reported were her constant demands for somebody to come to her, her continous shouting and her resistance when being helped. Her daughter spent a great deal of time at the home and whilst there her mother persuaded her to do everything for her. The daughter was so concerned about her mother that, as she told the staff, her marriage was still under strain, despite the fact that Mrs B had been removed from the scene.

The staff felt extremely angry with Mrs B – she played one off against the other – and made them look uncaring in front of visitors. It was as though she was trying to exercise over them the same enormous power she had over her daughter.

Fluctuations were noted in Mrs B's behaviour; for some staff she would dress herself, sometimes. When not being overtly observed it was felt she walked slightly better. When her daughter was present she lost all semblance of independence in her behaviour.

Mrs B's behaviour had been labelled as 'attention seeking' and – as is so often the case with such difficult patients – staff who were genuinely caring and warm to their residents were extremely angry with her. It would have been only too easy in what had become a tense home situation to establish a punitive plan; the suffering that other residents were undergoing in being deprived of *their* rights of attention could have made this seem justified.

The plan below, however, aims at building up positive behaviour, whilst not ignoring the negative feelings of the staff which it was important to have in the open to be discussed and acknowledged.

Plan

General	Specific
Increase mobility to unaided walking in home	Brief walking practice to be given, but staff support to be gradually withdrawn
Increase social interaction	Staff to employ 'chatty' conversation when she is sitting quietly – perhaps concerning past activities Mrs B to be invited to take on organisation of small tea party with three other residents
Improve dressing to self-care level	Staff to encourage her to do a little more for herself each morning, providing lots of time, only a few

	prompts which are withdrawn as soon as possible, but praising every effort made.
Increase physical independence from daughter	Daughter to be counselled to withdraw physical care and provide attention in alternative ways
Staff to feel less angry with her	Care for Mrs B to be shared among staff – staff to be free to hand over to someone else if they feel under stress with her Staff to discuss her difficulties and her qualities and seek to understand her point of view

Notice that no specific attempt is made to stop Mrs B shouting. One might consider ignoring her shouts, but the problem with this is that even if the staff manage this consistently other residents or visitors will respond from time to time and thus spur the shouting on even more. The plan aims to meet Mrs B's needs for her daughter's attention and that of the staff by increasing her positive behaviours and providing some attention for these. Mutual staff support is important too; not all patients are easy to love and yet care staff can feel guilty if there is an inward feeling of distaste, anger or active dislike for a particular person. Open discussion of these feelings helps to see that other people can experience the same emotions and negative feelings. Together it may be possible to see beyond the problem to more likeable attributes; here a previously highly competent lady, faced with the frightening reality of failing abilities, found a way of maintaining great power by taking on a demanding, dependent and manipulative role.

Mr C

Our third example is a moderately demented male resident, also in an EMI home. He had previously been interested in music, lived alone and had been an avid reader. Socially affable, he would willingly join in group activities, although he had yet to form any real relationship with any particular residents. Mobility and eating skills were generally good but his problem was that he became completely lost in the home. Occasionally he was incontinent, at night in particular. He joined in some domestic activities but required some verbal prompting for dressing and washing.

The one problem which concerned the staff was his temper and they reported that he 'was prone to temper outbursts and some aggression'. This was usually verbal, but at least once a day a blow was struck. These incidents occurred about once a day; usually they were when staff had *told* him to do something, upon which he would become angry and impatient. Afterwards he would be a little apologetic and then act as if the incident had never happened. There was no real evidence of fluctuations in his behaviour. A preliminary plan for Mr C could include the following:

Plan

General	Specific
Develop recreational interests	Explore Mr C's previous interests – obtain some of the music or books that he likes. Draw him into daily recreational activities.
Develop home orientation: aim to achieve independent ability to find his way	Guided tour of home–pointing out his room, toilet, dining-room, lounge etc. Indicating signs on doors, using colour as a clue, special pictures and particular characteristics as memory aids. Repeat this at least twice daily, gradually asking him to do the guiding, prompting with clues only when he is uncertain.
Develop independence in dressing and washing	Give praise to each phase of these performed correctly. Ensure there is an order in laying out the clothes. Gradually fade the prompts as the sequence is learned, eventually use mime as a clue until hopefully no prompt is needed.
Develop relationships with other residents	Introduce him to other residents. Slowly and appropriately – those sitting near him in the lounge, at the table. Ask him to repeat the names when introduced.

Basic approach to Mr C. Ask and do not tell him what to do. Praise him for co-operation.

Again there is no specific resolve to deal with the problem behaviour, instead attempts are made to avoid situations in which it might occur. This is achieved by the staff consistently adopting an approach that Mr C is able to accept.

Mr D

Mr D is 68 years old, he had a mild stroke which left him with some weakness in his left hand and leg. He has recovered from this weakness very well but there are other signs which cause his wife and family some concern. The cerebro-vascular accident has affected the right tempero-parietal areas so that although his speech is unaffected he does have difficulty in finding his way about, shows evidence of dressing apraxia, and has problems with maps and spatial organisation. Sometimes he has a little difficulty with finding his way around the house. He used to have a fairly responsible job with the Gas Board, used to drive one of the vans and was required to travel around the region. He had been a member of several clubs and Sports Associations and was regarded as an outgoing person. He has insight into the changes and is becoming increasingly depressed. His wife still works and so he is alone in the house during the day except when he goes to a day centre twice a week.

Plan

General	Specific
Help recent memory	Notice board (or chalk) in kitchen – Day, Month, and Weather every morning. Important information to be remembered. Also notebook always in top pocket. Memory games – name of newsreader on TV last night, one main headline from news, also written in number of things to remember as successful. Items from paper, TV, visitors etc. Games related to interests – cards, bought games etc.
Help dressing	Clothes placed in order. Tags denoting Front, Back, Left or Right. Practice with buttons, encouragement, written instructions if necessary. Modelling, verbal instructions, as little actual help as possible in order to build routine.
Help him to find his way about	Use of three dimensional games useful – 3D noughts and crosses. Drawing maps of increasing difficulty – starting with home, then street, then shopping street. Using words as cues, i.e. names of rooms, street names, house names, any signposts, shop names and commodities. At home use colour and words to denote toilet, bedroom etc. Play games e.g. Scrabble to increase confidence. Slowly move on to shapes, house colours, postboxes, buildings etc. Routine of putting away in set place – washing up, clothes etc.
Assist depression	All successes to be noted and encouraged. Bouts of 'low' behaviour to be ignored, but alternatives to be offered – 'let's go to the club'. Interests to be encouraged, friendships used. Routine way to the club, involvement in activities outside and at home.

Guidance should be given here to all the family (grandchildren included) on the use of RO, and a booklet can be helpful here. The overall aim is to use preserved abilities in order to increase function in the more impaired areas.

In each of these four cases fairly lengthy plans have been suggested: in the real-life situation these would be likely to evolve over a period of time, with particular parts of the plan being reviewed, changed, extended, or abandoned according to circumstances. In our view, the decision-making progress outlined above should be followed through, even if the ultimate decision is to attempt no change at all to the person's functioning or their environment. In this way patients are seen as individuals, and not just as part of a large group.

CONCLUSIONS

In this chapter we have sought to go beyond RO and outline an approach seeking to produce effects in specific areas of functioning. RO may be seen as one aspect of a behavioural approach and the plans outlined above show they can mesh well together. We suspect that the behavioural principle of rewarding appropriate behaviour also plays a part in the successes of other types of general treatment programmes outlined in Chapter 2. For RO this has been demonstrated (see Chapter 3); for the other approaches it is a reasonable assumption. The behavioural approach makes explicit what is often implicit in other programmes: this must help to bring about desired changes in a more efficient manner.

The setting of specific objectives tends to simplify the process of evaluating results and the ever-growing volume of knowledge of human learning, from experimental psychology, will in years to come generate techniques to be developed to facilitate learning further.

A danger of the 'individual plan' approach is that it may focus attention on changing the individual patient's behaviour and ignore the wider context in which that behaviour occurs. The person's behaviour is always an interaction between the person and the environment and we cannot ignore this interaction.

The environment is of course made up of many parts – the physical surroundings, other patients, the staff and their behaviour. Often in our individual plans we are changing aspects of the environment e.g. by changing our response to the patient in different situations.

Whenever we come across a person with a deficit of those skills needed for independent living we need to make a decision to try to at one extreme retrain these skills, or at the other end of the spectrum, change the environment so that these skills are rendered unnecessary. Thus for a dementing person living at home who cannot care for herself any more, do we retrain cooking skills, or provide meals on wheels so that the skills will not be required? The behavioural approach in the community would seek to identify those skills that are and are not retained; only supports that are necessary should then be provided. A general package of services should not be given; it may not meet the specific needs and may in fact deny opportunity for expression of some skills that are retained. For the elderly person living alone at home it is this environmental modification that will be of prime importance as there is no one present to repeatedly reinforce appropriate behaviour. What is needed is a prosthetic environment, an environment that fills in the gaps in the person's skills and abilities. The use of memory aids is part of this, as are home helps and meals on wheels. In the not too distant future the deteriorating person's environment could be monitored by a control system so the flat is kept at an even temperature, cookers are turned off automatically if left on or if saucepans boil dry and help is alerted if the person has a fall. Those controls the person can operate would be made as simple as possible. In this way risks to those living alone could be diminished, which would allow both personal choice and relief for worries of relatives.

In all this the behavioural approach is not to be seen as a cure for dementia. Rather we are seeking to change aspects of the dementing person's behaviour, partly by training, or retraining, the person's particular skills and partly by modifying their environment. The two assumptions are that firstly dementing persons can learn a limited amount and secondly that they can respond to some extent to their environment. In as far as these assumptions are valid the behavioural approach holds much promise for the future.

11

Concluding remarks

In previous chapters we have concluded that RO does have definite effects on verbal orientation in disorientated elderly patients. We have indicated that generalisation of improvements to other areas of functioning is problematic and in the previous chapter have suggested a means whereby wider ranging changes in functioning might be achieved. We do not, however, underestimate the difficulties of working with patients with dementia where progressive deterioration forms the normal pattern. We have argued that limited goals are possible in as much as the person is influenced by the environment in which he or she is living.

However, do these methods represent any change to the existing situation? We have come across many workers who have quite honestly been able to say that they were already carrying out RO, but had never given it a name! The value of RO is that it provides a structure in which staff can be helped to follow the practices of those who have been using it – perhaps unwittingly – for years. New staff can quickly receive guidance in the approach, and there is more chance of consistency of method and of all staff being involved.

We have focussed in this book on the use of RO with patients with dementia – surely the largest, most pressing problem facing Health and Social Services. We have also tried to indicate simple treatment methods for those with specific neurological dysfunctions. We are aware of RO programmes for patients who have been hospitalised for 40 years or more (usually with a diagnosis of chronic schizophrenia) with some success – indeed some of the American studies have been concerned mainly with this type of chronic population. Elderly people with depression as a component of their problems have also been suggested as benefiting from RO. In both cases it must be emphasised that RO should be considered alongside other treatment approaches. For example, with chronic psychiatric patients token economies have proved helpful, even where elderly people have been included. The RO approach – used flexibly – may provide useful stimulation and encourage interest in the person's surroundings in both the chronic long-stay and with some depressed patients, provided the level is appropriate. There is interest in the application of RO principles in areas such as rehabilitation following head injury as well as with elderly mentally handicapped. Once again there are other approaches and as yet there has been no research to evaluate RO in these settings.

With elderly people whose decision-making capacity is impaired for one reason or another it is important to make explicit the ethical issues involved as they form such a vulnerable group, perhaps unable to assert their rights and needs in a conventional manner. We are often asked if RO is harmful (see Chapter 9); whether in fact it treats patients like children; whether the person who is 'happily demented' should be 'disturbed' by being brought back to reality; whether it would be kinder to leave such people in their twilight world and not expose them to the reality of old age, infirmity, an unsatisfactory environment and so forth.

These and similar questions raise the important issue of the ethics of RO and other psychological approaches to people with dementia. Often these issues arouse a great deal of emotion, perhaps as those working with the elderly imagine themselves in the position of the dementing person, a fantasy that most people would find threatening and disturbing. Some people favour a passive approach, providing for physical needs until death occurs, keeping the person 'happy' by ensuring a 'no demand' situation. Others opt for a more positive, active approach encouraging awareness and independence. The ethical issues are complex. In some areas of behavioural intervention it is possible to arrive at an agreed treatment contract with the client, acceptable to both parties. This is extremely difficult – if not impossible – with the severely demented person. Thus there is a need for those working with this group to be clear about their own ethical position as a dementing person may not be capable of making a fully informed decision about treatment.

We will try to make clear the assumptions that we make as we outline the reasons for our preference for the positive approach.

Firstly, it must be emphasised that whether we do RO or not we are intervening in some way. Not doing anything with a patient still represents some kind of programme, ill defined as it may be. The advantage of RO is that it makes explicit what is being attempted and makes it more difficult to shirk responsibility and avoid ethical problems. This is of added importance as those with dementia are a particularly vulnerable group who are less likely to be able to use conventional means of self-protection.

Secondly, we see patients with dementia as people, with basic human needs – both physical and emotional. In our view attempts to meet both sorts of needs are the responsibility of those in the caring role. Emotional needs are more difficult to meet, but should not be ignored on this account. Thus elderly people who are deteriorating need to feel cared for and permitted to have opportunities to express care for others. We recognise that these needs may find expression in more restricted ways than in the non-dementing person, of course. In so far as RO aids communication and encourages self-respect then we would see it as helping in the satisfaction of these emotional needs.

Thirdly, we would draw a parallel with other disabilities, where increasingly the principle of 'normalisation' is being applied. This approach seeks to help a person lead as normal a life as possible, given the disability that is present. Thus a physically disabled person would work at a conventional job, despite being confined to a wheelchair; he might drive to work in a specially adapted (but otherwise conventional) car and live in an ordinary (but adapted) house. This is in contrast to a person living in an institution with other physically disabled people, driving an invalid carriage and working in a workshop for the disabled. Similarly mentally handicapped people are increasingly integrated into 'normal' society, rather than being placed out of sight and out of mind in a large country hospital.

We saw in Chapter 1 that 'normal' for elderly people is largely a continuation of previous patterns of living. If we apply this to the dementing person the implication is that independence in self-care should be encouraged. Previous activities and interests, social, recreational, domestic, occupational, etc., adapted where necessary, should be facilitated. Adaptations to the person's living arrangements so that previous life-styles can be continued are entailed.

It is, of course, quality of life that is the prime concern. This rather nebulous concept in this context could be assessed by the extent to which the person's life-style can continue despite the dementia, memory difficulties and so on. If this seems a far cry from the average long-stay ward, the normalisation principle does have its implications there also. Personalised, rather than shared, clothing; choice of food from a menu; space for personal possessions; choice of activities and so on all help to form the fabric of a 'normal' existence. Once more RO and the attitudes underlying it can be seen as part of the attempt to help the dementing person function in as normal a manner as possible.

To return to the original question of the 'happily' dementing person, it is difficult to judge to what extent this state *does* represent a high quality of life; this could be yet another assumption on the part of the onlooker as the people concerned are not capable of expressing their feelings and attitudes coherently. Indeed the situation may be a means of coping with the failures and difficulties of the dementing process. There may even be a sense in which, by withdrawing in this fashion, the person is missing out to some degree. What we would advocate is to provide opportunities to return to reality, and also to provide a choice. To force the issue is not acceptable, but to nurture and encourage still leaves the options open. In the final analysis elderly people will shut off the stimulation or will respond to it. Unfortunately they are not given the choice often enough and it is assumed that they would rather remain lost in fantasy. We have tried to make it clear that our approach is tactful, flexible and warm rather than pressurised and aggressive. There are dangers with RO and like approaches with the wrong attitudes; there is a need for discussion of ethical issues and monitoring of programmes by those outside the institution as well as those actively involved. Regrettably, advocates for the rights of the dementing elderly and their supporters are rare; discussion often centres on placement rather than on management and treatment.

The aspects of RO that work with the supporter and the nurse, the care attendant or relative should be considered. Here the ethical situation is simpler; staff members and relatives can make an informed decision about whether RO helps them in caring and communication with the elderly person.

A large component of these programmes is in changing the environment rather than necessarily inducing change in the individual. Again some sort of environment has to be provided: the issue is what the nature of this should be. We concur with Hanley (1980) in that the environment that RO provides with its emphasis on basic humanitarian values of respect, dignity and interaction is an improvement – psychologically – over many current settings. Although changes produced may not be of dramatic clinical significance, generally, there are arguments for utilising RO as a communication method to increase the person's quality of life by improving interaction with the staff. We would also argue that only by continuing to develop the approach – which remains relatively under-researched and conceptualised – can it be improved so that clinically important changes may occur more often. This applies particularly to 24 hour RO which raises difficult issues as to how it can, in fact, be successfully implemented and monitored.

Is it worth doing RO with a person when transfer to a setting in which RO is not in operation is intended? Again a quality of life consideration applies; if this can be increased in the present then it can be seen as valuable, whatever might or might not happen in the future. Ideally approaches would be consistent between different hospitals and old people's homes etc. – but for the moment this is nothing more than a pipe dream. Certainly if improvements are to be maintained continuing support is necessary, but it may be that this can be less intensive in some cases. Volunteers, suitably trained and with a good knowledge of RO methods, have an important part to play in this.

Used with the correct attitudes we consider that RO does have an ethical, humanitarian basis; it is indicated in Chapter 9 that abuses are possible, but we feel that where RO is used selectively and explicitly in settings that are open to external monitoring these can be guarded against.

It has been indicated – practically – how it may be possible to go beyond RO. Further work is necessary to design appropriate prosthetic environments for the confused elderly, for environments that aid rather than hinder orientation. Fundamental research on the nature of psychological functioning in dementia and related conditions is also required, to aid in the further rational development of programmes. Above all a positive approach combined with efforts to critically evaluate the effectiveness of these psychological programmes and their component parts is required if real progress is to be made in this field.

RO is exceedingly simple in concept; in practice there are many difficulties and obstacles to its successful implementation; there are many questions which remain to be fully answered. To be an RO therapist demands no formal qualification; all who care for the elderly can be involved, but to do so they need support. These programmes are hard work, require considerable imagination, the ability to keep things going, to forget about oneself, to plan, to remember, and even a willingness to make a fool of oneself if it achieves the aim! Yet many staff who have used the approach find it extremely satisfying as at last they communicate and make personal contact with the elderly person who has appeared so confused and disorientated.

Appendix 1:

TEST OF VERBAL ORIENTATION AND PERSONAL AND CURRENT INFORMATION

Instructions – ask questions conversationally, varying the exact words used as appropriate to ensure the person understands what is being asked; scoring may be lenient, but no help in giving answers may be offered.

1 What is your name?		0 1
2 How old are you?		0 1
3 When were you born?	All correct	0 1
	Date correct	0 1
	Month correct	0 1
	Year correct	0 1
4 Where were you born?		0 1
5 What school did you attend?		0 1
6 What was your occupation (or spouse's)?		0 1
7 Where did you (or spouse) work – which town?		0 1
8 Name of employers for whom you worked?		0 1
9 Name of spouse or sibling?		0 1

10 What is the name of this place?		0	1
11 What type of place is it? i.e. hospital, old people's home etc.		0	1
12 What is the address of this place? i.e. approximate location.		0	1
13 What is the name of this town/city?		0	1
14 What time of day is it now – morning, afternoon, evening etc.?		0	1
15 What time is it now? (accept answer if within 30 minutes of actual time.)		0	1
16 What day of the week is it today?		0	1
17 What season is it now – spring, summer, autumn, winter?		0	1
18 What month is it now?		0	1
19 What day of the month is it now?		0	1
20 What year is it now?		0	1
21 Recognition of persons (cleaner, doctor, staff-member, resident, relative – any two available) 1 point for each person.		0	1	2
22 Who is the prime minister at present?		0	1
23 Who was the prime minister immediately before this one?		0	1
24 Who is the president of the USA at present?		0	1
25 Who is on the throne at present?	1 point for name	0	1	2
26 Who was on the throne immediately before them?	1 point for number	0	1	2
27 What are the colours of the Union Jack?		0	1
28 When did the First World War begin, and end?	1 point for each allow 2 years error	0	1	2
29 When did the Second World War begin, and end?		0	1	2

30 Repeat this name and
address after me:
/Mr John/Brown/   0 1 2 3 4 5
42/West Street/Gateshead/
Ask for recall after five minutes; score 1
point for each segment recalled correctly.
Modify address to suit locality!

Total-score   (42 maximum)

As used in Woods' (1979) study.

Appendix 2:

CONCENTRATION TEST

Instructions – explain carefully what is required; prompt patient with first 2/3 items of each sequence; record time taken from the patient starting the task; record the number of errors made; discount errors the patient spontaneously corrects.

1. Count from 1–20 as fast as you can; 1..2..3.. off you go!
1 2 3 4 5 6 7 8 9 10 11 12 13 14 15 16 17 18 19 20
Time:
Errors:

3– all correct; 10 secs or less
2– all correct; 11–30 secs
1– one error; 30 secs or less
0– two or more errors, or more than 30 secs

2. Now count from 20 all the way down to 1 as fast as you can. 20..19..18.. off you go!
20 19 18 17 16 15 14 13 12 11 10 9 8 7 6 5 4 3 2 1
Time:
Errors:

3– all correct; 10 secs or less
2– all correct; 11–30 secs
1– one error; 30 secs or less
0– two or more errors or more than 30 secs

3. Now say the alphabet for me as quickly as you can; A..B..C.. start now!
A B C D E F G H I J K L M N O P Q R S T U V W X Y Z
Time:
Errors:

3— all correct; 10 secs or less
2— all correct; 11–30 secs
1— one error; 30 secs or less
0— two or more errors or more than 30 secs

4. Now the months of the year – going backwards from December to January; December, November, October....
Dec Nov Oct Sept Aug Jul Jun May Apr Mar Feb Jan.
Errors:

2— no errors
1— one or two errors
0— three or more errors

5. Now count again, starting at 1 and adding 3 each time; like this: 1..4..7.. now you try!
1 4 7 10 13 16 19 22 25 28 31 34 37 40.
Time:
Errors:

3— all correct; 20 secs or less
2— all correct; 21–45 secs
1— one error; 45 secs or less
0— two or more errors, or more than 45 secs

Total Score ———— (14 maximum)

This test was used in Woods' (1979) study of RO, in conjunction with a reading and writing test from the Clifton Assessment Procedure for the Elderly.

HOLDEN COMMUNICATION SCALE

Score:	0	1	2	3	4
Conversation					
1. Response:	Initiates conversation, deeply involved with anyone	Good for those familiar to him/her	Fair response to those close by. No initiation of conversation	Rather confused Poor comprehension	Rarely or never converses
2. Interest in past events:	Long full account of past events	Fairly good description	Short. Description a little confused	Confused or disinterested	No response
3. Pleasure:	Shows real pleasure in situation/ achievement	Smiles and shows interest	Variable response, slight smile, vague	Rarely shows even a smile	No response or just weeps
4. Humour:	Creates situation or tells funny story on own initiative	Enjoys comic situations or stories	Needs an explanation and encouragement to respond	Vague smile, simply copies others	No response or negativistic
Awareness and knowledge					
5. Names:	Knows most people's names on ward	Knows a few names	Needs a constant reminder	Knows own name only	Forgotten even own name
6. General orientation:	Knows day, month, weather, time and whereabouts	Can forget one or two items	Usually gets two right but tries	Vague, may guess one	Very confused
7. General knowledge:	Good on current events, generally able	Outstanding events only Fair on general knowledge	No current knowledge Poor general information	Confused about many things Gets anxious and upset	Confused about everything Does not respond
8. Ability to join in Game etc:	Joins in games and activities with ease	Requires careful instructions but joins in	Can only join in simple activities	Becomes anxious and upset	Cannot or will not join in

Score	0	1	2	3	4
Communication					
9. Speech:	No known difficulty	Slight hesitation or odd wording	Very few words, mainly automatic phrases	Inappropriate words, odd sounds. Nodding	Little or no verbalization
10. Attempts at communication:	Communicates with ease	Tries hard to speak clearly	Tries to draw – gesticulates needs etc.	Euphoric laughter, weeping, aggressive	No attempt
11. Interest and response to objects:	Responds with interest and comment	Despite difficulties, shows interest	Shows some interest, but rather vague	Weeps, rejects objects, shows aggression	No response No comprehension
12. Success in communication:	Clearly understood	Uses gestures and sounds effectively	Understanding restricted to a few people	Becomes frustrated and angry	Makes no attempt

Appendix 4:

A POSSIBLE PROGRAMME FOR THE STANDARD GROUP LEVEL
Two Month Schedule of suggestions – in addition to Basic Information. Notes should be kept on each session for continuity and progress.

First Week	*General Personal Information*
Day 1	Introductions. A little about each person – where each one is from. Discussion of Day, Month and Weather.
Day 2	Occupations. What are their interests. Other members of the family. Care should be taken in ensuring that everyone hears about their fellow group members.
Day 3	Using the interests and/or the occupations of the group, discuss.
Day 4 and 5	Previous planning will provide relevant equipment. If sessions continue through the weekend – use an extension of one of the best sessions during the week.
Second Week	*Way of Life*
Day 1	War experience. Use of gas/electric for light. Possible use of candles and oil lamps. Talk about experiences of this.

Day 2	Follow on from above. Prices then and now. Different commodities available, shopping. Use old newspaper advertisements, modern adverts. Money, pictures and 'antiques'.
Day 3	Pick on popular current topic. Compare with similar topic years ago. Relevant material – papers, old books e.g. old souvenirs, new ones.
Day 4	Travel and holidays. Use maps, travel brochures, post-cards then and now. Talk about free time from work. Costs. Transport. Boarding houses, hotels, caravans and camping. Changes.
Day 5	Evening entertainment. The family. What was it like without TV. The first radio. Weekends, special outings. Bank holidays. Sport, active or passive. Use old cigarette cards, Radio Times, holiday adverts. Did they drive, own a car or a bicycle. What special transport did they use and enjoy – models.

Third Week	*Using the senses*
Day 1	Smell. Use box of smells, fresh fruit and flowers. Food smells – spices, herbs, onions, yeast, coffee. Those without smell – ask them to recall the smell of wood shavings, burning wood, cooking, oils, and chemicals. Farmer – haymaking, cows, pig manure, fertilizer. Builders – the smell of damp.
Day 2	Sight. Shapes, colours, recognising faces. Reading, writing, watching TV. Getting clues for what is going to happen next. The dinner trolley arriving, the curtains being drawn, a bus conductor standing beside you. Appreciation of paintings, costume, design, lovely clothes and furniture.
Day 3	Touch and feel. Different cloth. Hot and cold. Rough and smooth. Hard and soft. Dry and wet. How to tell if goods are ripe or rotten. If materials are going to be warm or cool. If a piece of wood is ready for French polishing.
Day 4	Taste. Sweet and sour. Hot and cold. Nasty and nice. Use sweets, fruit, drinks and medicines. Likes and dislikes.

Day 5	Memory games using all the senses.
Weekend	Once again repeat the more successful sessions and enlarge upon the topics.

Fourth Week Notes can be consulted so that popular topics can be reintroduced and expanded. Other ideas based on interests that have emerged during the sessions can be employed. Outings and films are other approaches. A start could be made on self-help and care. Plans for tomorrow can be made with group discussion. Personal experiences, arguments about religion, politics and the 'difference' between the sexes are valuable. Discussions on Art, places, other countries and other cultures. Training them to do more for themselves.

Month 2 It is necessary to find out what each person can do for him/herself. What they could do for others. Outings – what they would like and enjoy – perhaps to parts of town under development, where they used to live, to be followed by a discussion of changes. What way would they like their lives to change or improve, what they could do for themselves. Discussions of history, politics, people and changes they have seen. Active suggestions about what they would like to do, or could do. Something half-learned that they would like to master. Therapists to set achievable targets and to make sure of success. Always keeping in mind the fact that aims must be realistic.

Regular planning sessions for the staff are needed. Preparations should be made before and after the sessions. Assessments of progress are needed. Help and materials from all sources can be sought.

References

Adams J, Davies J E, Northwood J 1979 Ridge Hill – a home, not a ward. Nursing Times 75: 1659–1661, 1725–1726, 1769–1770

Albert M L, Sparks R W, Helm N 1973 Melodic intonation therapy for aphasia. Archives of Neurology 29: 130–131

Ankus M, Quarrington B 1972 Operant behaviour in the memory disordered. Journal of Gerontology 27: 500–510

APA Task Force on Aging 1973 Recommendations to the White House conference on aging. In: Eisdorfer C, Lawton M P (eds) The psychology of adult development and aging. American Psychological Association, Washington DC, p ix

Atthowe J M 1972 Controlling nocturnal enuresis in severely disabled and chronic patients. Behaviour Therapy 3: 232–239

Baltes M M, Barton C M 1977 New approaches toward aging: a case for the operant model. Educational Gerontology 2: 383–405

Baltes M M, Lascomb S L 1975 Creating a healthy institutional environment: the nurse as a change agent. International Journal of Nursing Studies 12: 5–12

Baltes M M, Zerbe M B 1976a Re-establishing self-feeding in a nursing home resident. Nursing Research 25: 24–26

Baltes M M, Zerbe M B 1976b Independence training in nursing-home residents. Gerontologist 16: 428–432

Barnes J A 1974 Effects of reality orientation classroom on memory loss, confusion and disorientation in geriatric patients. Gerontologist 14: 138–142

Barns E K, Sack A, Shore H 1973 Guidelines to treatment approaches: modalities and methods for use with the aged. Gerontologist 13: 513–527

Barry A J, Steinmetz J R. Page H F, Rodahl K 1966 The effects of physical conditioning on older individuals. II – Motor performance and cognitive function. Journal of Gerontology 21: 192–199

Bayne J R D 1971 Environment modification for the older person. Gerontologist 11: 314–317

Benson D F 1979 Aphasia, alexia and agraphia. Churchill Livingstone, New York

Berger R M, Rose S D 1977 Interpersonal skill training with institutionalized elderly patients. Journal of Gerontology 32: 346–353

Bergert L, Jacobsson E 1976 Training of reality orientation with a group of patients with senile dementia. Scandinavian Journal of Behaviour Therapy 5: 191–200

Bergmann K, Foster E M, Justice A W, Matthews V 1978 Management of the demented elderly patient in the community. British Journal of Psychiatry 132: 441–449

Birkett D P, Boltuch B 1973 Remotivation therapy. Journal of the American Geriatrics Society 21: 368–371

Birren J E, Schaie K W (eds) 1977 Handbook of the psychology of aging. Van Nostrand Reinhold, New York

Blackman D K, Howe M, Pinkston E M 1976 Increasing participation in social interaction of the institutionalized elderly. Gerontologist 16: 69–76

Blessed G, Tomlinson B E, Roth M 1968 The association between quantitative measures of dementia and of senile change in the cerebral grey matter of elderly subjects. British Journal of Psychiatry 114: 797–811

Blundell J 1975 Physiological psychology. Essential psychology series. Methuen, London

Bodamer J 1947 Die prosop-agnosie. Archive Fuer Psyiatrie und Nervenkrankheiten Vereinigt Mit Zietschrift Fuer Gesamte Neurologie und Psychiatrie 179: 6–53

Bok M 1971 Some problems in milieu treatment of the chronic older mental patient. Gerontologist 11: 141–147

Botwinick J 1977 Intellectual abilities. In: Birren J E, Schaie K W (eds) Handbook of the psychology of aging. Van Nostrand Reinhold, New York

Botwinick J, Storandt M 1980 Recall and recognition of old information in relation to age and sex. Journal of Gerontology 35: 70–76

Bowen D M, Davison A N 1978 Biochemical changes in normal ageing and dementia. In: Isaacs B (ed) Recent advances in geriatric medicine. Churchill Livingstone, Edinburgh

Bowen D M, Davison A N 1980 Biochemical changes in the cholinergic system of the ageing brain and in senile dementia. Psychological Medicine 10: 315–319

Bower H M 1967 Sensory stimulation and the treatment of senile dementia. Medical Journal of Australia 1: 1113–1119

Bowers M B, Anderson G K, Blomeier E C, Pelz K 1967 Brain syndrome and behaviour in geriatric remotivation groups. Journal of Gerontology 22: 348–352

Broadbent D E 1958 Perception and communication. Pergamon, London

Brody E M, Cole C, Moss M 1973 Individualizing therapy for the mentally impaired aged. Social Casework (October): 453–461

Brody E M, Kleban M H, Lawton M P, Silverman H A 1971 Excess disabilities of mentally impaired aged: impact of individualized treatment. Gerontologist 11: 124–133

Brody E M, Kleban M H, Lawton M P, Moss M 1974 A longitudinal look at excess disabilities in the mentally impaired aged. Journal of Gerontology 29: 79–84

Bromley D B 1978 Approaches to the study of personality changes in adult life and old age. In: Isaacs A D, Post F (eds) Studies in geriatric psychiatry. J Wiley, Chichester

Brook P, Degun G, Mather M 1975 Reality orientation, a therapy for psychogeriatric patients: a controlled study. British Journal of Psychiatry 127: 42–45

Bunck T J, Iwata B A 1978 Increasing senior citizen participation in a community-based nutritious meal programme. Journal of Applied Behaviour Analysis 11: 75–86

Burnside I M 1971 Long-term group work with hospitalized aged. Gerontologist 11: 213–218

Burton M, Spall R 1981 Contributions of the behavioural approach to nursing the elderly. Nursing Times 77 (6): 247–248

Cameron D E 1941 Studies in senile nocturnal delirium. Psychiatric Quarterly 15: 47–53

Cautela J R 1966 Behaviour therapy and geriatrics. Journal of Genetic Psychology 108: 9–17

Cautela J R 1969 A classical conditioning approach to the development and modification of behaviour in the aged. Gerontologist 9: 109–113

Chien C P 1971 Psychiatric treatment for geriatric patients: 'pub' or drug? American Journal of Psychiatry 127 (8): 1070–1075

Christensen A L 1975 Luria's neuropsychological investigation. Munksgaard, Copenhagen

Citrin R S, Dixon D N 1977 Reality orientation: a milieu therapy used in an institution for the aged. Gerontologist 17: 39–43

Cluff P J, Campbell W H 1975 The social corridor: an environmental and behavioural evaluation. Gerontologist 15: 516–523

Collins R W, Plaska T 1975 Mowrer's conditioning treatment for enuresis applied to geriatric residents of a nursing home. Behaviour Therapy 6: 632–638

Conroy C 1977 Reality orientation: a basic rehabilitation technique for patients suffering from memory loss and confusion. British Journal of Occupational Therapy 40: 250–251

Constantinidis J, Richard J, de Ajuriaguerra J 1978 Dementias with senile plaques and neurofibrillary changes. In: Isaacs A D, Post F (eds) Studies in geriatric psychiatry. J Wiley, Chichester

Copeland J R M 1978 Evaluation of diagnostic methods. In: Isaacs A D, Post F (eds) Studies in geriatric psychiatry. J Wiley, Chichester

Cornbleth T 1977 Effects of a protected hospital ward area on wandering and non-wandering geriatric patients. Journal of Gerontology 32: 573–577

Cornbleth T 1978 Evaluation of goal attainment in geriatric settings. Journal of American Geriatrics Society 26: 404–407

Cornbleth T, Cornbleth C 1977 Reality orientation for the elderly. Journal supplement abstract service of the American Psychological Association MS 1539

Cornbleth T, Cornbleth C 1979 Evaluation of the effectiveness of reality orientation classes in a nursing home unit. Journal of American Geriatrics Society 27: 522–524

Corso J F 1967 The experimental psychology of sensory behaviour. Holt, Rinehart and Winston, New York

Cosin L Z, Mort M, Post F, Westropp C, Williams M 1958 Experimental treatment of persistent senile confusion. International Journal of Social Psychiatry 4: 24–42

Craik F I M 1977 Age differences in human memory. In: Birren J E, Schaie K W (eds) Handbook of the psychology of aging. Van Nostrand Reinhold, New York

Cumming E, Henry W E 1961 Growing old, process of disengagement. Basic Books, New York

Degun G 1976 Reality orientation: a multidisciplinary therapeutic approach. Nursing Times 72: 117–120

Diesfeldt H F A, Diesfeldt–Groenendijk H 1977 Improving cognitive performance in psychogeriatric patients: the influence of physical exercise. Age and Ageing 6: 58–64

Dimond S 1972 The double brain. Williams and Wilkins, Baltimore

Donahue W 1962 A brief report on the rehabilitation of long-term aged patients. In: Tibbitts C, Donahue W (eds) Social and psychological aspects of aging. Columbia University Press, New York

Drummond L, Kirchoff L, Scarbrough D R 1978 A practical guide to reality orientation: a treatment approach for confusion and disorientation. Gerontologist 18: 568–573

Eaton Griffith V 1975 Volunteer scheme for dysphasia and allied problems in stroke patients. British Medical Journal 3: 633–635

Eisdorfer C, Wilkie F 1977 Stress, disease, aging and behaviour. In: Birren J E, Schaie K W (eds) Handbook of the psychology of aging. Van Nostrand Reinhold, New York

Filer R N, O'Connell D D 1964 Motivation of ageing persons in an institutional setting. Journal of Gerontology 19: 15–22

Fine W 1972 Geriatric ergonomics. Gerontologia Clinica 14: 322–332

Finger S, Walbran B, Stein D G 1973 Brain damage and behavioural recovery: serial lesion phenomena. Brain Research 63: 1–18

Fishback D B 1977 Mental status questionnaire for organic brain syndrome, with a new visual counting test. Journal of American Geriatrics Society 25: 167–170

Folsom J C 1967 Intensive hospital therapy of geriatric patients. Current Psychiatric Therapies 7: 209–215

Folsom J C 1968 Reality orientation for the elderly mental patient. Journal of Geriatric Psychiatry 1: 291–307

Foxx R M, Azrin N H 1973 Toilet training the retarded. Research Press, Champaign, Illinois

Galliard P 1978 Difficulties encountered in attempting to increase social interaction amongst geriatric psychiatry patients: clean and sitting quietly. Paper presented at British Psychological Society Annual Conference, York

Garside R F, Kay D W K, Roth M 1965 Old age mental disorders in Newcastle–upon–Tyne Part III – factorial study of medical, psychiatric and social characteristics. British Journal of Psychiatry 111: 939–946

Gazzaniga M S 1970 The bisected brain. Appleton–Century–Crofts, New York

Gazzaniga M S 1974 Determinants of cerebral recovery. In: Stein D G (ed) Plasticity and recovery of function in the CNS. Academic Press, New York

Gazzaniga M S, Glass A V, Premack D 1972 Artificial language training in aphasics. Neuropsychologia 11: 95–103

Gazzaniga M S, Velletri A S, Premack D 1971 Language training in brain-damaged humans. Fed. Proc. Abstract 30 (2): 265

Geiger O G, Johnson L A 1974 Positive education for elderly persons — correct eating through reinforcement. Gerontologist 14: 432–436

Gilleard C J, Pattie A H 1977 The Stockton geriatric rating scale: a shortened version with British normative data. British Journal of Psychiatry 131: 90–94

Gilleard C J, Pattie A H 1980 Dimensions of disability in the elderly: construct validity of rating scales for elderly populations. Paper presented at British Psychological Society Annual Conference, Aberdeen

Ginsberg R 1953 Attitude therapy in geriatric ward psychiatry. Journal of American Geriatrics Society III

Goga J A, Hambacher W O 1977 Psychologic and behavioural assessment of geriatric patients: a review. Journal of American Geriatrics Society 25: 232–237

Goldstein A 1973 Structured learning therapy. Academic Press, New York

Goldstein K 1939 The organism. American Book Publishers, New York

Goldstein R S, Baer D M 1976 RSVP: a procedure to increase the personal mail and number of correspondents for nursing home residents. Behaviour Therapy 7: 348–354

Gottesman L E 1969 Extended care of the aged: psychosocial aspects. Journal of Geriatric Psychiatry 2: 220–237

Gottesman L E 1973 Milieu treatment of the aged in institutions. Gerontologist 13: 23–26

Gray P, Stevenson J S 1980 Changes in verbal interaction among members of resocialisation groups. Journal of Gerontological Nursing 6: 86–90

Greene J G, Nicol R, Jamieson H 1979 Reality orientation with psychogeriatric patients. Behaviour Research and Therapy 17: 615–617

Greene J G, Smith R, Gardiner M 1980 Reality orientation with psychogeriatric day hospital patients – an empirical evaluation. Paper presented at British Gerontological Society Annual Conference, Aberdeen

Grosicki J P 1968 Effects of operant conditioning of modification of incontinence in neuropsychiatric geriatric patients. Nursing Research 17: 304–311

Gubrium J F, Ksander M 1975 On multiple realities and reality orientation. Gerontologist 15: 142–145

Gupta H 1979 Group living in residential homes for elderly people in Northamptonshire. In: Positive approaches to mental infirmity in elderly people. MIND Annual Conference, London

Gurel L, Linn M W, Linn B S 1972 Physical and mental impairment of function evaluation in the aged: the PAMIE Scale. Journal of Gerontology 27: 83–90

Gustafsson R 1976 Milieu therapy in a ward for patients with senile dementia. Scandinavian Journal of Behaviour Therapy 5: 27–39

Hahn K 1980 Using 24 hour reality orientation. Journal of Gerontological Nursing 6 (3): 130–135

Halberstam J L, Zaretsky H H 1969 Learning capacities of elderly and brain-damaged. Archives of Physical Medicine 50: 133–139

Halberstam J L, Zaretsky H H, Brucker B S, Guttman A R 1971 Avoidance conditioning of motor responses in elderly brain damaged patients. Archives of Physical Medicine and Rehabilitation 52: 318–336

Hall J N 1980 Ward rating scales for long-stay patients: a review. Psychological Medicine 10: 277–288

Hanley I G 1980 Optimism or pessimism: an examination of reality orientation procedures in the management of dementia. Paper presented at the British Psychological Society Annual Conference, Aberdeen

Hanley I G, McGuire R J, Boyd W D 1981 Reality orientation and dementia: a controlled trial of two approaches. British Journal of Psychiatry 138: 10–14

Harris C S, Ivory P B C B 1976 An outcome evaluation of reality orientation therapy with geriatric patients in a state mental hospital. Gerontologist 16: 496–503

Harris H, Lipman A, Slater R 1977 Architectural design: the spatial location and interactions of old people. Gerontology 23: 390–400

Harris S L, Snyder B D, Snyder R L, McGraw B 1977 Behaviour modification therapy with elderly demented patients: implementation and ethical considerations. Journal of Chronic Diseases 30: 129–134

Hartie A, Black D 1975 A dry bed is the objective. Nursing Times 71: 1874–1876

Harvey T, Kinsman R 1981 Reminiscence. (Submitted for publication)

Havighurst R, Neugarten B L, Tobin S S 1968 Disengagement and patterns of aging. In: Neugarten B L (ed) Middle age and aging: a reader in psychology. University of Chicago Press, Chicago

Hécaen H, Albert M L 1978 Human neuropsychology. John Wiley & Sons, New York.

Hécaen H, Assal G 1970 A comparison of construction deficits following right and left hemispheric lesions. Neuropsychologia 8: 289–304

Hécaen H, de Ajuriaguerra J 1942–1945 L'apraxie de l'habillage, ses rapports avec la planotpokmesie et les troubles de la somatognosie, p 113–114

Hefferin E A, Hunter R E 1977 Reality orientation: how we turned the idea into a program. Nursing 7: 89–94

Hoedt–Rasmussen R, Skinhoj E 1964 Transneuronal depression of the cerebral hemispheric metabolism in man. Acta neurologica scandinavica 40: 41–46

Holden U P 1979a Return to reality. Nursing Mirror 149(21): 26–30

Holden U P 1979b A flexible technique for rehabilitating the confused. Geriatric Medicine 9(7): 49–50

Holden U P, Sinebruchow A 1978 Reality orientation therapy: a study investigating the value of this therapy in the rehabilitation of elderly people. Age and Ageing 7: 83–90

Holden U P, Sinebruchow A 1979 Validation of reality orientation therapy for use with the elderly. Unpublished manuscript

Hoyer W J 1973 Application of operant techniques to the modification of elderly behaviour. Gerontologist 13: 18–22

Hoyer W J, Kafer R A, Simpson S C, Hoyer F W 1974 Reinstatement of verbal behaviour in elderly mental patients using operant procedures. Gerontologist 14: 149–152

Hoyer W J, Labouvie G V, Baltes P B 1973 Modification of response speed deficits and intellectual performance in the elderly. Human Development 16: 233–242

Hoyer W J, Lopez M A, Goldstein A P 1980 Correlates of social skills acquisition and transfer by elderly inpatients. Unpublished manuscript

Hoyer W J, Mishara B L, Riebel R G 1975 Problem behaviours as operants: applications with elderly individuals. Gerontologist 15: 452–456

Hutt S J, Hutt C 1970 Direct observation and measurement of behaviour. Thomas, Springfield, Illinois

Inglis J 1962 Psychological practices in geriatric problems. Journal of Mental Science 108: 669–674

Jacoby R I, Levy R 1980 Computed tomography in the elderly. 2. Senile dementia: diagnosis and functional impairment. British Journal of Psychiatry 136: 256–259

Jenkins J, Felce D, Lunt B, Powell E 1977 Increasing engagement in activity of residents in old people's homes by providing recreational materials. Behaviour Research and Therapy 15: 429–434

Johnson C H 1979 Reality orientation: an evaluative study. Dissertation for British Psychological Society Diploma in Clinical Psychology.

Jones G H, Adam J H 1979 Towards a prosthetic memory. Bulletin of the British Psychological Society 32: 165–167

Kahn R L, Goldfarb A I, Pollack M, Peck A 1960 Brief objective measures for the determination of mental status in the aged. American Journal of Psychiatry 117: 326–328

Kanfer F H, Goldstein A P 1975 Helping people change. A textbook of methods. Pergamon Press, Oxford

Katz M M 1976 Behavioural change in the chronicity pattern of dementia in the institutional geriatric resident. Journal of the American Geriatrics Society 24: 522–528

Kay D W K, Beamish P, Roth M 1964 Old age mental disorder in Newcastle–upon–Tyne. Part I – a study of prevalence. British Journal of Psychiatry 110: 146–158

Kazdin A E 1975 Behaviour modification in applied settings. Homewood, Dorsey Press, Illinois

Kear Colwell J J 1973 The structure of the Wechsler Memory Scale and its relationship to 'brain damage'. British Journal of Social and Clinical Psychology 12: 384–392

Kempinsky W H 1958 Experimental study of distant effects of acute focal brain injury. Archives of Neurology and Psychiatry 79: 376–389

Kendrick D C, Gibson A J, Moyes I C A 1979 The revised Kendrick Battery: clinical studies. British Journal of Social and Clinical Psychology 18: 329–340

Kiernat J M 1979 The use of life review activity with confused nursing home residents. American Journal of Occupational Therapy 33: 306–310

King M R 1980 Treatment of incontinence. Nursing Times 76 (June 5): 1006–1010

Kleist K 1922 In: Schjernings O (ed) Handbuch der argblichen erfahrungen. Barth, Leipzig

Kochansky G E 1979 Psychiatric rating scales for assessing psychopathology in the elderly: a critical review. In: Raskin A, Jarvik L (eds) Psychiatric symptoms and cognitive loss in the elderly. Hemisphere Publishing Corporation, Washington

Kuriansky J, Gurland B 1976 The performance test of activities of daily living. International Journal of Aging and Human Development 7: 343–352

Kuriansky J, Gurland B, Cowan D 1976 The usefulness of a psychological test battery. International Journal of Aging and Human Development 7: 331–342

Labouvie G V 1973 Implications of geropsychological theories for intervention: the challenge for the seventies. Gerontologist 13: 10–14

Langer E J, Rodin J 1976 The effects of choice and enhanced personal responsibility for the aged: a field experiment in an institutional setting. Journal of Personality and Social Psychology 34: 191–198

Langley G E, Corder J M 1978 Workshop on the contribution of reminiscence theatre to reminiscence therapy with the elderly. Report on conference at Exe Vale Hospital, Exeter

Lawton M P 1970 Institutions for the aged: theory, content and methods of research. Gerontologist 10: 305–312

Lawton M P 1971 The functional assessment of elderly people. Journal of American Geriatrics Society 19: 465–481

Lawton M P, Brody E M 1969 Assessment of older people: self-maintaining and instrumental activities of daily living. Gerontologist 9: 179–186

Lemke S Moos R H 1980 Assessing the institutional policies of sheltered care settings. Journal of Gerontology 35: 96–107

Letcher P B, Peterson L P, Scarbrough D 1974 Reality orientation: a historical study of patient progress. Hospital and Community Psychiatry 25: 11–13

LeVere T F 1975 Neural stability, sparing and behavioural recovery following brain damage. Psychological Review 82 (5): 344–358

Libb J W, Clements C B 1969 Token reinforcement in an exercise program for hospitalized geriatric patients. Perceptual and Motor Skills 28: 957–958

Lindsley O R 1964 Geriatric behavioural prosthetics. In: Kastenbaum R (ed) New thoughts on old age. Springer, New York

Linsk N, Howe M W, Pinkston E M 1975 Behavioural group work in a home for the aged. Social Work 20: 454–463

Lipman A 1968 A socio-architectural view of life in 3 homes for old people. Gerontologia Clinica 10: 88–101

Lipman A, Slater R 1977 Homes for old people: toward a positive environment, Gerontologist 17: 146–156

Lipman A, Slater R, Harris H 1979 The quality of verbal interaction in homes for old people. Gerontology 25: 275–284

Lockyer M 1979 Reality orientation therapy: a comparison of the effects of combined classroom and 24 hour RO, 24 hour alone and occupational therapy on elderly residents in a large state mental hospital. MSc thesis, Leeds University

Lodge B, Parker F A 1977 Environmental modification in day care. Social Work Today 8: no. 24

Loew C A, Silverstone B M 1971 A program of intensified stimulation and response facilitation for the senile aged. Gerontologist 11: 341–347

Lopez M A, Hoyer W J, Goldstein A P, Gershaw N J, Spratkin R P 1980 Effects of overlearning and incentive on the acquisition and transfer of interpersonal skills with institutionalized elderly. Journal of Gerontology 35: 403–408

Luria A R 1963 Restoration of function after brain injury. Pergamon Press, Oxford

Lyle R C 1980 Prospect for an applied psychology of the elderly. Paper presented at the British Psychological Society Annual Conference, Aberdeen

McClannahan L E, Risley T R 1974 Design of living environments for nursing home residents. Recruiting attendance at activities. Gerontologist 14: 236–240

McClannahan L E, Risley T R 1975 Design of living environments for nursing-home residents: increasing participation in recreation activities. Journal of Applied Behaviour Analysis 8: 261–268

MacDonald M L 1978 Environmental programming for the socially isolated aging. Gerontologist 18: 350–354

MacDonald M L, Butler A K 1974 Reversal of helplessness: producing walking behaviour in nursing-home wheelchair residents using behaviour modification procedures. Journal of Gerontology 29: 97–101

MacDonald M L, Settin J M 1978 Reality orientation vs sheltered workshops as treatment for the institutionalized aging. Journal of Gerontology 33: 416–421

McFadyen M, Prior T, Kindness K 1980 Engagement: an important variable in institutional care of the elderly. Paper presented at British Psychological Society Annual Conference, Aberdeen

McGrath J 1960 The effect of irrelevant environmental stimulation on vigilance performance. Human Factor Problems in ASW Tech. Rep. No. 6 Human Factors Research Inc, Los Angeles

McGrath J J, Hatcher J F 1961 Irrelevant stimulation and vigilance under fast and slow stimulus rates. Human Factor Problems in ASW Tech, Rep. No. 7 Human Factors Research Inc, Los Angeles

Marsden C D 1978 The diagnosis of dementia. In: Isaacs A D, Post F (eds) Studies in geriatric psychiatry. J Wiley, Chichester

Marston N, Gupta H 1977 Interesting the old. Community Care (Nov. 16): 26–28

Matthews R, Kemp M 1979 Rooms of the past strike a chord in the mentally infirm. Geriatric Medicine 9 (June): 37–41

Melia A 1979 Research into staff attitudes and activities in psychogeriatric wards. In: Positive approaches to mental infirmity in elderly people. MIND Annual Conference Report, London

Merchant M, Saxby P 1981 Reality orientation: a way forward. Nursing Times 77: No 33: 1442–1445

Miller E 1975 Impaired recall and the memory disturbance in pre-senile dementia. British Journal of Social and Clinical Psychology 14: 73–79

Miller E 1977a Abnormal ageing: the psychology of senile and pre-senile dementia. J Wiley, Chichester

Miller E 1977b The management of dementia: a review of some possibilities. British Journal of Social and Clinical Psychology 16: 77–83

Miller E, Lewis P 1977 Recognition memory in elderly patients with depression and dementia: a signal detection analysis. Journal of Abnormal Psychology 86: 84–86

Mishara B L, Kastenbaum R 1973 Self-injurious behaviour and environmental change in the institutionalized elderly. International Journal of Aging and Human Development 4: 133–145

Mishara B L, Kastenbaum R 1974 Wine in the treatment of long-term geriatric patients in mental institutions. Journal of the American Geriatrics Society 22: 88–94

Mishara B L, Robertson B, Kastenbaum R 1973 Self-injurious behaviour in the elderly. Gerontologist 13: 311–314
confused elderly. Journal of Gerontological Nursing 4: 13–18

von Monakow C 1914 Die lokalisation im grosshirn und der abbau der funktion durch cortikale. Herde, Wiesbaden

Moos R H, Lemke S 1980 Assessing the physical and architectural features of sheltered care settings. Journal of Gerontology 35: 571–583

Mueller D J, Atlas L 1972 Resocialisation of regressed elderly residents: a behavioural management approach. Journal of Gerontology 27: 390–392

Nathanson B F, Reingold J 1969 A workshop for mentally impaired aged. Gerontologist 9: 293–295

Naylor G, Harwood E 1975 Old dogs, new tricks: age and ability. Psychology Today 1: 29–33

Nelson H E, McKenna P 1975 The use of current reading ability in the assessment of dementia. British Journal of Social and Clinical Psychology 14: 259–267

Neugarten B L 1977 Personality and aging. In: Birren J E, Schaie K W (eds) Handbook of the psychology of aging. Van Nostrand Reinhold, New York

Nihira K, Foster R, Shellhaas M, Leland H 1974 AAMD adaptive behaviour scale. American Association on Mental Deficiency, Washington

Oberleder M 1962 An attitude scale to determine adjustment in institutions for the aged. Journal of Chronic Diseases 15: 915–923

Pappas W, Curtis W P, Baker J 1958 A controlled study of an intensive treatment programme for hospitalised geriatric patients. Journal of American Geriatrics Society 6: 17–25

Parker F A 1974 Second childhood. Times Educational Supplement (9 August), London

Pattie A H, Gilleard C J 1979 Manual of the Clifton assessment procedures for the elderly (CAPE). Hodder and Stoughton Educational, Sevenoaks

Pearce J, Miller E 1973 Clinical aspects of dementia. Baillière Tindall, London

Perry E K 1980 The cholinergic system in old age and Alzheimer's disease. Age and Ageing 9 (1): 1–8

Peterson R F, Knapp T J, Rosen J C, Pither B F 1977 The effects of furniture arrangement on the behaviour of geriatric patients. Behaviour Therapy 8: 464–467

Pfeiffer E 1975 A short portable mental status questionnaire for the assessment of organic brain deficit in elderly patients. Journal of American Geriatrics Society 23: 433–441

Pincus A 1968 New findings on learning in old age. American Journal of Occupational Therapy 22: 302

Plutchick R, Conte H, Lieberman M, Bakur M, Grossman J, Lehrman N 1970 Reliability and validity of a scale for assessing the functioning of geriatric patients. Journal of American Geriatrics Society 18: 491–500

Pollock D P, Liberman R P 1974 Behaviour therapy of incontinence in demented in-patients. Gerontologist 14: 488–491

Post F 1965 The clinical psychiatry of late life. Pergamon Press, Oxford

Powell L, Felce D, Jenkins J, Lunt B 1979 Increasing engagement in a home for the elderly by providing an indoor gardening activity. Behaviour Research and Therapy 15: 127–136

Powell R R 1974 Psychological effects of exercise therapy upon institutionalized geriatric mental patients. Gerontologist 14: 157–161

Quilitch H R 1974 Purposeful activity increased on a geriatric ward through programmed recreation. Journal of the American Geriatrics Society 22: 226–229

Richman L 1969 Sensory training for geriatric patients. American Journal of Occupational Therapy 23: 254–257

Riegler J 1980 Comparison of a reality orientation programme for geriatric patients with and without music. Journal of Music Therapy 17: 26–33

Robinson R A 1977 Differential diagnosis and assessment in brain failure. Age and Ageing 6: 42–49 (supplement)

Rodstein M 1975 Challenging residents to assume maximal responsibilities in homes for the aged. Journal of American Geriatrics Society 23: 317–321

Ron M A, Toone B K, Garralda M E, Lishman W A 1979 Diagnostic accuracy in pre-senile dementia. British Journal of Psychiatry 13: 161–168

Sachs D A 1975 Behavioural techniques in a residential nursing home facility. Journal of Behaviour Therapy and Experimental Psychiatry 6: 123–127

Salter C L, Salter C A 1975 Effects of an individualized activity programme on elderly patients. Gerontologist 15: 404–406

Salzman C, Kochansky G E, Shader R I 1972 Rating scales for geriatric psychopharmacology – a review. Psychopharmacology Bulletin 8 (3): 3–50

Savage B, Widdowson T 1974 Revising the use of nursing resources. Nursing Times 70: 1372–1374, 1424–1427

Savage R D 1973 Old age. In Eysenck H J (ed) Handbook of abnormal psychology. Pitman, London

Scarbrough D R, Drummond L, Kirchhoff L 1978 Letter to the editor. Journal of Gerontology 33: 588

Schaie K W, Labouvie-Vief G 1974 Generational versus ontogenetic components of change in adult cognitive behaviour: a 14-year cross-sequential study. Developmental Psychology 10: 305–320

Schaie K W, Strother C R 1968 A cross-sequential study of age changes in cognitive behaviour. Psychological Bulletin 70: 671–680

Seidel H A, Hodgkinson P E 1979 Behaviour modification and long-term learning in Korsakoff's psychosis. Nursing Times 75: 1855–1857

Seligman M (1975) Helplessness: on depression, development and death. W H Freeman, San Francisco

Shaw J 1979 A literature review of treatment systems for mentally disabled old people. Journal of Gerontological Nursing 5 (5): 36–41

Shepherd G, Richardson A 1979 Organisation and interaction in psychiatric day-centres. Psychological Medicine 9: 573–579

Smith B J, Barker H R 1972 Influence of a reality orientation training programme on the attitudes of trainees towards the elderly. Gerontologist 12: 262–264

Smith J M, Bright B, McCloskey J 1977 Factor analytic composition of the geriatric rating scale (GRS). Journal of Gerontology 32: 58–62

Sommer R, Ross H 1958 Social interaction on a geriatric ward. International Journal of Social Psychiatry 4: 128–133

Sparks R, Helm N, Albert M L 1974 Aphasia rehabilitation resulting from melodic intonation therapy. Cortex 10: 303–316

Stephens L P (ed) 1969 Reality orientation: a technique to rehabilitate elderly and brain-damaged patients with a moderate to severe degree of disorientation. American Psychiatric Association Hospital and Community Psychiatric Service, Washington DC

Taulbee L R, Folsom J C 1966 Reality orientation for geriatric patients. Hospital and Community Psychiatry 17: 133–135

Toepfer C T, Bicknell A T, Shaw D D 1974 Remotivation as behaviour therapy. Gerontologist 14: 451–453

Townsend J, Kimbell M 1975 Caring regimes in elderly persons' homes. Health and Social Services Journal 85 (11 October): 2286

Turner R K 1980 A behavioural approach to the management of incontinence in the elderly. In: Mandelstam D (ed) Incontinence and its management. Croom Helm, London

Voelkel D 1978 A study of reality orientation and resocialization groups with confused elderly. Journal of Gerontological Nursing 4: 13–18

Wallis D, Cope D 1978 UWIST action research project on the job satisfaction of nursing and ancillary staff: report on research done in a psychogeriatric unit. Department of Applied Psychology, UWIST, Cardiff

Walsh K W 1978 Neuropsychology: a clinical approach. Churchill Livingstone, Edinburgh

Warrington E K, James M, Kinsbourne M 1966 Drawing disability in relation to laterality of lesion. Brain 89: 53–82

Warrington E K, Sanders H I 1971 The fate of old memories. Quarterly Journal of Experimental Psychology 23: 432–442

Wechsler D 1945 A standardised memory scale for clinical use. Journal of Psychology 19: 87–95

Woods R T 1979 Reality orientation and staff attention: a controlled study. British Journal of Psychiatry 134: 502–507

Woods R T 1980 Specificity of learning in reality orientation sessions: a single case study. Unpublished manuscript

Woods R T, Britton P G 1975 Psychological aspects of incontinence in a psychogeriatric population. Unpublished manuscript

Woods R T, Britton P G 1977 Psychological approaches to the treatment of the elderly. Age and Ageing 6: 104–112

Woods R T, Simpson S, Nicol R 1980 Reality orientation: the relative effects of 24 hour RO and RO sessions. Unpublished manuscript

Woodward S 1979 The effects of the reality orientation classroom on elderly confused people. Unpublished dissertation, University of Surrey

Index

WITHDRAWN